T0311017

THE SPIRIT OF ZEN

THE SPIRIT OF
ZEN

SAM VAN SCHAIK

PUBLISHED IN ASSOCIATION WITH
THE INTERNATIONAL SACRED LITERATURE TRUST

YALE UNIVERSITY PRESS
NEW HAVEN AND LONDON

For information about this and other Yale University Press publications, please contact:
U.S. Office: sales.press@yale.edu   yalebooks.com
Europe Office: sales@yaleup.co.uk   yalebooks.co.uk

Set in Arno Pro by IDSUK (DataConnection) Ltd
Printed in Great Britain by TJ International Ltd, Padstow, Cornwall

Library of Congress Control Number: 2018942946

ISBN 978-0-300-22145-9

A catalogue record for this book is available from the British Library.

10 9 8 7 6 5 4 3 2 1

INTERNATIONAL
SACRED
LITERATURE
TRUST

The International Sacred Literature Trust was established to promote understanding and open discussion between and within faiths and to give voice in today's world to the wisdom that speaks across time and traditions.

What resources do the sacred traditions of the world possess to respond to the great global threats of poverty, war, ecological disaster, and spiritual despair?

Our starting-point is the sacred texts with their vision of a higher truth and their deep insights into the nature of humanity and the universe we inhabit. The publishing program is planned so that each faith community articulates its own teachings with the intention of enhancing its self-understanding as well as the understanding of those of other faiths and those of no faith.

The Trust especially encourages faiths to make available texts which are needed in translation for their own communities and also texts which are little known outside a particular tradition but which have the power to inspire, console, enlighten, and transform. These sources from the past become resources for the present and future when we make inspired use of them to guide us in shaping the contemporary world.

Our religious traditions are diverse but, as with the natural environment, we are discovering the global interdependence of human hearts and minds. The Trust invites all to participate in the modern experience of interfaith encounter and exchange which marks a new phase in the quest to discover our full humanity.

To Aaron and Kristian

CONTENTS

PREFACE

In this book, I have tried to strike a balance between introducing readers to Zen, and providing a translation that brings something new even to those who are very familiar with the tradition. I have done this by looking at the continuities between one of the earliest Zen texts and the practice of Zen through the centuries, down to the present day. Traditional presentations of religions tend to emphasize constant truths, while academics often delight in discovering disjunctions and contradictions. I have sought a middle way here as well, showing the changes the Zen tradition has gone through over time and in different cultural settings, while tracing threads of continuity that make it possible for us to talk about a 'Zen tradition' at all.

Naturally, quite a bit of this book is about meditation. If readers who are new to Zen are interested in taking up meditation practice, there are some excellent books written by Zen teachers, some of which are listed in the References. I defer here to the advice given by James Ishmael Ford to anyone interested in beginning Zen meditation:

> if the Zen path sounds right for you, I would suggest you start by taking up the practice of Zen meditation pretty much right now. You can get the basics out of many good books: John Daishin Buksbazen's *Zen Meditation in Plain English* would be a good way to start, as would Robert Aitken's *Taking the Path of Zen*. A visit to a local Zen group of any flavor can provide some hands-on instruction that can clarify most beginning questions.

You don't have to sign up for anything other than an introductory class, nor, I strongly suggest, should you. Just check things out. If you like the group, perhaps keep going from time to time. But do begin to sit at home regularly. Cultivate a discipline.[1]

Turning to the scholarly side of this book, this is my first published translation of a Chinese text of some length, and I owe a debt of gratitude to those who have made it possible. First and foremost, for encouraging me to learn and translate Classical Chinese, and for reading and offering many helpful comments and corrections on this text, I offer grateful thanks to Imre Galambos. I am also grateful for Sinological advice offered by colleagues at the British Library, including Susan Whitfield, Emma Goodliffe and Mélodie Doumy. I would also like to thank Nathalie Monnet of the Bibliothèque nationale de France for her insights into the manuscripts from the Pelliot collection in Paris.

I am also immensely grateful for the work of scholars and practitioners whose work has helped my understanding of the history, texts, practice and indeed spirit of Zen. For this book in particular I would like to mention Wendi Adamek, Christoph Anderl, Charlotte Joko Beck, Marcus Bingenheimer, Jeffrey Broughton, Thomas and Jonathan Cleary, Huw Davies, Bernard Faure, James Ishmael Ford, Griffith Foulk, Taigen Dan Leighton, Carmen Meinert, John McRae, Jan Nattier, Bill Porter, James Robson, Morten Schlütter, Robert Sharf, Jonathan Silk, Kirill Solonin and Kazuaki Tanahashi. And for showing how the principles of Mahayana Buddhism are manifested in daily life, I owe immeasurable thanks to Lama Jampa Thaye.

There are an increasing number of excellent resources for studying and translating Classical Chinese. Two of the best are the Digital Dictionary of Buddhism and the Chinese Text Project, the results of the tireless work of Charles Muller and Donald Sturgeon respectively. Images of many of the manuscripts containing the *Masters of the Lanka* are available on the website of the International Dunhuang Project, and digital transcriptions have recently been made available by the Dunhuang Manuscript Full Text Digitization Project. In the original spirit of the internet, all of these resources are free to use.

My work on this translation was supported by the European Research Council, funders of the project *Beyond Boundaries: Religion, Region, Language and the State* (ERC grant agreement no. 609823) – a small example of the many good things that have come out of the European Union. The idea for the book was first suggested by Malcolm Gerratt at Yale University Press, and after his retirement the project was overseen by Robert Baldock; the editors were Rachael Lonsdale and Clarissa Sutherland, and the copy-editor was Beth Humphries. I am thankful for their professional work and guidance. At an early stage, Sarah Shaw offered sage advice which helped to shape the book. Finally, I thank my wife Ananda, daughters and family for their kindness, forbearance and support.

PART I

INTRODUCING ZEN

✦

CHAPTER ONE

THE PRACTICE OF ZEN

Peace of mind
Cannot be summed up in words;
True understanding of it
Comes from your own heart.

Daoxin in Masters of the Lanka

Peace of mind

The earliest Zen teachers talked about meditation in terms of peace of mind, a state free of the anxieties and irritations which afflict us all. They taught that this peace is not to be obtained through our usual preference of surrounding ourselves with what we like and banishing what we dislike. Instead, it is to be found by getting to grips with the nature of our own minds.[1]

This insight is at the heart of Zen. The Buddha's teachings are based on the principle that we want to be free from suffering, but are going about it in the wrong way. Thus the Buddha's four noble truths begin with suffering, though 'suffering' is really too narrow a translation for the word he used, *duḥka*. The dictionary translation of duḥka is wider, encompassing 'uneasiness, pain, sorrow, trouble, difficulty'.[2] Some translators prefer 'unsatisfactoriness'.

In any case, while most of us are not always suffering, if we stop and look within, there are few times that we can say we are free from a feeling of unease, or the sense of something missing, expressed by that awkward word 'unsatisfactoriness'. Ultimately, we can't escape suffering itself, because we cling to the things we want and need even though it is the nature of the universe to change, so at some point we have to lose them.

To have peace of mind, then, is to be free from suffering, to be able to face whatever happens with equanimity. Achieving peace of mind will not come about through trying to satisfy our attachment to ease and pleasure and aversion to discomfort and suffering. It is not the successful accomplishment of one pole of that neurotic dichotomy, but the peace that comes of letting go of all attachment and aversion. And that only comes from dissolving our attachment to 'I' and 'mine'.

The Buddha taught that everything is impermanent, in a process of constant change; yet we look for a sense of permanence in our idea of ourselves, our possessions, our friends. Because we invest in this solidity, we suffer when things change. In Zen this is sometimes taught through the metaphor of water freezing into ice. We attempt to 'freeze' the flow of the world into categories that make sense to us. This creates the illusion of the unchanging self that we feel ourselves to be, and the solid, essentialized phenomena that we feel we must control, whether grasping and keeping them or pushing them away.[3]

This is not just about our experiences of ourselves. This 'freezing' is also a solidification of our relationships – categorizing the fluid and subtle back-and-forth of our relationships into this 'self', that 'other person' and the things that we do to them, and they do to us. This blocks the intuitive, compassionate activity of which we are capable, and it reduces our personal interactions to an emotional calculus of help and hurt.[4]

This state of affairs – a frozen world – is what Buddhists call *samsara*. It is not a place, but the sum of all the ways of perceiving, reacting, thinking and behaving that bind us into patterns of suffering. Recognizing these patterns and working on them is the path; finally putting an end to them is enlightenment, or awakening. Anyone who has achieved this is an awakened one, a buddha.

The nature of mind

The path to awakening takes a variety of different forms in the many traditions of Buddhism. In Zen, the path from samsara to enlightenment is not a journey from A to B, but a gradual realization of something that has always been there in our day-to-day awareness. We have everything we need for awakening right here in our own minds, so there is no need to rely on gods or other supernatural aids. Even the Buddha cannot help us if we think of 'buddha' as something separate from what we are, for there is no buddha apart from the mind. To put it another way, 'the nature of mind has always been pure from the beginning.'[5]

To say our mind is pure from the beginning is only to say that the way we normally engage with the world is not fundamentally what we are. The ingredients of our anxieties and irritations – clinging to our own selfish needs, categorizing other people and things according to our own desires and fears – are part of a repeating pattern, but they are only one particular expression of our awareness, which is fundamentally pure. This awareness simply *is* – always present but obscured by our own confusion.

This pure awareness is there for everyone, but is like a pearl hidden by dirty water; only when the water is allowed to settle can we see the pearl. It is the practice of meditation, which is key to all Zen traditions, that allows the dirt to settle and the waters to become clear. Thus meditation is not primarily an intellectual activity, or an attempt to transform one's mind into something else. It is a way to let the mind be, so that the dirt stirred up by our own turbulent thoughts and emotions gradually settles.

This is why Zen teachers have often warned against becoming entangled in ideas of what the mind, the world or enlightenment really is. Many Zen stories express the idea that the mind, and indeed 'peace of mind', is not what we might think. A famous example is this dialogue between two of the founding figures of Zen, Bodhidharma and his student Huike:

> Huike said to Bodhidharma: 'My mind is anxious, please pacify it.' To which Bodhidharma replied, 'Bring me your mind, and I will pacify it.' Huike said, 'Although I've sought it, I cannot find it.' Bodhidharma then said, 'There, I have already pacified your mind.'[6]

This, like many Zen dialogues, points to the futility of seeking solutions to our problems within our usual frameworks. Intellectual analysis, though it has a crucial role in Buddhism, is often downplayed, and Zen teachers warn against too much concern with books and book learning. These statements must be taken with a pinch of salt, for the Zen tradition itself has made a huge contribution to the literature of East Asia. What the stories are getting at is that becoming fascinated by the literature, or by intellectual speculation, is to take a path away from awakening.

The path needs a guide. In Zen, as in most Buddhist traditions, the teacher–student relationship is key. While reading or hearing teachings and going away to put them into practice can be beneficial, it is akin to prescribing one's own medicine; it might have no result, or it might be dangerous. Buddhist literature often compares the teacher to a doctor, and the student to a patient. Those wishing to travel the path to awakening need to rely on a teacher's qualifications and knowledge, especially at the beginning, when it is easy to go off in the wrong direction entirely.[7]

Zen in practice

I am using the word 'Zen' here to encompass all the traditions of practice that came from the original Chinese Chan teachers. 'Zen' is the Japanese pronunciation of the Chinese character that is pronounced 'Chan' in China. We only know the tradition by the name Zen because it was introduced to the West from Japan, not China, and the same applies to other key Zen terms such as *zazen* and *koan*. In any case, the word 'Chan' or 'Zen' is itself just the Chinese rendering of the Sanskrit word *dhyāna*, 'meditation'. So 'Chan' and 'Zen' also just mean 'meditation'.

So the schools of Zen are by definition specialists in meditation practice. What is this meditation? It's important, first of all, to know that meditation is not just one thing. There are all kinds of meditation in Buddhism, and many of them have been taught by Zen teachers. Most fall into the category of zazen, sitting meditation. These days, students of Zen are likely to encounter two principal methods of zazen – the practice of 'just sitting' known as *shikantaza* and the contemplation of phrases and dialogues called 'koans'.

But before students get to these specialized Zen practices, they will often be taught a simple method of concentrating the mind, which is to focus on the breath. In this practice you sit in the lotus or half-lotus position, with hands in your lap and eyes open (but not staring ahead). While you sit, you try to keep your mind focused on the movement of your breath. As an aid to this focus, students are often told to count the breaths, usually from one to ten, before starting again. When the mind wanders off in thought, you bring it back to the breath and start counting again.

This simple practice is found in many other kinds of Buddhism, including Theravada and Tibetan Buddhism. It goes back to some of the earliest Buddhist writings, and came to China in the fifth century. The enduring popularity of the practice is due to its simplicity and effectiveness. It is easy to teach and practise, yet takes time to master, and is eventually very effective in calming the mind to the point where one can engage in other kinds of meditation. Yet it is not just a preliminary practice, as the Zen teacher Robert Aitken has written: 'Breath counting is not the kindergarten of Zen. For many students it is a full and complete lifetime practice.'[8]

In the practice of 'just sitting', one doesn't focus on the breath or any other object, and just lets the mind be. This may sound easy, but the point is to remain present and aware, and not to wander off in thought. This is not a state of mental blankness. Thoughts and emotions are not suppressed, but our habitual clinging to them relaxes, so that they pass over like clouds across the sky. One should not strive for peace of mind, nor cling to it when one experiences it. What's more, Zen teachers emphasize that one should not think of sitting as something that leads to enlightenment; to sit in the awareness of the present moment is to be a buddha in that very moment.[9]

A more specific kind of Zen practice is the koan. These are the apparently paradoxical questions and statements that Zen is well known for, the most famous being, 'What is the sound of one hand

clapping?' Most koans are longer than these, being dialogues taken
from the biographies of Zen teachers, and held up for special attention. In practice, koans are contemplated by students, who present
their interpretation of the dialogue or phrase to the teacher, who can
then judge the student's progress. Another use of the koan is to take a
very short phrase as the object of concentration, sometimes reciting it
like a mantra, in sitting meditation. This may result in a breakthrough,
a moment of awakening.

What is enlightenment?

Zen is not just about our own minds, our own practice, our own breakthroughs; Zen is very much about all living beings. This is because
Zen is part of the *mahayana* or 'greater vehicle' movement in Buddhism.
In the mahayana, every practitioner is a *bodhisattva*, someone who
aspires to liberate all living beings from the cycle of suffering. In order
to do so, the bodhisattva aspires to become a buddha, or in other
words, to experience enlightenment, or awakening (*bodhi* in Sanskrit).
This goal is expressed in the bodhisattva vow: the aspiration to
become a buddha for the sake of others.

Thus enlightenment is a moral imperative. To do it for one's
own benefit alone is to be stuck in the habitual pattern of self-interest
that keeps us in the cycle of suffering. Yet to become a buddha is
to become someone who has completely transcended this self-
interest, having let go of the emotional and cognitive tendencies
that keep us locked into the cycle of suffering. This is a lofty goal,
and few practitioners will expect to become buddhas in this life, but
the ideal informs the whole of the path – the *aspiration* is the key
thing.

As one travels the path, one's habitual tendencies may temporarily
weaken enough to allow brief glimpses of this state of awakening. In
Zen, particularly the Rinzai school of Japanese Zen, these glimpses are
what is known as *kenshō* or *satori*.[10] In some of the writing on Zen in
English, such glimpses of awakening are also called 'enlightenment'.
However, we should be careful to distinguish these different uses of

the English word 'enlightenment' which may cover quite different concepts in the original languages, ranging from a momentary glimpse to the state of being a buddha.

The modern Chinese Zen master Sheng Yen gives a helpful definition when he says that an experience of kenshō is 'the beginning of enlightenment'.[11] And in his interviews with Chan monks in China before the Communist Revolution, Holmes Welch reported a general view which distinguished between intimations of enlightenment (*kāiwù*) and full buddhahood:

> They make a distinction between enlightenment, nirvana and buddhahood. *K'ai-wu*, the Chinese phrase commonly translated as 'to attain enlightenment,' actually means to attain a *degree* of enlightenment. There are large and small degrees.[12]

Thus the path of Zen is a continuous path to awakening. The bodhisattva's aspiration to wake up in order to be able to save all sentient beings, though it may seem impossible, is fundamental to Zen practice. This is *bodhicitta* (*bodaishin* in Japanese), the state of mind with which one enters the practice of meditation. Without it, as Zen teachers have warned through the years, the practice is likely to lead to pride, and be derailed by desire for fame and gain. As the Japanese teacher Dogen wrote: 'But such things do not happen to those who have great compassion and whose vow to guide sentient beings is vast and mature.'[13]

As for the nature of enlightenment itself, this is something that can only be pointed out, but not really expressed. An awakened person does not freeze reality into solid categories, transcending even the fundamental difference between what is us (self) and what is not (other). Since this duality underlies our very language, the state of enlightenment cannot be expressed in words: 'full enlightenment is what is truly real, beyond language and speech'.[14] So in Buddhism this state is sometimes communicated through similes and metaphors, and in Zen through other kinds of linguistic play, bending and breaking the normal rules of language and communication.

The ethics of Zen

To follow the path of Zen is to follow the path of the bodhisattva. To practise Zen without the bodhisattva's altruistic aspiration would be to isolate meditation from the wisdom and compassion of Mahayana Buddhism. There are of course many presentations of Zen in the West that have done this, so it's important to realize that this is a radical innovation. The ethical grounding of Zen can be seen in the daily chants in Zen monasteries in Asia, which are now being translated and chanted in Zen centres in the West as well.[15]

These chanted verses include one that summarizes the practice of Buddhism in all traditions:

Refrain from unwholesome action.
Engage in wholesome action.
Purify your own mind.
This is the teaching of all buddhas.[16]

Here, ethics and the transformation of one's mind go hand in hand. Verses for taking refuge are chanted before each meditation session in monasteries and meditation centres, expressing dedication to the original teacher (the Buddha), his teaching (the *dharma*) and the community of fellow practitioners (the *sangha*). And at the end of each practice, any benefits accruing are dedicated to the welfare of all living beings.

Another brief verse is traditionally chanted in the morning by monks and nuns before putting on their robes:

Great is the robe of liberation,
A formless field of benefaction!
I wear the tathāgata's teaching
To awaken countless beings.[17]

In this and other ways, the ethical precepts of Mahayana Buddhism are expressed throughout the day. Another regular chant concerns the ten actions to avoid – not to kill, steal, misuse sex, lie or become intoxicated; not to slander others behind their backs or speak harshly to their faces; not to be mean-minded or angry; and not to speak ill of the Buddha, dharma or sangha.[18] These commitments are reasserted regularly in verses of confession, acknowledging all one's past misdeeds. And at other times of day, the bodhisattva's aspiration is restated in various ways, such as in verses chanted before meals:

The first spoonful is to end unwholesome actions.
The second is to cultivate wholesome actions.
The third is to awaken all beings.
Together may we realize the awakened way![19]

These daily recitations reaffirm that the path of Zen is not just about self-cultivation and freeing oneself from suffering, but grows out of boundless love and compassion, not limited by our self-interest and not directed by our personal preferences. Sitting and chanting like this might seem quaint, with little relevance to the modern world. But it is an act of commitment, and by stating one's basic ethical principles every day, they can be kept fresh, preventing the practitioner from wandering away from them through the inevitable need to make compromises.

Zen and emptiness

It is often said that the path of the bodhisattva is twofold, comprising wisdom and compassion. The compassionate aspiration to save all beings from suffering can only be actualized through wisdom. It is wisdom that sees where compassion can be applied and thus allows compassion to be turned into action. In Zen, as in other schools of Mahayana Buddhism, wisdom means to truly understand emptiness.

There is a great deal of philosophical writing about emptiness (in Sanskrit, *śūnyatā*), but it is not inherently a complex idea. Emptiness just means that all things are dependent upon other things for their existence. It does not mean nothingness, which is why the once popular translation 'the Void' is so misleading. All things, if you look at them closely, can be further broken down, or shown to depend on other things for their existence. Nothing, then, exists in its own right, outside this network of interdependence. Everything is just a brief coming together of causes and conditions, like a whirlpool, a rainbow or the reflection of the moon as it passes over a pool of water.

So emptiness is not a nihilistic philosophy, an assertion that nothing exists; it means that there is nothing that exists *as an immutable essence*, since everything can be broken down into other things. Thus all things are 'empty' of any such essence. So when Buddhists say 'form is empty', they don't mean there are not forms; they mean forms have no essential nature that makes them what they are.

Thus the way that we try to categorize the world is also fluid, not based on any permanent truths. The concept of 'long' depends on the concept of 'short', 'bright' depends on 'dark' and so on. They have no independent reality outside our own conceptual framework. This is taught in the *Laṅkāvatāra*:

> Long and short, is and isn't – from each in turn the other arises.
> Because one isn't, the other is; because one is, the other isn't.[20]

Emptiness means letting go of the clinging to our conceptual judgements about the world as if they were part of the very nature of the world, rather than our own constructions. This is why the Buddha often speaks of the world as being like a dream or an illusion. Yet emptiness does not point to some deeper, hidden reality behind the illusion. Things appear and pass away in dependence on other things, and this is always clear if we stop and look; everything lies open to view.

Emptiness doesn't just apply to the things out there in the world, but applies to ourselves as well. My thoughts, emotions and interactions with the world make me what I am, but is there an 'I' that is separate from these fluctuating things, an essential core that is just me? The Buddha taught that there is not. Our strong feeling that we do have a permanent identity, one that is whole and autonomous, is just evidence of our strong and habitual clinging. Like everything else, we are dependent things, dependent on external causes and conditions that allow us to be. My sense of myself relies on the various internal states that make up this bundle I call 'me'.

Such an understanding of emptiness does not lead to a nihilistic kind of relativism. Yes, there is no permanent, independent truth, yet we know that we suffer, and that others do too, and that we can do something about this. As the Buddha says in the *Laṅkāvatāra*, 'samsara is like an illusion or dream, but karma is relentless'.[21] That is to say, we still have to take responsibility for what we do. Thus the path of Zen is practised in the light of emptiness and is deeply informed by an understanding of emptiness, even if this is not always explicit.

Emptiness can be understood at two levels: as an intellectual understanding of how everything is interdependent, and as a deep and wordless dissolution of our habitual grasping at things as having a fixed and independent reality of their own. The intellectual investigation of emptiness was played out in the Madhyamaka school in India, and later carried through with equal rigour in Tibet. In China, though some of the texts of the Madhyamaka scholars were translated, there was more interest in the apparently paradoxical presentations of emptiness found in the sutras, and the Zen tradition became the main embodiment of this approach.

Giving without giving

How, then, does emptiness come together with compassion? If we consider an act of generosity, it can be divided into three aspects: the person who gives something, the person who receives it and the gift itself. All three of these are temporary labels that only apply at the moment of giving, each one dependent on the others. In other words, the act itself is empty. Thus a bodhisattva should not get stuck in the idea of him- or herself as a person who has given a gift, and the corresponding idea of the other person as a recipient.

There is nothing essential to you that makes you the giver, nothing essential to the thing you give that makes it a gift. This is just another way of freezing the flow of reality, which makes it more difficult to act with spontaneous compassion. True generosity comes from letting go of our self-interest entirely, which also means letting go of any idea of ourselves as being generous. In Mahayana Buddhism, generosity is the first of the six 'perfections'. It is perfect because it transcends rigid ideas about the act of generosity; in fact the Sanskrit word usually translated as 'perfection' (*pāramitā*) may be better translated as 'transcendence'.[22]

Thus in the mahayana every aspect of the path is always being undercut with the understanding of emptiness. In the *Laṅkāvatāra sūtra* the Buddha says, 'A statement about views is about no views. A statement about paramitas is about no paramitas. A statement about precepts is about no precepts.'[23] These ideas exist, indeed they are crucial for teaching the Buddhist path, but they are not to be grasped as if they were essential truths.

It is in this spirit, too, that Zen teachers have talked about killing the Buddha. The famous saying attributed to the ninth-century teacher Linji is, 'If you see the Buddha on the road, kill him.' This deliberately shocking injunction is meant to throw you into doubt. Why would I kill the Buddha? How would I ever meet the Buddha anyway? The saying is usually understood as a warning against clinging to a fixed idea of what a buddha is, because this is something that is only revealed to us through the practice of Zen.

This idea of killing the Buddha goes back to a mahayana sutra, which makes it clear that 'killing' in this sense means cutting through the idea that anything has an essential existence. Thus the Buddha says, 'you should kill the thoughts of a self, of a personal identity, of a sentient being, and of a life, eliminating the thoughts even of these names. You should kill in this way.' Likewise, in the thirteenth century Dogen wrote of killing the Buddha as a metaphor for destroying clinging to self and to the idea of sitting in meditation;[24] and the modern teacher Thich Nhat Hanh writes:

This is why it is necessary to 'kill' our concepts so that reality can reveal itself. To kill the Buddha is the only way to see the Buddha. Any concept we have of the Buddha can impede us from seeing the Buddha in person.[25]

Sudden and gradual

There is a popular Zen story about the eighth-century master Mazu and his teacher, which challenges the idea that meditation leads to enlightenment:

> Mazu was sitting down, when Huairang took a tile and sat on the rock facing him, and rubbed it. Mazu asked, 'What are you doing?' Huairang said, 'I'm rubbing the tile to make a mirror.' Mazu said, 'How can you make a mirror by rubbing a tile?' Huairang replied, 'If I can't make a mirror by rubbing a tile, how can you achieve buddhahood by sitting in meditation?'[26]

Now, this story could be read as a warning against the practice of sitting in meditation. But anyone familiar with the mahayana sutras would recognize in it the familiar act of cutting through the conventional understanding of a practice.[27] To think of any practice as the cause of becoming awakened is to categorize awakening according to our conventional way of thinking, and this itself separates us from awakening. Practitioners of Zen engage in meditation without thinking in terms of meditation as the cause and awakening as the result.

In Zen, meditation is not meditation and enlightenment is not enlightenment. This is not just a paradox: meditation is to be practised without a fixed idea of what meditation is; enlightenment is the goal of the bodhisattva, but there is no essence or definition of enlightenment. Getting stuck in such ideas is a mistake. Therefore to practise meditation with the idea that it is the cause of enlightenment is wrong, because the Buddha is right here as the true nature of our own minds.

This does lead to a kind of contradiction that underlies Zen and other Mahayana traditions: if enlightenment is already right here and now, why meditate or do any other practice? Such questions are often answered through images and similes: consider, for example, a poor family who don't realize there is a treasure chest hidden beneath their floorboards; or someone travelling in search of a gem that is sewn inside his clothes. That is to say, we don't know what we have. Meditation and other practices are the means by which we weaken the hold of the habitual grasping and distraction that hide our own nature from ourselves.

One might ask, if this is the case, what is the point of doing meditation or any other practice? Why do Zen monks spend a lifetime in monasteries? This brings us back to the difference between those experiences that allow a glimpse of reality and the state of enlightenment itself. Even if we are able to let go of our mental grasping and emotional distraction for long enough to have an 'enlightenment experience', our habitual patterns tend to reassert themselves fairly quickly. Thus practice continues. As Zongmi wrote: 'The sun rises all at once, but the frost melts step by step.'[28]

It is not that experiences of awakening are unimportant, but they are just that: temporary experiences. They are not the end of the path, and the practice that may last a lifetime is the gradual dissolving of those habitual patterns. We could say that the Zen path always exists in this state of uncertainty, suspended between the ever-presence of enlightened awareness and the need to gradually train so that we can live it.[29] This is expressed in a sutra quoted by Jingjue in his preface to the *Masters of the Lanka*:

> The path to awakening
> Is impossible to map.
> It is lofty but has no 'above';
> Impossible to reach its limit.
> Deep but has no 'below';
> Impossible to measure its depth.
> So large it encompasses heaven and earth,
> So tiny it enters where there is no gap;
> This is why we call it the path.

The spirit of Zen

If Zen can be summed up in a single phrase, it is this one: 'A special transmission outside the scriptures, not founded on words or letters, pointing to one's mind, so that we might see into our own nature and attain Buddhahood.' This formulation of the essence of Zen is from the twelfth century, but it expresses the principles of the earliest Zen texts as well.[30] Awakening is found not through study or intellectual exercises, but through directly engaging with reality itself. Moreover, this cannot be done alone; it is achieved through 'transmission' between teacher and student, the teacher pointing out the truth to the student, with or without words.

The classic story that accompanies this summary of the spirit of Zen comes from the time of the Buddha. It is said that, in one teaching session, when the Buddha's disciples were assembled, the Buddha simply held up a flower, without saying a word. Only one of the disciples, Kāśyapa, grasped the significance of this act and achieved enlightenment there and then. This first transmission, without words, between teacher and student marks the beginning of the Zen lineage.

It would be quite wrong to take this summary of Zen, and the story of the flower, to mean Zen practitioners have never read the Buddhist scriptures. In fact, the teachings of Zen are steeped in the learning of the scriptures, whether it is expressed directly (as in the *Masters of the Lanka* and *The Platform Sutra*) or through allusion (as in later records of dialogues between teachers and students).

So, like the act of sitting in meditation, and like the experiences of awakening, the Buddhist scriptures are not to be thrown out entirely; it is more that one should not become fixated on them, clinging to the words and losing the essential meaning.[31] In the *Masters of the Lanka* Hongren expresses this in various ways. He says that a picture of food does not make a meal and compares scholars to poor people who spend all of their time counting the wealth of others.[32]

Alongside this rejection of learning and philosophy as ends in themselves, there is a strong ethos in Zen of living a simple, humble life. Perhaps the best-known expression of this is the statement

'Before enlightenment, chop wood and carry water; after enlightenment, chop wood and carry water.' This phrase eloquently expresses
the idea that enlightenment is to be found in ordinary activities, and
even after enlightenment, the state of awakening is not something
separate from ordinary life.

Oddly, though, this statement is not found in classical Zen literature, and appears to be quite recent. The closest one finds is this poem
by Layman Pang (740–808):

> My day-to-day activities are no more
> Than whatever I happen to come across.
> There's nothing to acquire, nothing to abandon,
> Nothing to assert, nothing to deny.
> What are marks of high rank?
> Even the hills and mountains crumble to dust.
> I use my mysterious spiritual powers
> To carry water and haul firewood.[33]

Here Layman Pang elegantly demolishes any idea his students might
have about the activities of an enlightened master of meditation. Yet he
also communicates a state that is rather unusual, for he does not need
to obtain or get rid of anything, and feels no need to assert or deny
anything. Having fully taken on the impermanence of all things, he
does not hanker after recognition of any kind. In this state of peaceful
awareness, carrying water and hauling firewood might be totally ordinary, yet quite different as well.

✦

CHAPTER TWO

ZEN AND THE WEST

Is Zen Buddhism?

Alan Watts was one of the most successful exponents of Zen in the West in the twentieth century. In the first of many books on the subject – which also happens to be titled *The Spirit of Zen* – Watts introduced a version of Zen for Westerners 'weary of conventional religion and philosophy'. His Zen is free from all theorization, doctrine and formality, and what is more:

> is so markedly different from any other form of Buddhism, one might even say from any other form of religion, in that it has roused the curiosity of many who would not ordinarily look to the 'unpractical' East for practical wisdom.[1]

Watts wrote this in 1935, but the idea that Zen is not a religion, that it is not even really *Buddhism*, has proved surprisingly persistent in Western perceptions of Zen. As we have seen, Zen arose as a continuation of themes from Indian Mahayana Buddhism, as expressed in the *Laṅkāvatāra* and other sutras. But this is not how Watts explained the relationship of Zen to (other forms of) Mahayana Buddhism: 'Zen found the followers of the Mahayana looking for truth to scriptures, to holy men and Buddhas, believing that they would reveal it to them if they lived the good life.'[2]

For Watts, if Zen is similar to anything, it is to the mystical experiences expressed by some Christians, and he compares the experience of satori to the 'conversion experiences' related by William James in his

Varieties of Religious Experience. In his view, Zen is beyond religion because it is about a pure experience that is ultimately beyond all historically specific expressions of what it is. This was an idea of its time, popularized further by Aldous Huxley in *The Perennial Philosophy*, published in 1945. According to Alan Watts, and many who followed him, Zen offered the most direct approach to this universal experience.

This Western idea that Zen does away with all religious trappings and goes for a direct experience of reality made it well suited to the counter-cultural movements of the 1950s and 1960s. A new generation of Western Zen teachers emerged, who had trained in Japan with Japanese teachers and set up Zen centres to continue the tradition they had learned. One of these new teachers, Philip Kapleau, wrote another very influential book, *The Three Pillars of Zen*. Here, we find that the essence of Zen is the practice of zazen, sitting meditation. Kapleau distinguishes zazen from other, inferior, Buddhist sitting practices, which he dismissively terms 'meditation'.[3]

All of this tends towards separating Zen from its home in the Buddhist tradition, and suggesting that zazen is quite unlike, and superior to, anything going by the name 'meditation'. As David McMahan writes in *The Making of Buddhist Modernism*:

> The idea that the goal of meditation is not specifically Buddhist, and that 'Zen' itself is common to all religions, has encouraged the understanding of zazen as detachable from the complex traditions of ritual, liturgy, priesthood, and hierarchy common in institutional Zen settings. Today, while many traditional Zen monasteries around the globe still hold to largely traditional structures of doctrine and practice, zazen also floats freely across a number of cultures and subcultures, particularly in the West, where grassroots Zen groups with little or no institutional affiliation meet in homes, colleges, and churches.[4]

There is still a significant trend inspired by this separation of meditation from the context of Buddhism, or as it is sometimes put, separation of 'spirituality' from 'religion'. For example, the neuroscientist and popular writer on atheism, Sam Harris, writes in his book *Waking Up* of the need to 'pluck the diamond from the dunghill of esoteric religion'.[5] In recent years this approach has seen great success in the spread of a secular 'mindfulness' meditation, deriving from Buddhist models, but with minimal Buddhist context.[6]

The purification of Zen

The idea that true Zen is only about sitting meditation played an important role in popularizing Zen in the West. But the origins of the idea go back to Japan. In China, and until more recent centuries in Japan, the practices of Zen monks included burning incense and doing prostrations before images and stupas, chanting sutras and reciting buddhas' names, performing repentance rituals and turning pages or spinning rotating bookshelves to generate merit. Practices that are usually considered to belong to other Buddhist schools, such as chanting the name of the buddha Amitabha and performing esoteric rituals, were also practised in Zen monasteries in China and beyond.

As we will see later, the presence of this variety of practice in Zen monasteries did not come about as a degeneration, a falling-away from an earlier 'pure' Zen. Nor was it a kind of syncretism, combining practices from different schools. In fact, this sort of variety of practice was in Zen from as early as we can tell. The creation of a 'pure' Zen came much later, and was largely a product of the revival of the Japanese Soto and Rinzai schools in the eighteenth century, and the modernization agenda that began in the Meiji period (1868–1912).[7]

In Japan during the Meiji period, Buddhism came under heavy criticism, and there was great pressure to show its relevance to modern scientific thinking, and to the Japanese national interest. One of the new branches of Zen that developed out of this was called Sanbo Kyodan. The teachers of this school minimized ritual practices, brought zazen and koan practice to the fore, and emphasized the importance of the kenshō 'enlightenment' experience. They also tried to take Zen out of the monasteries by bringing these practices to the laity. It so happened that some of the most influential Japanese Zen masters in the Western absorption of Zen were from this school, including Philip Kapleau's teacher Yasutani Hakuun.[8]

There is an irony here – the Zen that came to the West, and was embraced as an alternative to the Western tradition, had already been radically reshaped by an agenda of Westernization in Japan, as Robert Sharf has pointed out:

> The irony, as we have seen above, is that the 'Zen' that so captured the imagination of the West was in fact a product of the New Buddhism of the Meiji. Moreover, those aspects of Zen most attractive to the Occident – the emphasis on spiritual experience and the devaluation of institutional forms – were derived in large part from Occidental sources. Like Narcissus, Western enthusiasts failed to recognize their own reflection in the mirror being held out to them.[9]

In a similar way, Alan Watts and other popularizers of Zen in the West owed a great debt to the Zen priest and scholar D.T. Suzuki (1870–1966), who tailored his presentation of Zen to a secular, philosophically minded Western readership. Half a century after his death, Suzuki's writings on Zen are still among the most influential books on Zen in the English language, and his *Introduction to Zen Buddhism* (with a foreword by Carl Jung) is still in print.

Zen and the art of...

The idea that Zen is beyond Buddhism, even beyond religion, has gone a long way towards embedding Zen in Western popular culture. Most often the word 'Zen' is used to evoke a calm, unruffled state of mind, or a state of total absorption in an activity. It is also used to denote a minimalist Japanese aesthetic, and in some way all of these meanings overlap and merge into a fairly vague whole. Though it has perhaps faded in recent years, Zen also acquired a coolness from the sixties onwards that resulted in the word being attached to almost anything.

An interesting example is in the discourse of programming and hacker culture. Here it is the total absorption aspect of Zen that seems to appeal. A popular compendium of hacker slang, 'The Jargon File', contains many examples, like *hack mode*, defined as 'a Zen-like state of total focus on The Problem that may be achieved when one is hacking (this is why every good hacker is part mystic)'.[10] We also find a number of programming languages aligning themselves with Zen; for example, the overarching guidelines of the Python language are called 'The Zen of Python', while the Ruby language is taught through modules called 'koans'. Exponents of the Lisp language have also invoked Zen in explaining the usefulness of this niche language:

> Lisp is worth learning for the profound enlightenment experience you will have when you finally get it; that experience will make you a better programmer for the rest of your days, even if you never actually use Lisp itself a lot.[11]

This illustrates another feature of Zen that has entered secular Western culture – the idea of a flash of inspiration, a state of 'getting it' which comes from the explanations of sudden illumination in kenshō and satori by Zen popularizers like Alan Watts. It is perhaps this aspect of Zen that is behind the title of Robert Pirsig's hugely popular book *Zen and the Art of Motorcycle Maintenance*, published in 1974. Pirsig wrote in the author's note to the first edition of his book that 'it should in no way be associated with that great body of factual information relating to orthodox Zen Buddhist practice. It's not very factual on motorcycles, either.'[12]

Nevertheless, Pirsig took one genuine aspect of Zen, the idea of a nonconceptual and direct apprehension of the nature of reality (in Pirsig's terminology, *Quality*), and used it in a critique of the Western philosophical tradition. The title of the book is a play on an earlier one, *Zen in the Art of Archery* by Eugene Herrigel, an account of a Westerner's training in archery with a Japanese teacher who applies a form of Zen – though a highly idiosyncratic one – to his teaching.[13]

The application of Zen principles to the arts of battle is sometimes called 'Samurai Zen', and is a particularly Japanese phenomenon that developed during the Tokugawa shogunate (1603–1868). For some, this was a troubling development that resulted in Japanese Zen becoming separated from its moral grounding in Buddhist ethics.[14] In any case, the idea that Zen could be applied to various other disciplines was promoted in the West by D.T. Suzuki, who suggested that Zen was equally applicable to other Japanese cultural practices, such as flower arranging and the tea ceremony.

Suzuki's lectures on Zen at Columbia University had a profound effect on a generation of American avant-garde artists, including John Cage and Allen Ginsberg. Later influential artists such as Bill Viola also explicitly incorporate aspects of Zen into their work. The cross-fertilization between Zen (or an idea of Zen) and artistic creation in the twentieth century shows us that a tradition does not have to be fully understood and assimilated before it can have profound effects on another culture.

Beyond this life

One major stumbling block for a secular adaptation of Zen (and other forms of Buddhism) is the central role of karma and rebirth in Buddhist discourse. Exponents of explicitly secular Buddhism, such as Sam Harris and Stephen Batchelor among others, have downplayed the importance of rebirth to Buddhism. They see the doctrines of karma and rebirth as part of the religious accretions to the core teachings of the Buddha, which ought to be discarded, or at least radically reinterpreted.[15] But karma, understood as the inevitability of cause and effect as applied to an individual, need not be superstition; rather it is the extension of the concept of dependent origination.[16]

In Buddhism, we have no essential self and are always in a process of change. What we are now is not what we were, but there is a causal connection, and that is the definition of karma. Furthermore, if we are not singular and autonomous beings from birth to death, but constantly changing, and existing through our relationships with other people and the world around us, then the idea of extinction at death is far less compelling. In the *Masters of the Lanka*, Daoxin teaches a meditation practice in which one mentally takes apart and analyses the constituents of one's own body. This leads to an understanding that one's physical existence is merely a temporary assemblage of parts which does not hold some kind of unchanging essential 'me'. Daoxin concludes: 'Then you will realize that your own body, for past immeasurable aeons, has ultimately never been born, and in the future there is ultimately no person who dies.'

We should also consider how our secular Western emphasis on the singularity of an individual lifetime derives from the Judaeo-Christian concept of a single, individual soul. This concept of the nature of the person carried on into the thinking of the European Enlightenment, despite critiques of other aspects of religion in the seventeenth and eighteenth centuries. As Mary Midgley has put it, 'the Enlightenment notion showed the individual as essentially an isolated will'.[17] This way of understanding people and their relationships to each other is still prevalent. Yet it is a very specific view of humanity that we have inherited, one that we should examine with the same scepticism that we turn on the concept of rebirth.

The secular atomistic model of persons involves not only a fundamental separation between sentient beings, but also an unchanging personal identity that begins at some point between conception and birth and continues through to the time of death. A Buddhist would argue that this is not merely a philosophical concept, but proof of our deeply embedded attachment to our own sense of ourselves as persistent through time; and it is this concept of an unchanging, autonomous self that is the target of the concept and practice of non-self in Buddhism.

The model of rebirth also extends our commitment to others through time. The concept of karma is that every action determines what we will become in future lifetimes, which vastly extends our responsibility for those actions into distant futures. As the philosopher Annette Baier has pointed out, our ethical commitments to future generations are not well established in the West.[18] Thus the model of rebirth should perhaps be appreciated better for its ethical effect; giving everyone a place in the universe from beginningless time to the endless future. As understood in Buddhism, this vastly increases our connections and responsibilities to all living beings; also, one could argue, our future responsibilities to safeguard the environment. So if we choose to discard the idea of rebirth, we should consider what we are losing in terms of the ethical breadth of Buddhism.[19]

A popular Mahayana Buddhist practice involves contemplating the infinite cycle of rebirth and considering that we have been every type of living being; this encourages not only the kindness to animals that Buddhism is known for, but empathy and compassion across all perceived barriers of race, gender and social class. It is part of the practice of Buddhism to break down our identification of ourselves with this particular life that we find ourselves in. Further to this, there should be no attachment to what we might have been in the past, or what we might hope to become in the future.

Embedded in this kind of practice, rebirth is not a doctrine of comfort; it is perhaps more comforting to embrace the prevalent view of our time that 'you only live once'. The popularity of that phrase may owe less to hard-headed realism than to the desire to feel free of responsibilities, to believe that whatever we do, it won't matter much in the end. The teachings of the Buddha are the polar opposite of this: in the end, all that continues beyond this life is our responsibility to others.

Zen centres

There have of course been many Westerners who have engaged with what it means to practise Zen Buddhism in a traditional way. Traditional Zen practices were brought to the West by teachers emigrating from Japan, and later Korea and Vietnam as well. An early example is Yeita Sasaki, also known as Sokei-an (1882–1945), a teacher in the Rinzai school who travelled from Japan to America in 1906 to establish a Zen community in San Francisco.

After settling in New York, Sokei-an taught Zen to American students, including Ruth Fuller Everett, whom he married shortly before his death. Ruth Fuller Sasaki, as she was known after her marriage, became one of the first Western teachers to be ordained as a Zen priest and to teach the traditional forms of Zen practice. After the death of her husband, she moved to Kyoto to continue her practice at the Daitokuji temple.

Here Ruth Fuller Sasaki founded a sub-temple for teaching Westerners and, at the age of seventy-five, was ordained as a priest. Late in life, she wrote *Zen Dust*, the most authoritative work in English on the koan. Perhaps more importantly, among those she taught in Kyoto, several returned to establish centres for Zen meditation in the West. These centres have since spread across the world, usually growing through the efforts of Zen teachers and their local students.[20]

Zen centres are places where people come together to practise Zen. They can be anything from urban flats hosting drop-in meditation sessions to large temple-style buildings with resident teachers and students. Though many centres are led by ordained Zen priests, most students are not ordained. Zen in the West is overwhelmingly a lay movement. Yet most Zen centres are deeply informed by the monastic heritage of Zen, in their daily schedules, prayers and study of the literature of the tradition.

Most Zen centres are associated with a specific lineage, that is, with a teacher whose lineage is traced back through successive past teachers; thus the centre is also the continuation of a tradition. For example, the San Francisco Zen Center, which was founded by the influential Soto Zen teacher Shunryu Suzuki, has the following mission statement:

The purpose of Zen Center is to express, make accessible, and embody the wisdom and compassion of the Buddha. The ideals are based on the example of the Buddha and guided by the teachings and lineage of the Soto School as conveyed to us by our founder, Shunryu Suzuki Roshi, and other Buddhist teachers. Our central value is to express the non-duality of practice and awakening through the practice of Zen and the Sixteen Bodhisattva Precepts.[21]

There are a great variety of Zen centres in the West, continuing lineages not only from Japan, but also from China, Korea and Vietnam. Nevertheless, this formulation of a vision is fairly typical of mainstream Zen centres, situating Zen in the wider context of the Buddha's teachings, and emphasizing what is special about Zen ('the non-duality of practice and awakening') as well as its ethical foundation in the compassionate aspiration of a bodhisattva.[22]

Life in the monastery

To those who have encountered Zen in the works of popular writers like Alan Watts, the serious and highly regulated rhythms of a Zen centre might come as a surprise. Yet this is the way Zen has been cultivated and transmitted down the generations in Asia. Thus the traditional life of a Zen monk is a life governed by rules. For example, an account of life in Tofukuji, a Rinzai Zen monastery in Kyoto, states:

> Above the back entrance of the meditation hall is hung a large tablet on which the severe rules of the monastic life are written. They deal not only with zazen meditation but also with seemingly trivial actions such as how to walk, how to drink tea, how to take off sandals. The daily rules are purposefully very strict to put the monk's life in good order, so that his inner being may attain right awareness. For this reason the initiate's daily life is filled with admonitions from the elder monks.[23]

The daily schedule of the monastery is signalled by the striking of a gong or wooden sounding board. The board is first struck at dawn, traditionally when it is first possible to see the lines on one's own palm. By this time, the monks will already have been awake for some time, washing and dressing for the day. At morning services, each monk bows down in front of images of the Buddha and the Zen patriarchs before sitting down and beginning a session of reciting from scripture. After this there are further sessions of chanting; in Tofukuji, scriptures are chanted for the bodhisattva Mañjuśrī in the meditation hall.

The dominance of chanting in Zen monasteries might come as a surprise to those whose idea of the Zen monk is of a figure in silent meditation, but this has always been a major part of Zen monastic practice. As Dogen wrote in the thirteenth century:

> There are a variety of occasions for reciting a sutra. For example: a donor comes to the monastery and asks the assembly of monks to recite a sutra regularly or on a particular occasion; the assembly aspires to do so on their own; or the assembly recites a sutra for a deceased monk.[24]

The early morning sessions are followed by breakfast, cooked and served by the monks for the monks, and eaten in silence. After breakfast there is a tea ceremony, and announcements of the day's tasks allotted to each of the monks. These include working in the monastery gardens, cleaning the buildings, doing the begging round in the town and attending the daily lecture by the monastery's head priest. Menial work is considered to be a part of the path, and is not optional; the saying is, 'A day without work is a day without food'.[25]

The main meal of the day, lunch, is served to all the monks, who gather to chant scripture before receiving their portions. After lunch there are further tasks to be done, including chopping wood for cooking, working on the vegetable fields, and heating water for baths. In the late afternoon, evening services, with further chanting of scripture, begin. Once these are finished, some monks attend to cleaning the meditation hall and other monastic buildings for the evening, and then once the evening bell is rung, gather to chant scriptures again and retire for the night.

In a Rinzai monastery like Tofukuji, sitting meditation is mainly practised in special training weeks called *sesshin*. During these weeks monks sit together in the meditation hall, while the head monk of the hall watches the meditators and occasionally taps them with an 'encouraging stick' (*keisaku*); a monk who is feeling sleepy may ask to be struck with the stick. During this period, the monastery's head priest will call monks into his room individually to ask them questions and assess their progress. The priest will also give a lecture during the day addressed to all the monks.

The monastic routine is broken up by other regular events. In Japan, there is the *shukushin* ceremony, which happens twice a month. This is a ritual for the protection of the emperor and the state, in which all the monks gather in the main temple hall. As described in the account of Tofukuji temple:

> People are sometimes surprised to see Zen monks engaged in such an elaborate ceremony. The main hall is decorated in a manner similar to that of a Catholic church, with images, candles and other decorations. Priests of various temples wear colorful robes and chant long scriptures. While chanting, they walk around the hall, following the Rōshi. This provides those adherents who attend this ceremony with a strong impression of the Zen tradition.[26]

The shukushin ritual has generally not been part of the export of Japanese Zen to the West. More significantly perhaps, the role of chanting scriptures – both sutra and dharani – that is evident in accounts of life in Asian Zen monasteries, has been downgraded in the West, with greater emphasis on meditation.[27] The reason for the dominance of chanting from scripture in Asian monasteries is partly economic, since monasteries derive significant income from the sponsorship of chanting by lay supporters. Despite these differences, the routines of most Zen centres in the West are influenced by the rituals, liturgies and daily rhythms of Asian Zen monasteries.

✦

CHAPTER THREE

THE HISTORY OF ZEN

Three stories about Zen

There are three key moments among the stories told about Zen, all of which concern the transmission of the teachings. The first story is in the time of Śākyamuni Buddha, set at a teaching session on Vultures' Peak, where the Buddha was seated surrounded by his disciples. At this particular session, instead of beginning to speak, the Buddha simply raised a lotus flower that he was holding in his hand. Only one person in the audience, his student Kāśyapa, understood this wordless teaching, and smiled in recognition. Then the Buddha spoke, telling the whole audience that he entrusted the transmission of his enlightened state to Kāśyapa.

This story is a vivid embodiment of the principle that Zen Buddhism is ultimately beyond sermons and other discursive teaching methods. The personal relationship between teacher and student leads towards the student's realization of the nature of reality, and the teacher's recognition that the student has woken up. The story of the flower sermon is important to the Zen tradition because it takes that principle right back to the time of Śākyamuni himself, so that every Zen teacher can, in theory at least, trace the transmission of their teachings back to the Buddha.

The second key moment is the arrival of the Indian monk Bodhidharma in China, specifically at the court of Emperor Wu of the Liang dynasty in the sixth century. The emperor was a devout Buddhist, who had performed the classic good works of building temples, publishing scripture, and supporting monks and nuns. In conversation with Bodhidharma, the emperor asked about the merit of these activities, and Bodhidharma replied, 'None at all.' So the emperor asked what the true meaning of Buddhism was, and Bodhidharma replied, 'Emptiness, nothing sacred.' The emperor, becoming discomfited, asked, 'Who are you?' Bodhidharma replied, 'I don't know.'

After this performance, Bodhidharma was dismissed by the emperor and left to practise meditation on his own, until years later he met a student who was able to grasp his teaching. This is a story about the transmission of Zen from India to China. It tells us that the essential teaching of Mahayana Buddhism – that everything, even religious activity, is ultimately empty – was not appreciated in China before Bodhidharma. The story suggests that Zen did not gain the support of the royal courts, but had to get by through the power of dedicated practitioners alone.

The third key moment in Zen history is about a young lay practitioner called Huineng, who came to study with a monk from Bodhidharma's lineage, Hongren, in the seventh century. Huineng was from a humble background, couldn't read or write, and hadn't had much time to study Buddhist scripture or even practise meditation. When the time came for Hongren to appoint his successor in the Zen lineage, he asked the monks to write verses to show their understanding. Only one of them, the head monk Shenxiu, wrote a verse:

> The body is a bodhi tree,
> The mind a mirror clear.
> Strive to polish it at all times,
> And don't let dust adhere.

The next day, the young illiterate monk Huineng heard the verse read out aloud, and thought it could be improved. He asked for another poem to be written beside it:

> Original bodhi has no tree,
> The mirror has no stand.

Our buddha nature is always pure,
So where could dust motes land?

Thanks to the superiority of the second verse, Huineng received the transmission of the Zen lineage, at first in secret, and became Hongren's successor. Through to the present day Huineng is considered the sixth Zen patriarch. This story communicates the same truths as the previous two – that realization goes beyond words, and that all religious formulations are ultimately empty. It also tells us that meditation itself is empty; since 'buddha nature is always pure' there is nothing to be gradually cultivated through meditation.

What really happened?

These historical accounts, and many others, have been key to the way Zen Buddhism is taught to students, and presented to outsiders as well. The stories are evocative, pithy and offer much to contemplate. However, over the last century or so, with a greater concern with historical evidence, and better access to early sources, it has become apparent that they are just stories. While the individuals in the stories usually did exist, the tradition has developed around them for centuries after their death.

The story of the Buddha holding up a flower was first written down in the eleventh century in China. It probably does not date from much earlier than this, and was never known in India. The eleventh century was a time when the specific figures in the lineages of Zen transmission all the way back to Śākyamuni were being formalized. Thus the story is enduringly popular because it is both an evocative image of a transmission beyond words, and at the same time works as a justification for the legitimacy of the Zen transmission.[1]

As for Bodhidharma, historical enquiries into this key figure of the Zen lineage have turned up only one source from the time of Bodhidharma himself, which doesn't mention his meditation teachings. As we will see later, a version of his basic teachings was preserved by one of his disciples, yet the first account of that meeting with

Emperor Wu does not appear until some two centuries after the event was supposed to have occurred. Earlier biographies, like the one in the *Masters of the Lanka*, do not tell this story.[2]

The story of Huineng's verse and his elevation to the position of the sixth patriarch of Zen is even more troublesome. Huineng's opponent in the story, Shenxiu, was indeed considered one of the main successors to Hongren, but the latter had no interest in nominating a single successor to the Zen lineage, and Shenxiu did not present himself in this way either. Huineng was a little-known teacher until his students compiled his oral teachings into a text called the *Platform Sutra*. The text begins with this story, which purports to prove that Huineng had been secretly appointed as the sole successor of Hongren.

Thus the story of Huineng's accession to the role of sixth patriarch was almost certainly a fabrication, one that helped his successors to claim that they were the true inheritors of Zen's lineage.[3] The story, which is an inspiring and vivid teaching on gradual and sudden approaches to enlightenment, was also a political device to claim authenticity for a particular Zen tradition in eighth-century China. This might seem shocking, and these critical approaches to revered Zen figures have caused some strife between academics and practitioners.

Yet for many modern Zen teachers and students, whether these stories 'really happened' is of secondary interest. Their value is in the work they do in the present moment, in the acts of teaching and contemplation. This view is eloquently expressed by a twentieth-century Japanese Zen teacher, Shibayama Zenkei:

> Whether the story of 'Sakyamuni Holds Up A Flower' can be supported by history or not is a matter of historical and bibliographical interest and has nothing to do with the fact of teacher–disciple transmission of Zen. That is to say, the fact of transmission in Zen transcends historical concern, and in this sense the koan has a profound Zen significance for us even today.[4]

Some academics also see the danger of focusing purely on a historical critique of Zen traditional stories. John McRae writes on the traditional images of Bodhidharma:

> Those images are not true, and therefore they are more important. More precisely, those images were used by generations of Chan practitioners and enthusiasts, and therefore they are more important than a simplistic reconstruction of historically verifiable events might be.[5]

This is not to say that historical enquiry into Zen, and indeed other religious traditions, can be safely ignored. But a mature historical analysis should not stop at questioning the traditional stories. As McRae points out, the importance of the stories is itself a historical fact, as well as their being central to the Zen traditions as they are practised today. For modern practitioners, the challenge is to accept this historical scrutiny, while valuing the importance of the stories to their own practices.

Meditation and visualization

The story of Bodhidharma's arrival in China in the sixth century reflects a more general change in how Buddhism was being taught there. Before this time, those who came to China from India and Central Asia were either translators or ritual specialists, with only a very few teachers specializing in the practice of meditation. Only in the fifth century do the sources begin to speak of famous teachers who were specialists in meditation living in temples that became centres of meditation instruction.[6]

At this point in time, 'meditation' meant a variety of things, including, as Erik Zürcher pointed out, 'such practices as the preparatory technique of counting the respirations leading to mental concentration (ānāpānasmṛti); the contemplation of the body as being perishable, composed of elements, impure and full of suffering; the visualization of internal and external images or various colours, etc.'[7]

It is important to realize that meditation was never just about sitting concentrating on the breath. Visualization played a key role in many of the early meditation instructions that were brought to China, especially the imaginative deconstruction of one's own body into its parts. This visualization, which is meant to cut attachment to the body, can be very detailed; in a fifth-century meditation text, the *Meditation Essentials*, one begins with the toes and moves on upwards:

> First, fix your thoughts on the tip of your left big toe. Carefully contemplate one half of the toe bone and imagine a swelling. Contemplate carefully until this is very clear. Then imagine a burst-open swelling. When you see the half bone underneath make it extremely white and pure, as if glowing with white light.[8]

Once all the rest has been peeled away the meditator's own body is just a skeleton, pure white and glowing. Other techniques include visualizing that one's body is being consumed by fire, resulting in a realization of nonself: 'When contemplating this fire he contemplates that his own body is entirely without self, and seeing that there is no self the fire spontaneously goes out.' Images of light also play a major role, and some of the visualizations are more positive in nature, involving blessings from the buddhas:

> He sees a real buddha appear and pour a pitcher of water into his head, filling the inside of his body. When his body is filled, the bones too are filled, and the water then flows out through his navel onto the ground, while the buddha continues to pour water. Having finished pouring water over the head the buddha disappears. The water that emerges from the navel is like beryl, its color like the glow of purple beryl. The cloud of its light fills the entire cosmos.[9]

These visualization practices were often done as part of the ceremonies of repentance (*poṣadha*) carried out twice a month in

Buddhist monasteries. At these ceremonies the monks or nuns recited the monastic rules, admitted any breakages and performed the ritual of repentance.[10] These meditation practices were meant to purify recent transgressions and, more importantly, those of countless previous lives as well. The meditation texts also discuss the spontaneous visions that might appear, as signs of the progress of the meditator. Such visions, and their use in interpreting whether repentance rituals had been effective, were one of the main reasons for the popularity of these meditation practices in China.[11]

Some of these visualizations, especially those involving light, are similar to those of later Buddhist tantric practices, and are an obvious influence on them. But what is important here is to understand that meditation meant many things when the Zen tradition first emerged in China, and that 'just sitting' is only one of them. Bodhidharma and his successors were part of a new wave of teachers who specialized in meditation.[12] As we see in early Zen teachings such as the *Masters of the Lanka*, what they offered was not just teaching techniques of meditation, but a way of understanding the sometimes bewildering world of meditation practices that were in circulation in China.

Pioneers in the art of meditation

The Tang dynasty, which ruled China and much of Central Asia from the year 618 to 907, is generally seen as one of the high points of Chinese culture. This is also the period of the foundational teachers of Zen, teachers regarded by the Zen tradition as living exemplars of enlightenment. As we have seen, little is really known about Bodhidharma, the first of these iconic figures. He arrived in China at a time when interest in meditation was on the rise. However, he didn't receive support from any emperor or local ruler, and didn't write down any of his teachings, which were only passed on to his students. Just one brief treatise, *The Two Entrances and Four Practices*, is considered a fairly reliable record of his teachings.

It is interesting to compare Bodhidharma to his contemporary Zhiyi, another meditation teacher of a quite different type. While

Bodhidharma's *The Two Entrances and Four Practices* is a modest presentation of some Indian Buddhist methods of contemplation, Zhiyi's voluminous writings represent an ambitious attempt to synthesize the array of meditation practices that had begun to circulate in China. He brought them together under the headings of calmness (*śamatha*) and insight meditation (*vipaśyanā*). The former involves all sorts of practices to calm the mind, including breathing meditation; the latter features different types of investigation into the nature of reality, including the deconstruction of the body and contemplation on the emptiness of all things.

Also popular in China at the time of Bodhidharma's arrival were the devotional practices known as Pure Land Buddhism. These practices focused on a celestial buddha, most commonly the buddha Amitabha, who resides in the pure land of Sukhāvatī in the west. Sutras from India, which had been translated into Chinese, spoke of how devotion to Amitabha could result in rebirth in his pure land. These devotional practices and beliefs, which spread in China from the fourth century onwards, included the meditation technique called *niànfó* ('mindfulness of the Buddha') which involved visualizing the Buddha and reciting his name. These practices were especially popular at the time of the early teachers of Zen, and became part of Zen practice at an early stage.[13]

As we have seen, Bodhidharma himself was an obscure figure at the time, and only seems to have taught a handful of students in China. One of them, Huike, is traditionally regarded as his successor, though he is equally obscure. It is not until the seventh century, and the fifth figure in the classic line of Zen patriarchs, Hongren, that we see the beginnings of a movement. Hongren established a temple on Dongshan, the East Mountain, where he taught meditation to a large group of students. His teachings later came to be known as 'the East Mountain tradition'. One of Hongren's students, Shenxiu, gained the highest level of support for the East Mountain teachings when he gained the patronage of the empress Wu Zetian.

At that point, this Zen lineage went from obscurity to the highest of profiles, and in the following generations came the inevitable political struggles over who was the true inheritor of Bodhidharma's teaching. One of the outcomes of these struggles, as we saw earlier, was the removal of Shenxiu from the traditional line of Zen patriarchs and his replacement with a rival figure, Huineng. The transmission of the Zen lineage continues from Huineng in an unbroken line; however, as scholars have pointed out, this line is very much a retrospective creation, a 'string of pearls' with only one representative for each generation. This has a lot to do with tracing authority back through time, and cannot be taken to reflect the complex reality of how Zen actually spread through China and beyond.

With each generation, many teachers of meditation continued to teach across China, and different flavours of Zen developed in different regions. Quite how many versions of Zen were being taught is made clear in the works of an eminent scholar of the ninth century, Guifeng Zongmi. In a preface to a collection of Zen texts, he wrote:

> Chan has various lineages that conflict with one another. In fact the writings collected herein are like the one hundred contending schools of China's classical age. However, differences in the principles of their axioms involve only ten houses.[14]

Thus Zongmi identified ten 'houses' of Zen teaching as a way of simplifying the variety that was out there. Though scholarship on Zen often misses this point, he was not talking about ten different schools of Zen. Rather, as Zongmi himself says, this was just a convenient way to talk about different approaches to teaching meditation, some of which he associated with particular teaching lineages. What Zongmi is showing is differences in emphasis: how much should a teacher draw on the traditional scriptures? Should the specifics of practice be taught, or just the fact of the buddha nature being always present within? Should the mind be restrained or given free rein when meditating? And so on.

In any case, a couple of generations after the modest success of the East Mountain meditation temple, Zen was spreading across China.

One of the reasons for this was the popularity of ceremonies where the bodhisattva vow was taken by large groups of people. When these ceremonies were led by Zen teachers, they gave sermons which, as well as expounding on the ethical precepts of the bodhisattva, taught that the Buddha was present in the true nature of one's own mind, and how to sit in meditation. Since these bodhisattva ceremonies could be attended by both monks and laypeople, they helped to both spread the message of Zen and secure financial support.[15]

Zen roots and branches

Though the most famous Zen teachers date to the Tang dynasty, it was during the next major dynasty, the Song, that Zen became a significant player in Chinese Buddhism. The rulers of the Song dynasty were generous in their grants to Buddhist monasteries, bestowed imperial favour on individual monks, and sponsored the translation and printing of Buddhist scriptures. Zen monks became abbots of most of the public monasteries in China.[16] Great collections of biographies and sayings of the iconic Zen teachers were published, and these are the ones still used today. The social conventions of life in the monastery, which continue to inform Zen monasteries across the world today, also took shape in the Song dynasty.

As for meditation, it was in the Song that the two main styles of Zen meditation practised today were formalized: the sitting practice called 'silent illumination' (*mòzhào*) and the koan practice called 'viewing the phrase' (*kànhùa*). The first of these is a continuation of older Zen practices, in which one sits in meditation without a particular technique or goal. The great exponent of silent illumination, Hongzhi, wrote:

> Completely and silently be at ease. In true thusness, separate yourself from all causes and conditions. Brightly luminous without defilements, you directly penetrate and are liberated. You have from the beginning been in this place; it is not something that is new to you today.[17]

This presentation of meditation was mainly taught in the Caodong school, known as the Soto school when it was brought to Japan in the thirteenth century. Despite the clear relationship between silent illumination and earlier Zen meditation instructions, it was criticized by contemporary exponents of the practice of 'viewing the phrase'. Their practice was the contemplation of key phrases drawn from the classic stories of Zen masters. Unlike silent illumination, the teachers of this practice did emphasize effort and meditation, as this instruction from Dahui shows:

> You must in one fell swoop break through this one thought – then and only then will you comprehend birth and death. Then and only then will it be called accessing awakening.[18]

Thus the practice of contemplating key phrases was part of a radically sudden approach to enlightenment. Students were warned not to understand the phrase logically, or in accordance with Buddhist doctrine or indeed any specific method. The literature associated with the practice is also suggestive rather than instructive, introducing and elaborating on the key phrases with the poetic and metaphorical language of the Chinese literati. The school which specialized in these practices was called Linji, which became known as Rinzai when it travelled to Japan.[19]

Following this peak in the Song dynasty, the fortunes of Zen ebbed and flowed. After a long period of decline, the seventeenth century saw a revival of the Linji lineage in China, with an emphasis on returning to the principles and practice of the 'golden age' of the Zen teachers of the Tang dynasty. This movement also had a significant impact on Zen in Japan, Korea and Vietnam, as Chinese monks travelled to these countries to promote the new dispensation. Zen remained an important aspect of Chinese Buddhism through to the great cataclysm of the Communist era, and has begun to recover in recent decades.

Zen was an organic part of Buddhist life in China, but never developed into a separate school, unlike elsewhere in Asia. Zen monks lived in the same monasteries and carried out the same monastic rituals as other monks, and, unlike in Japan and Korea, Zen in China never became identified with one or two specific meditation practices.[20] It is still common practice to describe Chinese (and sometimes Vietnamese and Korean) Zen as 'eclectic' or 'syncretistic'. Yet this is taking things backwards. It was the later Zen schools that narrowed the range of Zen meditation practices.[21]

Zen in Japan

It was in the thirteenth century that Zen schools first began to develop in Japan, though monks had been teaching and practising Zen there for centuries. The two main schools of Japanese Zen, Soto and Rinzai, both come from that period. The Soto school's founder was Dogen (1200–53), a monk who travelled to China to discover the true teachings on Zen, which he felt were not available in Japan. On his return to Japan he began to teach sitting meditation (zazen). Dogen gathered a devoted group of students who built a monastery for him, and wrote extensively on all aspects of Zen and the Buddhist path. The book that is considered his masterwork, *Shōbōgenzō*, is a collection of his sermons, written down between 1231 and his death in 1253.[22]

The same period saw the emergence of the Rinzai school, which was introduced to Japan by the monk Esai (1141–1215), who specifically sought the patronage of the ruling samurai class. Esai wrote in his book *Promoting Zen for Protecting the Country* that 'rituals performed at Zen monasteries commemorating imperial birthdays, invoking the names of the buddhas, repaying the emperor's kindness, and so on, are all designed to enhance the imperial cause and the fortunes of the Japanese state'. After Esai's death, Rinzai teachers continued to gain the support of the samurai class. During the Muromachi period (1336–1573), Rinzai monasteries were favoured by the shoguns and the court, and Zen monks worked in government roles.[23]

Meanwhile, the scholarly writings and strict meditation practices expounded by Dogen and his successors remained a minority interest, and by the seventeenth century, rigorous meditation had largely been abandoned in Zen temples, as Griffith Foulk has shown:

> The typical Zen temple thus became a place where a resident priest or abbot and a few assistant monks performed funerals and memorial services for their lay parishioners and perhaps engaged them in other Buddhist practices as well, such as receiving the precepts or repentances or celebrating the Buddha's birthday or his nirvāṇa.[24]

In the eighteenth century, a new wave of Chinese Zen teachers arrived in Japan; they called themselves Obaku, and set up monasteries in which monks followed the monastic code (*vinaya*) and engaged in regular meditation sessions. Both the Soto and Rinzai schools had to respond to this challenge, and were subjected to reforms. As had happened in China, these reforms were based on the idea of returning to the principles of the 'golden age' of Zen, and as well as bringing back dedicated periods of meditation, emphasized monastic discipline and activities such as regular work in the monastery gardens for monks.

At the same time, the practice of examining koans in the Rinzai school was revitalized by Hakuin Ekaku, who emphasized the psychological aspect of grappling with a koan, which he called 'great doubt'. Hakuin was also the originator of what is now the most famous koan, 'What is the sound of one hand clapping?' In Hakuin's autobiographical works he often wrote of his own experiences of awakening, which were linked to breakthroughs in his contemplation of koans. He taught widely, and to laypeople as well as monks, helping to popularize the Rinzai school once again.

In the present day, Soto remains the largest Zen school in Japan, followed by Rinzai. The school that came from China in the seventeenth century, Obaku, is the third largest. As we have seen, one way that Zen in Japan differed from its Chinese ancestor was the specialization of Zen schools in specific meditation practices. Another was the discarding of the traditional monastic code of conduct, the vinaya.

Instead, Zen schools used the bodhisattva precepts as the vows of ordination.

The bodhisattva precepts emphasize self-discipline and compassionate activity, but they do not include the celibacy that is at the centre of the vinaya tradition. Instead, Zen monks are bound by the rulebooks of their particular monastery.[25] This situation did not immediately lead to abandoning monastic celibacy, but it did open the door to that option. Ordained monks who were married householders became increasingly common, and in the Meiji reformations of the late nineteenth and twentieth centuries the banning of celibacy among all monks made this the rule. This has led to a unique situation in Japan, put succinctly by Richard Jaffe:

> The departure of Japanese Buddhism from the monastic and ascetic emphasis of most other forms of Buddhism is striking. The Japanese Buddhist clergy are unique among Buddhist clerics in that the vast majority are married, but they continue to undergo clerical ordination and are considered members of the sangha (*sôgya*) by both the Buddhist establishment and parishioners alike.[26]

As Jaffe and others have discussed, it may be misleading to continue to use the term 'monk' (and indeed 'nun') in this situation. He suggests 'cleric' or 'minister' as alternatives, and the term 'priest' is probably the most commonly used alternative, despite the Christian connotations that it still evokes.[27]

Zen in Korea and Vietnam

There have been Korean practitioners of Zen since at least the eighth century, when a popular teacher called Reverend Kim was active in China. The Reverend Kim's meditation teachings, which were popular with Chinese students, included reciting the sound of a single syllable until it died away and one rested in a state of nonthought. There is even a place for Kim in the story of how Zen came to Tibet.[28] Other Korean teachers travelled to China as well, with some returning to teach and establish Zen temples in Korea. But it was in the twelfth century that a specifically Korean form of Zen developed in the writings of a teacher called Pojo Chinul (1158–1210). In his time a split had developed between the Buddhist schools which emphasized study of the scriptures, and the Zen schools that dismissed the scriptures and stressed the inherent nature of realization.

Chinul looked to China, and in particular the work of the ninth-century scholar Zongmi, to find an approach to Zen that could unite the immediate realization taught by the Zen school with the central role of the scriptures insisted on by other Buddhist teachers. Like Zongmi, Chinul found the balance in the idea that realization is instantaneous, but practice is gradual; as Zongmi had said, 'the sun rises all at once, but the frost melts step by step'.[29]

In Korea, as in China, Zen monks live and practise in monasteries with monks of other lineages, and their practice is not restricted to one specific form of meditation. Perhaps the most specifically Zen form of meditation practised by these monks is the contemplation of a key phrase from a koan. Unlike in Japan, where monks are expected to work through many koans, in Korea a monk or nun is given a single phrase and will often stay with it for the whole of his or her life. The most common form of this practice is contemplation of the phrase, 'what is this?'[30]

In Vietnam there has always been a strong influence from Chinese Mahayana Buddhism, and it is only in the twentieth century that Theravada gained a significant following in the country. There is a tradition that Zen teachings were brought to Vietnam by an Indian monk as early as the sixth century. However, Zen only achieved a level of popularity and influence in the eleventh century; after this, several Zen lineages were brought to Vietnam by Chinese monks.

The only Zen school established by a Vietnamese was Trúc Lâm ('Bamboo Grove'), which was founded by the emperor Trần Nhân Tông (1258–1308). This courtly Zen incorporated Confucian and Daoist teachings as well. Though the school was relatively short-lived, the idea of the fusion of religious and secular realms was a powerful one, and there have been several revivals of the school up to the modern era. The most important Zen schools in Vietnam today, Lâm Tế and Nguyen-Thieu, were founded in the new dispensation of Zen that was spread by Chinese monks in the seventeenth century. Like the Obaku school in Japan, their monastic rituals came from the Chinese Linji lineages, and included devotional practices for the buddha Amitabha.[31]

In the modern era, Vietnamese Zen has been brought to a global audience by the monk Thich Nhat Hanh. In his teachings and publications on Zen, Thich Nhat Hanh has emphasized Zen's continuity with other forms of Buddhism, and focused on the practical applications of mindfulness and loving kindness. In one of his early publications in English, *Zen Keys*, he begins by writing about a book that was given to him when he first entered the monastic life:

> There is no philosophy at all in this book. All three parts discuss only practical problems. The first part teaches how to calm and concentrate the mind. The second discusses the precepts and other practices essential to monastic life. The third is a beautiful exhortation to Zen students to encourage them to remember that their time and life are precious and should not be vainly dissipated. I was assured that not only young novices begin with this book, but that monks [of] even forty and fifty also followed its prescriptions.[32]

This illustrates the tradition of monastic Zen in Vietnam which Thich Nhat Hanh has adapted to teach lay students in the West. Here, realizing the nature of one's mind is important, but so is cultivating calmness, behaving in an ethical way and contemplating basic Buddhist teachings such as impermanence. He goes on to say that he initially thought that this book was just for preparation and was the beginning of his practice of Zen, but that fifty years later he realizes that it is the very essence of Zen Buddhism.[33]

✦

THE LOST TEXTS OF ZEN

A hidden cave

At the very beginning of the twentieth century, a Chinese monk opened up a hidden cave containing a cache of ancient manuscripts. The hidden cave was part of a spectacular complex of temples and shrines carved into a sandstone cliff, near the town of Dunhuang, in eastern Central Asia. In time, this treasure trove of manuscripts, numbering in the tens of thousands, would revolutionize our understanding of the history of Buddhism in Asia – and Zen Buddhism in particular.

In the decade after the hidden cave was discovered, expeditions from Britain, France, Russia, Japan and the Chinese capital arrived and took bundles of manuscripts back to their own museums and libraries. The town of Dunhuang was a major trading hub, and the manuscripts from the Dunhuang cave are written in a variety of languages, including Chinese, Tibetan, Sanskrit and the forgotten languages of the Silk Road.

As scholars began to work on the manuscripts, they realized that the cave must have been sealed by the beginning of the eleventh century, and the manuscripts sealed within it came from as far back as the fifth century. This means that they offer a unique view into the past of over a thousand years earlier. Most of the manuscripts from the cave are Buddhist, and the picture they present of Buddhism is sometimes quite different from the traditional view today.

Thus in the same period that Zen was being transmitted to the West, the roots of Zen were being questioned by scholars working on the Dunhuang manuscripts. Two very different pictures of Zen were emerging, as James Robson puts it:

> It is now no secret that the Chan/Zen tradition was initially imagined as the pinnacle of Eastern transcendental spiritualism and marketed as an antidote to Western rationalism and materialism by a slew of Chan/Zen apologists fired by Orientalist fantasies and ideological agendas. Their idealized images of an iconoclastic, anti-institutional 'pure' Chan/Zen Buddhism began to receive critical scrutiny at the turn of the twentieth century with the important discovery of thousands of documents in the Dunhuang caves.[1]

Considering the importance of the Dunhuang manuscripts to understanding the roots of Zen, it's worth looking a little more closely into why they were put in the cave and why it was sealed up. Perhaps surprisingly, there is no agreement about this. Marc Aurel Stein was the first explorer to reach the caves and gain access to the manuscripts. In his immense reports of the expedition, *Serindia*, he speculates about why the manuscripts were placed in the cave. He suggests that they were essentially discarded books, which nobody needed any more but which could not be destroyed because of their sacred, Buddhist content. They were, in his influential phrase, 'sacred waste'.[2]

This idea was widely accepted by Dunhuang scholars like Akira Fujieda, and many still argue for it. In China it has a name: *feiqi shuo*, the 'waste theory'. Yet this theory doesn't easily explain all the nonreligious manuscripts in the cave, or the many beautiful and complete manuscripts (and paintings too). Moreover, this apparently pragmatic explanation doesn't really engage with Buddhist ritual practice.

Stein actually had a more nuanced view than this. In *Serindia* he mentions that some of the bundles of manuscripts looked as if they had been picked up and deposited in the cave as a religious (or as he put it, 'superstitious') act. This touches on a truth that the description 'sacred waste' does not – that the act of depositing manuscripts can itself be a religious act. But what kind of religious act might lie behind depositing manuscripts in a cave? We know that in many ancient Buddhist cultures, scriptures and other texts were considered to be equivalent to relics. Richard Salomon writes of the Gandhari scrolls discovered in Afghanistan, the earliest Buddhist manuscripts:

> It can be safely assumed that the manuscripts in question, regardless of their specific character or condition, were understood and treated as relics. The status of their written representations of the words of the Buddha as dharma-relics, functionally equivalent to bodily relics of the Buddha or other Buddhist venerables, is widely acknowledged in the Buddhist tradition. Thus, the essential motivation for interring manuscripts is obvious; it was a form of relic dedication.[3]

Understanding the Dunhuang cave manuscripts as relics in this way brings us closer to the world of the Buddhist monks who lived there. If the manuscripts were 'functionally equivalent' to the body of the Buddha, every time someone deposited a manuscript in the cave it was a ritual act, pregnant with symbolism and operating in the system of merit creation and dedication. To understand why this particular cave came to have this function, we need to look at who it was made for in the first place.

The abbot's story

In Dunhuang during the eighth and ninth centuries there was a monk called Hongbian. He was Chinese, but he grew up at a time when Dunhuang was ruled by the Tibetan empire. So, like everybody else in the city, he wore Tibetan clothes, and learned to read and write the Tibetan language. Because he was from the wealthy Wu family, he quickly rose in the ranks, eventually becoming one of the most senior monks in Dunhuang. This brought him into contact with orders that came from the emperor of Tibet himself.

More than once, the Tibetan emperor commanded that the city of Dunhuang should make hundreds of copies of Buddhist sutras in Tibetan. The copying of these sutras was a massive undertaking, almost turning the whole city into a scriptorium. Hundreds of (mostly Chinese) scribes copied the sacred Tibetan syllables onto loose-leaf pages and scrolls. The result was a series of monumental volumes of the *Perfection of Wisdom Sutra*, and many hundreds of scrolls of the *Sutra of Aparimitāyus*. Many of these mass-produced sutras survive today because several thousand of them were placed in the Dunhuang cave.

So Hongbian's home was one of the major centres of copying Buddhist scriptures for the Tibetan empire. He was still there when the Tibetan rulers were forced out of Dunhuang in 848. A few years later, he rose to the eminent position of head of the Buddhist sangha in the whole of Hexi, roughly equivalent to the modern Gansu province. Around the same time, Hongbian and his wealthy relatives paid for the excavation of a large cave shrine in the Dunhuang cave site. It was actually the third cave that he had commissioned, and all three now formed three storeys of a cave temple.

This large new cave temple (now known as Cave 16) contained a small antechamber (Cave 17). It might have been a meditation retreat, or perhaps it was just for the storage of supplies. In any case, after Hongbian's death in 862, it was converted into a memorial shrine with a statue of the revered monk in meditation, perhaps with his ashes beneath it. An inscribed stone recording his achievements was also placed in the cave. Over the next one hundred years, Cave 17 came to be filled to bursting with manuscripts, and Hongbian's statue was taken out and put in the cave temple above.

The massive volumes of Tibetan *Perfection of Wisdom* sutras found in the Dunhuang cave were of so little interest to Chinese scholars in the twentieth century that most of them remained untouched in the stores of the Dunhuang city museum. Yet they might be the key to understanding the manuscript hoard. The cave also held a collection of Tibetan letters addressed to Hongbian. Both sets of manuscripts represent Hongbian's official responsibilities, and they may have been interred in the cave at the same time as the statue and stone inscription, or some years later.

So, perhaps the first batch of manuscripts placed in the cave were those that belonged to Hongbian himself. These could have been the seed for future deposits of manuscripts and paintings collected by other monks who had passed away, until the cave gradually became a repository for manuscripts. In other words, the old abbot who built the cave died, a statue of him was placed inside it, and then his letters and books, and those of other people too, and then so many more manuscripts that his statue had to be taken upstairs. Other people, born long after the cave was first made, came and performed rituals there, and more manuscripts were deposited, until the cave was filled to the brim, and was closed.[4]

We still don't know why the cave was sealed. Several people have suggested that it was done to protect Buddhist manuscripts from the threat of invasion. By the end of the tenth century, Islamic armies were threatening the Buddhist kingdoms of the Silk Road, and the monks of Dunhuang might have feared the destruction of their books. But there are problems with this theory. For one, there never was an Islamic invasion, so one wonders why the monks didn't open up the cave again to retrieve their manuscripts.

It is also worth noting that after the cave was sealed up, the resulting wall was painted with a new mural of Buddhist images. Such a treatment implies a considered and time-consuming process, rather than a sudden retreat. So it is quite possible that no real or imagined invasion was behind the sealing of the cave. A more prosaic explanation could suffice: by the beginning of the eleventh century Hongbian's cave was almost completely full and had outlived all of its uses. The main motivation for covering it and painting the wall may have been that a patron was willing to sponsor a new set of murals.[5] Sometimes the least exciting explanation works best. In any case, the result of the sealing of the cave, and its uncovering 900 years later, was one of the most dramatic finds in the history of archaeology.

Rethinking Zen's history

Since the manuscripts from the Dunhuang cave date from the tenth century and earlier, they are from just before the time when Zen really came to prominence in China. As we have seen, it was during the Song dynasty, mainly in the eleventh and twelfth centuries, that the classic compilations of stories of the Zen masters were published, fixing in place the version of Zen's history that has been passed down to the present day. What the Dunhuang manuscripts show is that this version did not really describe that history, but reimagined it based on earlier texts that were later forgotten.

Of the thousands of manuscripts found in the Dunhuang cave, some 350 are related to Zen Buddhism. These texts include collections of sayings by famous teachers, dialogues between teachers and students, scholarly treatises, commentaries and prefaces, and historical and biographical accounts of Zen monks. It is the last group of texts that has been the focus of most modern scholars, who have used these early accounts to challenge and complexify the later, traditional histories.[6]

Since the middle of the twentieth century, scholars have used these Dunhuang Zen texts to discover the works of nearly forgotten Zen teachers, to show the flimsy ground on which claims about the most celebrated figures are based, and to cast a sceptical eye on the political activities of some Zen masters. One of the things that these histories show is that the lineage of Zen was not the orderly succession of enlightened masters that one finds in later literature. Rather, there were struggles between factions, bitter criticism and the creative fashioning of lineages by some factions to assert their authority over others. One of the harshest critics of these early Chan texts, Alan Cole, puts it like this:

> To offer a slightly humorous analogy for the challenge that the Dunhuang texts present, imagine that you moved to a small town in Virginia, and once you became a regular at the corner bar, you began hearing from the locals how the town mayor was related to

George Washington and that was why his tenure as a mayor was so successful. That was interesting enough, but then one day when you ventured across town to another bar, you heard that it was actually the previous town mayor who was really Washington's descendant, a mayor who happened to be the bartender's cousin. Then, a short time later, when the campaign warmed up for the next mayor, it was widely rumoured that the new figure contesting the incumbent mayor was, in fact, the one really related to George Washington. What would you do with all these stories about the connection between leadership in the present and some distant ancestor?[7]

Time and again, it seems that most of the details of the stories of Zen masters cannot be verified the further back we go, until there is very little left at all that is historically verifiable. This goes for Bodhidharma, the founding figure of Zen, and for many others who followed him. The exposure of the Zen tradition to historical analysis has resulted in some disenchantment, yet this challenge is not really any different from that which has been faced by any religious tradition that has been placed under the scrutiny of historians.

And as with these other traditions, academic scholars and believers are often pitted against each other, the former accusing the latter of naivety, while the latter accuse the former of missing the point entirely. As we have seen, some Zen practitioners and scholars (and some who are both) have proposed a way of avoiding a stand-off between those inside and those outside the tradition by suggesting that history does matter, but that it makes little difference to the way the stories of Zen teachers are used in actual practice.

There are also more positive aspects of the discovery of early Zen texts, in that we now know more about how Zen came to be. The story of how Huineng bested Shenxiu in a poetry competition has been shown to be a fiction that helped elevate one lineage of Zen at the expense of another. Yet we now know much more of Shenxiu's lost lineage of Zen, the teachers and practices of what came to be known as 'the Northern School'. Although they were forgotten, these early Zen teachings can help us understand the roots of Zen from which the traditions of today have grown.

One of the most important things the *Masters of the Lanka* and other early Zen manuscripts show us is that teaching Zen is about how best to approach meditation, without falling into the extremes of clinging to one specific kind of practice or denying the value of practice entirely. This way of teaching continued through the centuries, though it is sometimes obscured by rhetoric (never more so than in the Western appropriation of Zen) and it can be seen as the 'family resemblance' that all Zen traditions have, up to the present day.

Introducing the *Masters of the Lanka*

The canonical account of the lives and teachings of the main teachers or 'patriarchs' of the Zen tradition is the *Record of the Transmission of the Lamp* (*Chuandeng lu*). The image of 'the transmission of the lamp' is a metaphor for the passing down of the state of realization from teacher to student through the generations. This English translation is a little clumsy, suggesting a kind of handing over of a lantern from one person to another. It should actually be thought of as lighting one lamp or torch from another, so the flame continues, though there is nothing that can be grasped in the act of transmission.

The *Transmission of the Lamp* is a massive work in some thirty volumes. It coherently traces the teachers in the Zen lineage through every generation in India and China, with a single representative for each generation. By contrast, what we get from the Dunhuang manuscripts are several different works presenting competing versions of the early Zen lineage in China. The *Record of the Masters and Students of the Lanka* (*Lenqie shizi ji*) is one of these lineage histories, dating back to the early eighth century. Two other significant lineage texts were also discovered among the Dunhuang cave manuscripts: one written slightly earlier, the *Record of the Transmission of the Dharma Jewel* (*Chuan fabao ji*), and one written several decades later, the *Record of the Genealogy of the Dharma Jewel* (*Lidai fabao ji*).[8]

The *Masters of the Lanka* begins with a preface by a Zen monk called Jingjue, in which he writes about how he came to Zen Buddhism, and achieved a level of realization thanks to the Zen teacher Shenxiu. He goes on to offer an eloquent and profound exposition of the path to awakening. After this, the *Masters of the Lanka* goes back to the beginning of the lineage in China. Unlike virtually all other Zen lineage texts, in this one Bodhidharma is not considered the teacher who brought the transmission to China. That honour goes to Guṇabhadra, the Indian Buddhist scholar who travelled to China in the fifth century and worked on the first Chinese translation of the *Laṅkāvatāra sūtra*.

There is no personal teacher–student connection between Guṇabhadra and the next in the line, Bodhidharma; instead, the connection is the *Laṅkāvatāra sūtra* itself. The *Laṅkāvatāra* is still held in high regard by many Zen teachers. Some continue the tradition of the *Masters of the Lanka* in considering it the most relevant sutra for practitioners of Zen. But why this sutra in particular? The translator Red Pine, in the introduction to his own translation of the sutra, writes:

> If there ever was a sutra that presented the underlying teaching of Zen, this is it. It is unrelenting in its insistence on the primacy of personal realisation and is unlike any other teaching attributed to the Buddha in this regard.[9]

The *Laṅkāvatāra* is one of hundreds of Mahayana sutras, scriptures of the greater vehicle of Buddhism, all said to be the word of the Buddha, though modern scholarship suggests that they were written later, mostly from around the first century BC to the fifth century AD. The *Laṅkāvatāra* is one of the most revered of the sutras, and also one of the most complex. In it, many of the fundamental doctrines of Mahayana thought are laid out clearly, including the division of reality into three levels and consciousness into eight aspects.[10]

In the *Masters of the Lanka* we hear about Bodhidharma taking the *Laṅkāvatāra* as the basis for his teachings, and handing it on to his student Huike. The next chapters take one figure in each generation who carries forward the lineage of the *Laṅkāvatāra*. After Bodhidharma comes his student Huike, and then his student Sengcan. Apart from their place in the Zen lineage, these two teachers are obscure, and little is known about the content of their teachings.

In contrast, the section on the next teacher, Daoxin, is by far the longest, as it contains his own writings on meditation practice. This is really the centrepiece of the *Masters of the Lanka*. Next comes Hongren, who founded the East Mountain teaching tradition. Out of his many students, the *Masters of the Lanka* focuses on Shenxiu, who was favoured by the Empress Wu. The final part of the text looks briefly at some of Shenxiu's students, taking us to the generation of Jingjue, the author of the preface.

The *Masters of the Lanka* differs from all the other early Zen lineage texts in its focus on teaching over biography. The life stories of the teachers are relatively brief, and most of the work is given over to their teachings. There is no single orthodox teaching, no rejection of one way of practising over another; instead, the *Masters of the Lanka* brings together several different trends that were emerging in Zen practice at the time.[11]

Teachers of the Northern School

The *Masters of the Lanka* begins with the preface by Jingjue, and for this reason he is usually considered the author of the text. Yet Jingjue's preface is not found in the Tibetan translation, which is earlier than the surviving Chinese versions. Even if the preface was originally part of the text, it seems to have been put together from different sources, possibly by students of Jingjue. And much of the rest of the *Masters of the Lanka* is also derived from other sources, most of which are now lost. In the manuscripts themselves, the *Masters of the Lanka* is said to have been 'compiled' by Jingjue, rather than composed by him.[12]

Furthermore, when we work from manuscripts, we need to keep in mind that what we have are always copies of copies of copies (and so onwards). At each stage in copying, a scribe may have added or omitted some parts of the text, intentionally or by mistake. In the Buddhist context we know that monks copying sutras tried to reproduce the text exactly, though they were not always successful. But for texts that were not the words of the Buddha, there was much less scruple about adding explanatory glosses, suitable quotations from scripture or bits of texts found in other sources.

The *Masters of the Lanka* looks as if it developed in just this way. The various Chinese manuscripts and the Tibetan translation of the *Masters of the Lanka* all differ from each other, and missing text at the end of some of the chapters in the Tibetan translation suggests that copyists added passages to the ends of chapters at different stages in the transmission of the text. Thus the *Masters of the Lanka* is interdependent in both senses of this Buddhist concept: it is a composite thing, based on parts coming from different sources, and it changed over time as it was copied again and again from one manuscript to another.[13]

For these reasons I will avoid referring to Jingjue as the 'author' of the *Masters of the Lanka*. This in itself is misleading, but to take the further step of speculating about Jingjue's authorial practice and motivations would really be to build an elaborate structure on a basis of shifting sands. Still, even if we can't in all honesty call Jingjue an author as we usually understand the word, he is still a key figure in the *Masters of the Lanka*, and his preface contains some of the most poetic and pithy teachings on the path of Zen in the text. He also lived at the centre of a turbulent and creative period in Chinese history, when the Empress Wu brought an end (if only temporarily) to the Tang dynasty.

Jingjue was from one of China's noble families, rivals to Empress Wu; his sister, the princess Wei, had risen to become a threat to the empress. When Wu took power, Jingjue's sister was exiled, and his brothers were killed. Later, after the death of Empress Wu in 705, her son became emperor again, but his wife (who was Jingjue's sister) was the true ruler, becoming known for a time as Empress Wei. During her reign, Jingjue returned to the capital, where he was offered a political appointment. However, he turned this down, choosing to be ordained as a Buddhist monk under Shenxiu instead.

Along with other students of Shenxiu, Jingjue came to be known as a follower of the Northern School of Zen in China. However, this name was not used by Jingjue or his teachers and actually originated in criticisms of these teachers by a radical monk called Shenhui, who called his own teaching lineage 'the Southern School'.[14]

In his sermons and writings, Shenhui attacked the most successful exponents of Chinese Zen: Shenxiu and his disciples. In particular, Shenhui attacked the Northern School for its practices, which he claimed fostered the idea that enlightenment was to be gradually cultivated. He claimed that his Southern School was for those who understood the truth, that enlightenment is a sudden revelation. Needless to say, this was an oversimplification. The tension between the cultivation of practice, which unfolds over time, and the experience of enlightenment, which is timeless, is present in all Zen traditions, and many other Buddhist traditions as well.[15]

In any case, it is wrong to talk about 'schools' of Zen in China. In fact, it is misleading to think that there were distinct, institutionally separate schools of Buddhism in China at all. The actual situation has been well summarized by Morten Schlütter:

> Differences between Chinese Buddhist schools did not develop into strict sectarian divisions, and sects or denominations like those known in later Japanese Buddhism or in Protestant Christianity were never established. Although distinct trends within Buddhist thought and practice did emerge in China, they were rarely understood to be mutually exclusive, and many monastics studied within several of the schools. Throughout Chinese history, anyone becoming a monastic was ordained into the wider Buddhist order, not into any particular school or tradition.[16]

The clearest distinction between different approaches to Zen in the period is made by Zongmi in his preface to a compendium of Zen texts in a passage I quoted earlier:

Chan has various lineages that conflict with one another. In fact the writings collected herein are like the one hundred contending schools of China's classical age. However, differences in the principles of their axioms involve only ten houses.[17]

Here Zongmi's 'schools' are clearly schools of thought rather than religious institutions. Furthermore, Zongmi tells us that what he calls 'ten houses' is his own artificial construction to make sense of the vast range of teachings and practices going by the name of Zen in his time; these are not historical schools as we understand them. So if Zongmi was writing about different doctrinal approaches to Zen rather than social groups, what was the social situation?

The picture was more like this: there were social groups with a meditation teacher at their centre. One of these teachers, Shenxiu, achieved high visibility thanks to the patronage of the empress. The success of Shenxiu and his students meant that other teaching lineages had to struggle for prominence. From the eighth century onwards, some of these groups followed Shenxiu, while others had accepted the alternative figure of Huineng as the true successor to Bodhidharma's teaching. In both cases, the idea of lineage and transmission came to be much more important than it was before.[18]

The more successful of these groups received some patronage and were able to circulate texts of their teachers' works, and increasingly those of the lineage as well. These successful teachings tended to go into a melting pot of Zen instruction, as the Dunhuang manuscripts show. The manuscripts contain many collections of Zen texts, drawn from teachers who supposedly represented different schools. This suggests that there was little or no concern for school affiliations when using teachings for the purpose of practice. That is, if there were schools of Zen that adhered only to texts and practices of their own tradition, there is no evidence of this.[19]

So what of the Northern School? Since there never really was a tradition that called itself by this name, it is more like a catch-all term for the teachings of the *Masters of the Lanka* and other texts associated with Shenxiu's lineage. We know about most of these texts because so many of them survived in the cave of manuscripts in Dunhuang.

It is often said that Shenhui's polemics spelled the end of the Northern School of Zen, which was over by the early ninth century. Yet there is no sign from the Dunhuang manuscripts that the works associated with Shenxiu and his students were any less popular than other Zen writings, even up to the end of the tenth century. In other words, there is no reason to think that this teaching tradition died out before the Song dynasty, when so much of earlier Zen teaching was either forgotten or reformulated into something new. So in the *Masters of the Lanka,* we see not so much the specific teachings of the 'Northern School' but rather a window into the teachings of Zen before the Song dynasty. These are the roots of Zen.

Critical views of the *Masters of the Lanka*

Recent studies of the *Masters of the Lanka* and other early Zen lineage texts have taken a highly critical view of the literature. Much academic scholarship has argued that these texts are primarily political, that they were written to validate the role of a particular teacher and his lineage. In the case of the *Masters of the Lanka*, scholars have taken a suspicious view of Jingjue, arguing that the text is his way of inserting himself into Shenxiu's East Mountain lineage.

The most extreme example of this tendency to apply the least charitable, and most suspicious, interpretation of the text and the motives of its author is Alan Cole's *Fathering Your Father*. In this book Cole paints Jingjue as an 'arriviste' who fabricated a lineage of Zen teachers by plagiarizing previous texts. Cole even argues that Jingjue's teacher Xuanze never existed, but was invented by Jingjue as part of the latter's attempt to insert himself into the lineage.[20]

Though this critique might seem hard-nosed and realistic, it is actually based on a series of assumptions and speculations that render it quite flimsy. The first is the assumption that the modern model of publishing, where there is an author and a reading public, applies to pre-modern China. As we have seen, even to identify Jingjue as 'author' in the sense that we use the word today is highly speculative and almost certainly misleading. As for the 'reading public', it is not clear who this would be in pre-modern China – the elite literati, or the more educated Buddhist monks? The argument that Jingjue was duping innocent readers by fabricating a Zen lineage for himself relies on the idea of an avid but ignorant lay audience. But there is no evidence at all that such an audience existed. As James Robson has written in a review of the book, 'Cole's repeated claims about a complicit public "readership" or "adoring audience" are merely unproven suppositions.'[21]

Scholars like Cole sometimes castigate pre-modern writers like Jingjue for being poor historians, as if they were academic colleagues. Yet the reasons for the existence of a text like the *Masters of the Lanka* do not include 'history' as we understand the word. Even if we take the leap and call Jingjue an author, he was certainly never a historian. Likewise, accusations of plagiarism are commonly levelled at Jingjue and other authors of these Chan lineage texts, but this is completely anachronistic, as Robson points out:

> Whereas the practice of building upon previous texts without attribution was standard in Chinese writing, Cole presents the authors as plagiarists and forgers. Modern conceptions of plagiarism and standards of citation did not, however, apply to early historical writing. As Marc Bloch noted, plagiarism 'was at this time universally regarded as the most innocent act in the world. Annalists and hagiographers shamelessly appropriated entire passages from the writings of earlier authors.'[22]

This was true for most forms of writing in China, and indeed in other pre-modern cultures as well. Historical texts are created as a patchwork of what has been written before; there is no intellectual property, and therefore no plagiarism.

Since Cole spends little time on the actual Dunhuang manuscripts – the only surviving sources of the *Masters of the Lanka* – he misses some of the more pertinent questions. Why was the text circulating in several copies in Dunhuang in the ninth and tenth centuries? Who was using it? For what purposes? One clue is in the manuscript containing the Tibetan translation of the *Masters of the Lanka*. On the other side of the manuscript there is another text, written for teachers, about how to guide students learning and practising meditation. Could the *Masters of the Lanka* have served the same pragmatic purpose, as a resource for meditation teachers?

As I have mentioned, what distinguishes the *Masters of the Lanka* from other early Zen lineage histories is the amount of the text that is dedicated to what the masters of the lineage taught. Whereas other accounts focus on life stories and miracles, the majority of the *Masters of the Lanka* passes briefly over these and concentrates on teaching and practice. Whether or not these teachings are accurate representations of what these masters actually taught, they were certainly some of the earliest Zen teachings to be put into writing. So reading the *Masters of the Lanka* in order to understand something about the practice of Zen in its formative period is not necessarily naive.

But this is not an either/or decision. The sphere of religious (or 'spiritual') practice cannot be separated from the sphere of social interactions and political manoeuvring, as Wendi Adamek has written in her study of another early Zen lineage text:

> In Zen contexts, realisation of emptiness and 'just sitting' are characterised as nondual. How pure! At the same time, inevitably, disputes arise over how to *teach* people to experience nonduality. How to express and transmit the inexpressible is a challenge in all soteriological contexts. Paraphrasing the famous *Heart Sutra* phrase, 'form is emptiness, emptiness is form,' we could say, 'soteriology is politics, politics is soteriology'.[23]

✦

CHAPTER FIVE

EARLY ZEN MEDITATION

Principles and practice in the *Masters of the Lanka*

We know surprisingly little about the actual practices taught by the teachers of the classic period of Zen. Most early writings on Zen are about principles rather than practice. Even Zongmi, the most perceptive commentator on the Zen teachings of his time, has little to say about practice.[1] This makes the *Masters of the Lanka* especially important. Presenting the Zen masters mainly in terms of their teachings, it contains clear and specific instructions on how to sit in meditation. Each section of the *Masters of the Lanka* gives us a different view of Zen, a different angle on the principles and practices that inform Zen.

Jingjue

Much of Jingjue's preface is concerned with explaining the concept of emptiness. This ties in with his other known work, a commentary on the *Heart Sutra*, one of the key texts of the perfection of wisdom literature, in which emptiness plays a key role. For Jingjue, it is important to understand that emptiness is not nothingness; rather, emptiness is seen in the very functioning of life. Emptiness and activity are the same thing. In terms of practice, the inseparability of emptiness and function means that mental stillness is not privileged over mental activity. That is, meditation practice is not the suppression of thoughts and emotions, but just sitting in the emptiness of thoughts and emotions as they arise.

Guṇabhadra

The teachings of Guṇabhadra as presented in the *Masters of the Lanka* almost certainly don't originate with the translator himself. What we have is a picture of an Indian monk arriving in China, and being dismayed by the misrepresentations and abuses of the Buddha's teaching that he sees there. In this chapter, Guṇabhadra comes across as a fire-and-brimstone preacher, warning his audience of dire consequences if they continue in their misguided ways. He categorizes those who seek peace of mind into four types: (i) ordinary people, (ii) hearers (i.e. hinayana practitioners), (iii) bodhisattvas and (iv) those who recognize the buddha in their own mind. Guṇabhadra, who apparently was also known by the name 'Mahayana', also gives a teaching on the nature of the greater vehicle, giving the six perfections in a Zen interpretation.

Bodhidharma

The *Two Entrances and Four Practices* is the only text attributed to Bodhidharma that is generally accepted in modern scholarship as representing Bodhidharma's actual teachings. It is presented in its entirety in the *Masters of the Lanka*. This brief teaching brings together the sudden and gradual approaches to enlightenment in a single system. The two entrances are: (i) entrance by principle, which is to practise sitting meditation with a firm confidence that one's own mind is the same as the Buddha's, and (ii) entrance by practice, a series of four contemplations, which act as antidotes to harmful mental states. These four are (i) when one is suffering, contemplating that this is the result of one's past actions, (ii) when one is experiencing good fortune, contemplating the fact that this too is only temporary, and cannot be relied upon, (iii) as an antidote to attachment, contemplating that suffering is inevitable in existence and ceasing to seek anything, and (iv) practising the dharma itself, which is the practice of the six perfections without conceptualization.

Huike

Little is said about actual practice in the chapter on Huike. But, more than Bodhidharma, he emphasizes the role of sitting meditation above any other kind of practice. In Huike's teaching here, sitting meditation is a way of recognizing the buddha nature which has always been present in oneself. The only difference between ordinary people and buddhas is that the latter have recognized their own nature in meditation. The other main thrust of Huike's teachings here is a negative one: not to get distracted by books and ideas. A picture of food, he says, will not assuage your hunger, and always talking about food leaves no time for eating. The main thing is to realize that the enlightened state is already present in one's own body and mind.

Sengcan

The teachings of Sengcan are given here in his own words, through a commentary on a contemporary Zen master's teachings. Though this teaching does not deal with practice, it sets out some fundamental principles that inform meditation practice. At the centre of this work is the image of Indra's net, a network of jewels, each of which contains reflected images of every other jewel in the net. This is a metaphor for the fundamental interconnectedness of all things, the Buddhist concept of dependent origination. The teaching states that 'a single atom contains all the phenomena of the universe; a single moment contains all the times of past, present and future'. This is why the categories that we use to understand and interact with the world do not define the nature of reality, as nothing can exist independently of anything else.

Daoxin

The long chapter on Daoxin reproduces a complete work called *Methods for the Bodhisattva Precepts*, followed by some of his teachings intended for beginners on practising sitting meditation. The *Methods for the Bodhisattva Precepts* is a record of a sermon, which according to its title was given to groups who had gathered for the ceremony of taking the bodhisattva vow. These ceremonies could be attended by both monastics and laypeople, and usually involved a sermon as well as the ritual of taking the vow. So this is an early example of Zen sermons given in the context of the bodhisattva precepts ceremony, of which the *Platform Sutra* is the most famous. Daoxin's meditation teachings are by far the most detailed in the *Masters of the Lanka*, and for that reason I will discuss them separately below.

Hongren

While the chapter on Hongren is mainly concerned with his life and his students, there is a brief passage on his meditation teachings. These involve visualizations: first, of a single syllable as a focus for concentration, and second, visualizing oneself sitting on top of a mountain, and seeing the whole world around. There are some similarities between Hongren's instructions and the tantric meditation practices that were beginning to arrive in China around the same time.

Shenxiu

As in the chapter on Hongren, there is little direct teaching on meditation attributed to Shenxiu (though there are other sources for his teachings found among the Dunhuang manuscripts). Most of the teaching given by Shenxiu here is in the form of questions along the lines of, 'When you see forms do they have form?' He is also said to have pointed to things like a bird flying past and asked 'What is this?' A similar style of questioning is attributed to Guṇabhadra and others in the *Masters of the Lanka*, but since those passages are not found in the Tibetan translation, they may be later additions. It is more likely that this method of asking questions emerged around the time of Shenxiu and his students. In any case, this method of teaching through questions seems to be an early forerunner of the Zen koan, even if it is not the fully formed practice of koan contemplation.

Mindfulness of the Buddha

As I mentioned earlier, the most detailed instructions in the *Masters of the Lanka* on how to sit in meditation are found in Daoxin's chapter. This chapter includes the complete texts of Daoxin's *Dharma Teachings for the Bodhisattva Precepts*, which begins with a teaching on a meditation practice called 'single practice concentration'. This is a form of meditation that is focused on a single buddha. Why would that need to be emphasized? In the mahayana there are, of course, many buddhas, and therefore many different practices focused on those buddhas. The point of the single practice concentration is that it is not necessary to perform the meditation practices of all buddhas in order to attain enlightenment; this needs emphasizing in a situation where new practices featuring different buddhas and bodhisattvas are being translated and taught all the time.

Daoxin begins his teaching on this practice with a quote from a sutra; this is the key passage from the sutra describing the actual 'single practice concentration':

> Focus your mind on a single buddha and only recite his name. With an upright posture, facing towards the place where the buddha resides, stay constantly mindful of this single buddha. In this state of mind, you will be able to see every buddha of the past and future clearly manifest.

This passage gives us a clear picture of the practice that Daoxin is teaching here. One focuses one's mind on a buddha of choice; this would probably involve visualization, a practice that was already well known in China at the time. At the same time, one recites the name of that buddha over and over again.[2] One sits upright, and faces in the direction of where that buddha resides – the pure realms of buddhas are associated with a particular direction, the most famous being Amitabha's pure land in the west.

Through being constantly mindful in this way, the meditator will be granted visions of all the buddhas – not just the one who has been the subject of this meditation. This is possible because there is no difference between the buddhas and the totality of the world itself (the term is *fǎjiè* in Chinese, *dharmadhātu* in Sanskrit). So to be mindful of one buddha is to be mindful of all buddhas, and to be mindful of all buddhas is to be at one with the nature of reality itself.

To some extent, Daoxin wants to revise these meditation instructions in his own version of the single practice concentration. For one thing, he sees no reason to face in any specific direction:

> Once you know that mind, from the start, has never arisen or ceased to be, and has always been pure, then you know that it is identical with the pure lands of the buddhas, so there is no longer any need to face the pure land in the west.

That is to say, if the pure land is found in your own mind, it doesn't matter which way you face. On the other hand, Daoxin does not apply this to every meditator: it is only for those who have understood the nature of mind. For those people, the key point is that the pure land is present here and now. Daoxin goes on to say, 'it is exactly the same as this realm but entirely free from clinging'. So, when one's mind is no longer grasping, one is experiencing a pure land.

While Daoxin questions the idea that one has to face in the direction of the pure land, he does not challenge the basic practice itself – reciting the Buddha's name while visualizing his or her form in one's mind. This practice of mindfulness of the Buddha is *niànfó* in Chinese (pronounced *nembutsu* in Japanese).[3] It is a practice that is strongly associated with the 'pure land' schools, and whenever it is encountered in Zen, there is usually talk of syncretism, of Zen incorporating pure land practices. For example, Andy Ferguson writes: 'By combining Zen practice with more broadly appealing acts of religious piety, Daoxin created a religion that took root in the broad population of Chinese society.'[4]

However, and this can't be stressed enough, *we have no surviving instructions on how to do Zen meditation practice before Daoxin.* So, to the best of our knowledge, from the very beginning of the thing that we call Zen practice, it included visualizing and reciting the name of a buddha. Nobody combined a pre-existing pure form of Zen with other types of practice; Zen emerged out of these practices.

For Daoxin, the purpose of practising mindfulness of the buddha is to get to the point where one is meditating without focusing on anything, a state of mind called 'mindfulness without an object':

> When you are mindful of the buddha continuously through every state of mind, it will simply become clear and calm, and mindfulness will no longer be based on perceptual objects.

This state is perhaps closer to what is taught as 'mindfulness' nowadays. So it is interesting to see that seasoned meditation teachers in the early years of Zen Buddhism did not teach mindfulness without an object straight away. Mindfulness without an object was the culmination of the practice of mindfulness with an object – the visualized form of a buddha and the recited sound of that buddha's name.

The progression to mindfulness without an object is organic, for Daoxin explains that the Buddha is no different from one's mind. Therefore mindfulness of the Buddha is really mindfulness of one's mind, which is mindfulness without an external object:

> Mindfulness of the Buddha is the same state of mind as that which we call 'mindfulness without an object'. There is no separate mind distinct from the Buddha, nor is there a separate buddha distinct from the mind.

This mindfulness without an object leads to a state of mind free from grasping and dualistic thinking. Daoxin concludes: 'When you reach this stage mindfulness of the Buddha fades away, as it is no longer needed.' So the meditation technique of visualizing a buddha and reciting his or her name is to be practised, but it is also eventually left behind, in the realization of nonduality.

Observing the mind

According to Daoxin's meditation teaching in the *Masters of the Lanka*, the meditator eventually reaches a point where all techniques are dropped. There remains a kind of technique that is not a technique, which he calls *observing the mind* (in Chinese, *kànxīn*). As Daoxin makes clear, 'observing' here does not mean examining or analysing. In a pithy instruction written in a four-character metre, Daoxin explains what it means:

> Don't be mindful of the Buddha;
> Don't control the mind;
> Don't examine the mind;
> Don't speculate about the mind;
> Don't deliberate;
> Don't practise analysis;
> Don't become distracted;
> Just let it be.

Obviously, most of these instructions are about what not to do. The meditator has dropped the practice of mindfulness of the Buddha. Having done so, that space is not to be filled with trying to control, examine or analyse the mind. But also, one is not to wander off in distraction. The key phrase here is 'just let it be'; the Chinese term (*rènyùn*) literally means to accept one's fate.[5] Thus this practice of observing the mind means remaining in a state of awareness without getting distracted, but also without attempting to control the mind. This comes very close to how meditation is taught in Zen monasteries and centres to this day.

Later in his sermon, Daoxin refers to a kind of meditation he calls 'to be always aware without interruption', which seems to be the same thing. 'Awareness' here translates the Chinese character *jué*, which has several different meanings in Buddhism. It can mean 'feeling' or 'sensation' (*vedanā* in Sanskrit), a technical term for one aspect of the mind's activity in samsara. Here, and in later Zen texts, it is closer to the latter, denoting a clear and wakeful awareness that is present at all times.

Daoxin considers this practice of observing the mind to be an advanced one, not appropriate to all students of meditation. It results in a direct realization of the nature of mind; as Daoxin says: 'If you can truly observe the mind in this way, you will directly apprehend mind's luminosity and clarity, which is like a bright mirror.' The crucial role of the meditation teacher is to decide whether this kind of advanced practice is appropriate for a particular student or not:

> Thus the way students attain this realization is not always the same, and these differences are due to the fact that currently their inner faculties and outer conditions are not the same. A person who wants to be a teacher must be capable of recognizing these differences.

This eminently practical advice is crucial for understanding early Zen teachings. All we really need to do is rest in the flow of awareness, without analysing or controlling it, or becoming distracted. But this is difficult, and so other methods, such as visualization and intellectual analysis, are taught as preliminaries to help students reach the point where they can simply be aware.

This practice continued to be transmitted by Zen teachers in the generations after Daoxin; for example, the teacher Moheyan, who lived in Dunhuang and was involved in the Tibetan court in the late eighth century, wrote these instructions for meditators:

> When they engage in meditation, they should view their own mind. Since nothing exists there, they have no thoughts. If conceptual thoughts move, they should experience them. 'How should we experience them?' Whatever thoughts arise should not be designated as moving or not moving. They should not be designated as existing or not existing. They should not be designated as virtuous or nonvirtuous. They should not be designated as afflicted or pure. They should not be designated as any kind of phenomenon at all. If the movement of mind is experienced in this way, it has no nature.[6]

Analysis and calmness (vipaśyanā and śamatha)

In his *Dharma Teachings for the Bodhisattva Precepts*, Daoxin describes five main types of meditation practice:

- to recognize mind's essence;
- to recognize mind's activity;
- to be always aware without interruption;
- to see the physical body as empty;
- to maintain oneness without wavering.

Daoxin does teach something that looks very much like the first three types of meditation – especially 'to be always aware' – in the first half of *Dharma Teachings for the Bodhisattva Precepts*. But in the second half, he teaches a meditation method that begins with the fourth, seeing the emptiness of the body, and continues and culminates in the fifth, maintaining the state of oneness.

Seeing the physical body as empty has two perspectives, first from the point of view of an ordinary being, and second from the point of view of a buddha. So first of all the meditator performs a classic Buddhist deconstruction of the body into its physical and mental components. The emptiness of the body means that it has no essence, nothing that constitutes 'me'. When the meditator divides up the body into all these different parts, nothing remains but the parts, and all of these parts are impermanent.

Then the meditator looks at the body from the point of view of enlightenment, imagining their own body as empty and clear like a reflection, endowed with wisdom, which is also like a reflection. This enlightened body, the body of a buddha, spontaneously responds to the needs of beings, without being limited by space and distance.

What we perceive with our six senses (in Buddhism, these are the five physical senses and the mind) are also like reflections in a mirror. As Daoxin puts it: 'Just as a mirror reflects the image of a face with the greatest clarity, forms manifest within emptiness like reflections.' He wants us to imagine a mirror in which reflections appear, but where there is no object causing the reflections; our sense of things being 'out there' is just an objectification of what we experience.

These images and ideas appear in the *Laṅkāvatāra sūtra*. For example:

(Ch.1, IV): Our perceiving consciousness functions like a clear mirror in which shapes and images appear.

(Ch.2, LXIV): Because the various projections of people's minds appear before them as objects, they become attached to the existence of their projections.

(Ch.3, LXXIV): Who doesn't know the mind or conditions / gives rise to projections of duality / once they know projections and the world / projections no longer arise.

In the *Laṅkāvatāra* and in Daoxin's discussion, mind is not like a mirror in the sense that it accurately reflects reality (a concept popular in European philosophy, discussed and criticized in Richard Rorty's *Philosophy and the Mirror of Nature*). Rather, the mirror-like mind is what gives rise to our false assumption that what we perceive is really 'out there'. The enlightened mind is like a mirror too, but it does not grasp the forms that arise within it, projecting them into the outside world as real.[7]

Thus, in this practice, the meditator is imagining what it is to be a buddha, to have that mirror-like mind. When forms appear, they do not grasp them, and so they are naturally empty. As Daoxin says, this emptiness is not contrived; it is the natural state of things. Once the meditator attains the state of enlightenment, all the phenomena of the senses arise free from clinging. When Daoxin says, 'in this sense there is no hearing or seeing', he is referring to frequent statements in the sutras that buddhas do not see or hear. He is saying that this does not mean that enlightened beings exist in a state of blankness, but that they do not see or hear as we understand it. They see and hear without imposing the distinction between what they are and what is out there.

Once the meditator has completed this preliminary practice, they should do the main practice, known as 'maintaining oneness without wavering'. Daoxin teaches this in a clear and direct passage:

> Concentrate your attention on a single object without concern for the passing of time. Continue to focus your energy without moving. If your mind wants to wander off, quickly take it in hand and gather it back, again and again, like using a string attached to a bird's foot to pull it back and catch it when it wants to fly away.

This is a classic form of the calming meditation practice known as 'śamatha' (in Chinese, zhǐ). Found in some form in almost all Buddhist traditions, it is usually paired with the practice of analysis called 'vipaśyanā' (in Chinese, guān). Daoxin's teaching also pairs the two, as the analysis of the body which precedes this meditation is certainly a form of vipaśyanā.

So what does 'maintaining oneness' mean? From Daoxin's instructions, 'oneness' is clearly not meant to be a mystical 'Oneness' with 'the One' as is found in the Daoist tradition. Rather, oneness here is a more prosaic single-mindedness. Indeed, in other traditions, meditation is often described in terms of one-pointed concentration (e.g. in Pali, ekaggata; in the Tibetan tradition, rtse gcig).[8]

While Daoxin does teach the classic pair of śamatha and vipaśyanā, he does it in a particular way, best summed up in his own words: 'This is not an ordinary activity, it is the ultimate truth itself.' That is to say, meditation is not a practice that creates or leads to enlightenment; it is an expression of the inherent enlightenment of our own mind. These practices do not take the meditator anywhere else, since 'aside from the mind, there is no buddha'.

Questions without answers

The koan is one of the quintessential practices of modern Zen, and definitely the practice that has least in common with other Buddhist traditions. Almost every koan comes from a story of an encounter between a teacher and a disciple, and most are an exchange of questions and answers. The *Masters of the Lanka* happens to contain the earliest examples of this kind of teaching; these are not koans, but they appear to be the seeds out of which the koan literature grew.[9]

In the *Masters of the Lanka* we have questions, but not answers – we only hear about what the master asked, not any of the students' responses. These questions appear at the end of the chapters on Guṇabhadra, Bodhidharma, Hongren and Shenxiu. For several reasons, not least that the questions are missing in the Tibetan translation, it is doubtful that Guṇabhadra or Bodhidharma actually used this teaching technique. It is more credible that it might have begun with Hongren or Shenxiu, and it was certainly becoming more widespread in the generation of Shenxiu's students.[10]

The questions in the *Masters of the Lanka* are like some later koans in that they do not allow an easy answer. They are clearly meant to throw the students off track, to challenge their conventional understanding of things. A teaching technique attributed in the text to Bodhidharma illustrates how this would work:

> The great teacher would point his finger at something and ask what it really was. He would just point at a single object, and call upon someone to stand up, and question them about that object. Then he would ask the whole group about the object, substituting another name for the object and asking whether it had changed.

Pointing at an object and asking the students what it 'really is' poses an unanswerable question. Changing the name of the object looks like a way of breaking down the students' conventional understanding of the link between signifier and signified. This technique also appears in the chapters on Guṇabhadra, Hongren and Shenxiu, where the question is always 'What is this?'

> He used to go up to objects and ask a question. For example, he would point to a leaf on a tree and ask, 'What is this?'

'There is a little room that is completely full of excrement, earth and hay. What is this? We sweep and clean away the excrement, earth and hay until it is all gone and not a thing remains. What is this?'

Also, seeing a bird fly past, he would ask, 'What is this?'

The simple question 'What is this?' (in Chinese, *héwù*)[11] is applied to an everyday object or an image such as Hongren's room, and in the teaching context it is clear that the obvious answer ('a bird', 'a leaf') will not suffice. This brings about a situation of uncertainty or doubt, turning the focus back to the question itself. This procedure looks very much like an ancestor of the later koan contemplation on 'key phrases' (*hùatóu*). The most famous of these is the contemplation on the word 'no' (*wú*), as an answer to the question 'Does a dog have the buddha nature?' The conventional answer should be 'Yes', so the 'No' brings about a state of doubt and brings the focus to the nature of the answer.

In contemporary Zen, 'What is this?' also features as a key phrase.[12] It comes from a story about Huineng and his student Huairang. When the latter first visited Huineng, he was asked, 'What is this that comes?' Having contemplated the question for years, Huairang eventually gave his answer: 'To explain or demonstrate anything would miss the mark.' Thus, 'What is this?' is a question which points to the lack of an answer.[13]

Martine Batchelor describes the practice as it is taught in modern Korean Zen:

Whether you are walking, standing, sitting, or lying down, you ask repeatedly, *What is this? What is this?* You have to be careful not to slip into intellectual inquiry, for you are not looking for an intellectual answer. You are turning the light of inquiry back onto yourself and your whole experience in this moment.

She goes on to say that her teacher, Master Kusan (1909–83), told his students that the answer to the question was not an object, because you could not describe it as long or short, this or that colour.[14]

Another kind of question challenges the students' assumptions about the distinction between conventional categories like inside and outside, as in the following questions attributed to Guṇabhadra and Shenxiu:

> In this room there is a jar. Isn't this jar outside the room as well? Isn't the water in the jar? Isn't the jar in the water? Indeed, from the greatest to the smallest of the various rivers and streams, aren't each and every one of them in this jar?

> Does the sound of a bell being struck only exist inside the monastery, or does the sound of the bell pervade the whole universe as well?

Again, the fact that there is no possible answer except the most obvious and banal ('No, the jar is not outside the room as well') throws the attention back on the students' basic assumptions. A similar question, with a striking resemblance to another famous koan, is attributed to Shenxiu:

> It is taught in the *Nirvana Sutra* that the bodhisattva's body has no periphery, yet he came from the east. Since the bodhisattva's body has no periphery or boundary, I ask again, did he come from the east? Why could he not come from the west, or from the south or north? Are they not equally possible?

The famous koan that this brings to mind is the question 'Why did Bodhidharma come from the west?' The question refers to Bodhidharma's journey from India (which was considered to lie to the west, along the Silk Road). On the other hand, Shenxiu's question refers to the Buddha himself, who is said, in the *Mahāparinirvāṇa sūtra*, to have come from eastern India. Yet the Buddha, as the embodiment of the enlightened state, cannot be restricted to any place or time. As we have seen in the visualization practices of Daoxin and Hongren, the body of a buddha is limitless space.

Other questions in the *Masters of the Lanka* target basic concepts and categories more directly (the first is attributed to Bodhidharma, the rest to Shenxiu):

'Does this body exist? Is this body a body?'

'Does this mind have a mind? Is your mind really a mind?'

'When you hear a bell being struck, does the sound exist when it is struck? Does it exist before it is struck? Is sound really sound?'

'When you see forms do they have form? Are forms really forms?'

In the background of these questions, there is emptiness. In Mahayana Buddhism, all categories, including existence and nonexistence, are empty, in that they only work in dependence on each other. This is pointed out in a teaching attributed to Hongren:

Once he picked up two fire tongs, one long and one short, held them up side by side and asked: 'Which one is long? Which one is short?'

These metal tongs are used in hearths and braziers, and in modern Japan they are still used in tea ceremonies. They vary from 25cm to 40cm in length, so in this example Hongren might have had two tongs of different sizes from different sets. In any case, we can imagine him holding them up and asking his students, how are you sure that this one is long and this one is short? Isn't the long one only long when we hold it up next to the short one?

Zen and the art of archery

The title of the famous *Zen and the Art of Motorcycle Maintenance* was inspired by the slightly less famous but still well-known book *Zen in the Art of Archery*. In the latter, Eugen Herrigel described his lessons in archery with a Japanese teacher, Awa Kenzō, as a way of attaining Zen realization. In recent years, Japanese scholars have shown that

Herrigel's account is a mixture of misunderstandings and wishful thinking. His teacher, Awa Kenzō, might have had an interest in Zen, but never taught archery as a way to attain an understanding of it.[15]

So it is interesting to see archery appearing in Daoxin's *Dharma Teachings for the Bodhisattva Precepts*:

> Listeners, do your practice properly and without even a moment of doubt! Be like a person learning to shoot an arrow. They begin with a large target, then aim at a small target, then aim at a large circle, then aim at a small circle, then aim at a single piece of twine, then split the piece of twine into a hundred threads and aim at one of the hundred threads.

This is not an instruction to practise archery, or to find the essence of Zen contemplation in archery. Rather, archery here becomes a metaphor for gradual practice. Daoxin is advising his audience, composed of people who have just received the vows of a bodhisattva, and therefore are just beginning in their meditation practice, to take it slowly. As somebody learning archery begins with large targets, and gradually moves on to smaller and smaller ones, beginners in meditation should not try to do the most advanced practices from the start. And if hitting a single thread seems difficult, Daoxin goes on to describe an even more advanced stunt:

> Then they shoot their arrow into the previous one so that the arrow is fixed in the nock, preventing both arrows from falling.

The image here is of the archer hitting the previous arrow which he or she has already shot into the centre of the target. In the West this feat is known as a 'robinhood' after the fictional achievement of Robin Hood in nineteenth-century versions of the tale, shown in the 1938 film *The Adventures of Robin Hood*. Apparently it is very hard to split a wooden arrow all the way down with another arrow, but hitting the nock of the previous arrow so that both arrows stay fixed without falling to the ground is quite a common occurrence in modern archery, as modern arrows are hollow tubes – like ancient Chinese bamboo arrows.

What does this have to do with meditation practice? Daoxin explains that 'as the stream of consciousness flows through the mind, every moment of mind is continuous, without the briefest interval'. Thus consciousness is like a sequence of arrows stuck in the nock of the previous arrow; there is no break. This is also true of mindfulness: 'true mindfulness is uninterrupted – true mindfulness is always there'.

Daoxin employs other images to emphasize the need to practise meditation constantly, rather than stopping and starting. If you want to make a fire, you will have to keep rubbing the sticks together; if you stop and start, the fire will not come. Or in a more uncomfortable archery metaphor, the meditator should be like someone who has been shot with a poison arrow – in agonizing pain, they cannot forget the arrow even for a moment. Thus, for Daoxin, meditation practice requires complete dedication. Yet at the same time, it is just a means to an end:

> Though the ocean of dharma may be immeasurable, it can be crossed with a single teaching. Once you have grasped the intention, the teaching can be forgotten, for even a single teaching is of no use any more.

Once the intention of the teachings is understood, the words can be forgotten, for words themselves are provisional. This recalls Ludwig Wittgenstein's penultimate passage in the *Tractatus Logico-Philosophicus*:

> My propositions are elucidatory in this way: he who understands me finally recognizes them as senseless, when he has climbed out through them, on them, over them. (He must so to speak throw away the ladder, after he has climbed up on it.)[16]

Rather closer to home for Daoxin, and in a passage which he would certainly have read, the Daoist classic *Zhuangzi* expresses a similar sentiment:

> A fish trap is there for the fish. When you have got hold of the fish, you forget the trap. A snare is there for the rabbits. When you have got hold of the rabbit, you forget the snare. Words are there for the intent. When you have got hold of the intent, you forget the words.[17]

This is the spirit of Zen. The methods taught by the buddhas are a means to an end. Once awakening has happened, there is no point in holding on to them. Thus there is no point in clinging to one particular practice, whether it is contemplating koans or just sitting, as the 'true' Zen practice. On the other hand, completely rejecting meditation is another kind of attachment. So the Zen approach is to practise diligently but lightly, without attachment, confident that enlightenment is already here.

PART II

THE *MASTERS OF THE LANKA*

CHAPTER SIX

MANUSCRIPTS AND TRANSLATION

The *Masters of the Lanka* has only survived thanks to the manuscripts preserved in the Dunhuang cave. The Chinese text is found in thirteen manuscripts, none of which is entirely complete, so what we have has to be put together from different sources. These manuscripts are from four major collections of Dunhuang scrolls: the British Library, the Bibliothèque nationale de France, the National Library of China and the Institute of Oriental Manuscripts in St Petersburg.[1] The popularity of the text is shown by the number of manuscript versions and the fact that there are quite considerable differences between them, suggesting that there were several lines of transmission of the text, even among manuscripts found in a single location.

The most complete scrolls containing the text are:

- Pelliot chinois 3436, which contains the preface through to the end, missing just the first part of the preface. This is rendered in neat handwriting.
- Or.8210/S.2054, which contains the preface through to the middle of the Daoxin chapter, with a few lines missing at the start. This is written in neat cursive handwriting.
- Pelliot chinois 3703, which begins in the middle of the Hongren section and continues to the end of the whole text. This is written in a less careful cursive hand.
- Three other manuscripts seem to have been originally one single scroll, written in a neat hand: (i) Pelliot chinois 3294, which is a single panel with the beginning of the preface (and also Pelliot

chinois 3294 Pièce, which has part of what looks like the title); (ii) Pelliot chinois 3537, which has the second half of the Guṇabhadra chapter and the beginning of the Bodhidharma chapter; (iii) Or.8210/S.4272, which has the end of Bodhidharma chapter through to the beginning of the chapter on Sengcan.[2]

There are also smaller scroll fragments:

• Pelliot chinois 4564, also from the very beginning of the text, with the title and four columns of text;
• Dh 1728, a small fragment from the preface, corresponding with the beginning of the text in S.2054;
• Dh 5464 and 5466, a fragment with part of the preface, overlapping with Pelliot chinois 3436 and Or.8210/S.2054;
• BD 9933 and 11884, two tiny fragments from the Bodhidharma section;
• Dh 18947 and 8300, two tiny fragments from the Bodhidharma section;[3]
• BD 9934, a tiny fragment from the Guṇabhadra section;
• BD 10428, a tiny fragment from the Huike section.

A version of the *Masters of the Lanka* appears in the *Taishō Tripiṭaka* (vol. 85, no. 2837). This version of the text is based on Or.8210/S.2054, followed by Pelliot chinois 3436 for the latter part of the text which does not appear in S.2054. Oddly, the earlier part of the preface which appears in Pelliot chinois 3436 was not included in the Taishō version.

There is also one manuscript from the Dunhuang cave with a Tibetan translation of the *Masters of the Lanka:* IOL Tib J 710. What is interesting about this translation is that it was probably made in the latter part of the eighth century. Since the Chinese manuscripts of the *Masters of the Lanka* were written down in the tenth century, this means that the Tibetan translation probably represents an earlier version of the text.

The Tibetan translation lacks the preface found in some of the Chinese manuscripts, and ends abruptly in the chapter on Daoxin's teachings. Since the title of this Tibetan translation states that it is the first volume, there was probably more of it in existence once, though we don't know where the complete translation would have ended (for example, whether it contained the brief final chapter on Shenxiu's successors).[4]

Intriguingly, certain other parts of the text are missing from the Tibetan translation, including the rhetorical questions that come at the end of the chapters on Guṇabhadra and Bodhidharma. Scholars have plausibly concluded that these were added in the century or more that elapsed between the making of the Tibetan translation and the Chinese versions from Dunhuang.[5] One thing that has not been noticed before is that the Tibetan translation contains a few passages that are not found in any of the Chinese manuscripts. These may have been lost in the manuscript transmission of the Chinese text.

For this English translation, I have compared all the original manuscripts, with reference to the edition of Yanagida Seizan (1971). Where the text diverges so significantly between different manuscript versions that I have had to make a choice between different translation options, I have noted this. I have also taken account of translation choices made in J.C. Cleary's English translation (1986) and Bernard Faure's French translation (1989). Faure relied on Yanagida's edition of the text, while Cleary based his translation on a single modern edition derived from a limited selection of the Chinese manuscripts: the *Jiangyuan congshu* compiled by Kim Kugyŏng.[6]

Since this is primarily a translation of the Chinese text, I have generally followed the Chinese manuscripts when they diverge from the Tibetan translation, but I have noted interesting differences. In the few cases where the Tibetan translation contains passages that seem to have been lost in the transmission of the Chinese text, I have included these passages in the translation, and noted that they occur only in the Tibetan.

✦

CHAPTER SEVEN

JINGJUE
Student of Emptiness

The preface to the *Masters of the Lanka* is by and about Jingjue. The preface does not appear in the Tibetan translation (which is earlier than the extant Chinese manuscripts of the *Masters of the Lanka*) and does not mention the rest of the text. Furthermore, the *Masters of the Lanka* is, like many pre-modern texts, largely put together from texts that came before it. And, like many texts in the age of manuscripts, it developed over time as it was copied out over and over again. Thus Jingjue's role with respect to the *Masters of the Lanka* is not entirely clear, and it is better not to consider him its 'author' in the modern sense of the word.

Still, Jingjue is very much part of the *Masters of the Lanka*, even if he is not in the main lineage of teachers that the text presents us with.[1] Jingjue lived at the centre of a turbulent and creative period in Chinese history. Born in 683, Jingjue grew up during the reign of one of China's greatest rulers, Wu Zetian. Wu was the power behind the throne for much of the latter part of the seventh century, and in the year 683 became China's first female ruler. She declared the beginning of a new dynasty, the Zhou, and instituted sweeping reforms.

In military terms, Empress Wu was one of the most successful Chinese rulers, reversing the advances of the Tibetan empire across Central Asia, and extending her empire into the Korean peninsula. She is famous for her support of Buddhism and Daoism over Confucianism, which earned her the lasting resentment of Confucian historians.[2] Traditional portrayals of Empress Wu as corrupt, murderous and licentious are largely due to this, and to the restitution of patriarchal norms after the anomalous ascent of a woman to the highest position in the empire.

It was also Empress Wu who brought Zen into the mainstream of Chinese Buddhism through her patronage of Shenxiu. According to the *Record of the Transmission of the Dharma Jewel*, Wu invited Shenxiu to teach at the capital, Luoyang, received him as an honoured guest, and ceremonially bowed down before him. It was during Shenxiu's time in Luoyang that Jingjue met and studied with him. Jingjue was from one of China's noble families; his sister, the princess Wei, had been married to the previous emperor (Wu's son), and had risen to become a rival to Empress Wu. When she took power, Jingjue's sister was exiled, and his brothers were killed.

After the death of Empress Wu in 705, her son became emperor again, but his wife, Jingjue's sister, was the true ruler, becoming known for a time as Empress Wei. During her reign, Jingjue returned to the capital. He was offered a political appointment but turned it down. Instead, he was ordained as a Buddhist monk under Shenxiu. According to his preface in the *Masters of the Lanka*, it was in this period that he met his main teacher, Xuanze, who had been invited to teach at the court. And it was a good thing that Jingjue had refused a political role, as five years later Empress Wei and her supporters fell to another palace coup and were executed or sent into exile.

After his sister's reign came to an end, Jingjue retreated from public life entirely. Little is known of him after this time, except that he lived in his monastery at Mount Taihang, teaching and writing. Two texts that survived in the Dunhuang cave are attributed to him, the *Masters of the Lanka* and a commentary on the *Heart Sutra*. He died sometime in the 750s, and an account of his funeral suggests that he was held in high regard:

> From the gates of the city to the opening into the valley, banners and platforms made an uninterrupted sequence, and his dharma companions in their white mourning dress accompanied the

inhabitants of the capital. People beat on their chests, tore at their hair, sprinkled themselves with water, spotted themselves with dust.[3]

Yet, despite his position in one of China's ruling families, and in the most prominent lineage of Zen teaching at the time, Jingjue was almost completely forgotten, and would still be, were it not for the discovery of the Dunhuang manuscripts. This is not really surprising; the names that are forgotten by tradition are far more numerous than those that are preserved. In Jingjue's case, his own involvement with Shenxiu and what came to be known as the Northern School of Zen is probably the main reason why his name and writings fell into obscurity.

The preface to the *Masters of the Lanka* is, like the whole text, a collage of different sources: first-person and third-person accounts, teachings and quotations from scripture. From the parts of the preface that present Jingjue's own teachings, he seems to have been an eloquent and educated writer. Not quite all of the preface survives, and the translation here is pieced together from four different manuscripts.[4]

After an opening prayer, Jingjue begins with an account of his discovery of the teachings of Bodhidharma, stating that before this, 'despite all that I had seen and read, my knowledge was like someone peering through a tube'. He then describes how he met Shenxiu during the reign of Empress Wu, received Shenxiu's teachings in meditation, and achieved 'something resembling realization'.

Then Shenxiu died, leaving Jingjue bereft. The preface goes on to describe Xuanze, whom Jingjue next took as a teacher. Abruptly, we hear about Xuanze's death, when five-coloured rays of light emerged from the point between his eyes, which was taken as a sign that he had attained enlightenment. Then we move back in time, hearing about how Jingjue met Xuanze when the emperor summoned him to the court.

This narrative, in which Jingjue is referred to in the third person, was probably added to Jingjue's own, incomplete account of his relationship with Xuanze. It ends with Xuanze giving Jingjue a pointing-out instruction, informing him that 'within one's own heart there is all the reality one needs'. After this, the preface continues with some teachings from the *Awakening of Faith in the Mahayana* and the *Laṅkāvatāra sūtra*; perhaps these are meant to explain the transmission that Jingjue received, and the realization that he experienced. The preface then returns to Jingjue's first-person account, where he describes what he did after receiving the pointing-out instruction from Xuanze:

> After this, I devoted myself to solitude, and cultivated my nature deep in the mountains. In solitude, I maintained the purity of my mind; embraced by oneness, I left the valleys behind. I will now commit this preface to words so that others, basing themselves in this realization may traverse the path as I have done, with the sole aspiration of knowing their minds.

Thus Jingjue tells us that he went on a solitary meditation retreat after receiving Xuanze's transmission, developing and strengthening his own realization. What follows in the rest of the preface seem to be his own teachings. Much of Jingjue's teaching is about the samsara and nirvana being one and the same. The Buddhist path is not a journey from one place (samsara) to another (nirvana). Rather, it is the discovery of nirvana in samsara: 'The true essence of reality is not far away, it is here in the midst of samsara.'

To illustrate the sameness-in-difference of samsara and nirvana, Jingjue uses the example of ice and water. They are not different, yet they function differently – ice obstructs while water flows. All that one needs to go from samsara to nirvana is a change in the way one's mind functions. Our experience is a manifestation of our mind, and at the source of mind is a profound stillness. This stillness is always there in all movement, for 'where there is movement, there is always stillness'. It is present in all our thoughts, for 'where there is thought, there is always thusness'.

This might make the transformation of samsara into nirvana seem easy and quick, but in these passages Jingjue also bemoans the low quality of his contemporary students of Buddhism, who start out on the path with enthusiasm, but give up when their past karma causes difficulties to arise. He also criticizes contemporary teachers for not understanding how emptiness goes beyond the concepts of existence and nonexistence at the same time:

> If there are people under heaven who cannot know how to practise the path, it is because they are attached to existence and nonexistence.

The philosophy of emptiness is not just about challenging the concept of independent existence; it also challenges the concept of nonexistence. Jingjue writes, 'If existence was the source of existence, then existence would itself always be, but things only exist after arising dependently.' That is to say, things do exist, but only in one sense – they exist in dependence on their conditions. Likewise, things cease to exist when those conditions are no longer present, and there is no metaphysical 'nonexistence' beyond that ordinary fact.

What Jingjue is explaining here is the view of the Madhyamaka as set out by Nāgārjuna, Āryadeva and other Indian Buddhist scholars. In this view, emptiness challenges the idea that any thing – whether particular objects like pots, or universal concepts like 'green' – exists independently. In the Madhyamaka view, everything, from particular objects to our most general concepts, owes its existence to other things. Pots owe their existence to the clay that was used to make them, the actions of the potter and so on. Even more fundamentally, the categories we use to establish a picture of the world are all dependent on each other; the concept 'long' cannot exist without the complementary concept 'short', and so on.

So, Jingjue says, emptiness is not nonexistence, and we should not be attached to the nonexistence of things any more than to the idea of their existence. As it says in the *Heart Sutra*, on which Jingjue wrote a commentary, 'Form is nothing other than emptiness; emptiness is nothing other than form.' Here, Jingjue puts that thought in slightly different terms:

Though empty, it is always functioning, though functioning, it is always empty.

So emptiness is expressed in the activity of dependent arising. Furthermore, this union of emptiness and function is not a concept for philosophy alone, but is to be observed in one's own mind. Addressing his students, or readers, Jingjue says, 'Now, go and sit in meditation and verify them for yourself, rather than depending on what is expounded in the three vehicles.' Emptiness is to be fully understood through meditation, which reveals the true nature of one's own mind.

Jingjue's preface does not say much about the actual practice of meditation, but we can see that he taught a practice of turning one's attention to the mind's source:

> If we look closely at samsara, we can see that it is nothing more than repeated acts of grasping. When one contemplates the mind that grasps, it is originally pure. In this state of stillness there is no deluded thought. Where there is movement there is always still-ness. Where there is stillness there is no striving.

In this meditation practice, one's attention is turned away from the perceptions and thoughts that usually occupy our attention to their source, the nature of mind. This nature is a state of stillness that is always present, even in the midst of the mind's movements. Since this is the very nature of mind, stillness does not need to be sought or imposed upon movement – it is expressed through movement. This way of teaching meditation was known as observing the mind (*kànxīn*), and features prominently in the *Masters of the Lanka*, especially in the meditation instructions of Daoxin.[5]

✦

RECORD OF THE MASTERS AND STUDENTS OF THE LANKA

Preface

Buddha nature is emptiness without categories,
Reality is peace beyond words.
When taught through spoken words of written letters,
Both are conceptualizations of meditation.[6]
The pure dharma of final nirvana
Is a secret not taught to everybody:
'Mind is always everywhere, whether still or active.'[7]
This is only granted in the records of those who have attained
    liberation.
The followers of the two vehicles do not know it.[8]
Non-Buddhists have never heard of it.
Among those of lesser ability, many criticize it.
So I vow not to disseminate it.[9]

* * *

We sentient beings spend a long time in samsara, entirely because of the imprints of our past actions.[10] Despite all that I had seen and read, my knowledge was like someone peering through a tube. Though I had contemplated purity and emptiness, my explanations had been those of a petty man. So I made this aspirational vow: 'Till the end of this life I will propagate the remaining works of Bodhidharma throughout the world', and this is the path I trod.

I left in the first year of the Dazu era (701) for the Eastern Capital, where I met Master Datong, whose personal name was Shenxiu.[11] He transmitted extensive teachings on meditation to me, and I achieved something resembling realization. But even though he had shown me the basis of my mind, he always said, 'Exert yourself!' When my merit is so meagre, how could my devotion to him not be sincere? This monk then, in accordance with the ways of the world, suddenly passed away and I no longer had recourse for my questions and doubts.

Then another who possessed the seal of approval appeared, a great monk of Shoushan in Anzhou whose personal name was Xuanze and whose family name was Wang.[12] He came from Qixian in Taiyuan, but as his grandfather had the role of district prefect, he was born in the fertile land of Yunmeng. He was one of the disciples to whom Hongren, the great master of Dongshan in Qizhou, passed on the flame.[13] One day when this great monk was living at Shoushan, in the head monk's quarters, he entered the state of purity. From between his two eyes rays of light for each of the five colours appeared as relics.[14] Consequently we understood that the great teacher had already completed the path a long time ago.

* * *

Emperor Zhongzong Xiaohe of the Great Tang, in the second year of the era of Jinglong, summoned Xuanze by imperial decree to the Western Capital (Chang'an).[15] However, he already was teaching meditation widely in the Eastern Capital (Luoyang). Jingjue publicly avowed that he would bring him quickly back.[16] He took up this business single-mindedly, coming and going between both capitals, and finally brought them together for an imperial audience. Jingjue decided to commit himself to practice for the rest of his life, and soon he had a clear vision of the way the mind's ground manifests.[17]

The Patriarch Hongren, made a prediction about this great teacher: 'There is one person from Anzhou who will be a great monk.' And indeed, though Xuanze did look like any ordinary monk, he was actually at the same stage of development as a buddha. He was also an

Imperial Preceptor, the jewel of the state, and lay people took refuge with him as well. Since Jingjue possessed the conditions accumulated over many previous lives, Xuanze personally gave him the pointing-out instruction. Only then did Jingjue understand that within one's own heart there is all the reality one needs. Whatever he had not known before, he now finally understood.[18]

* * *

Thusness is without categories,
And knowing is without knowing.[19]
When knowing is without knowing,
Why abandon knowing?
When categories are without categories,
Why abandon categories?

Persons and dharmas are thusness,
Speech is thusness too.
Thusness itself has no explanation;[20]
If explained, it is not thusness.
At the source of thusness there is no knowing,
So knowing is not thusness.

The Treatise on the Arising of Faith says:

As for the thusness of mind: in brief, it is the one nature of reality, which encompasses all dharma teachings.[21] That which we call the nature of mind is unborn and unceasing. All of the various entities are different merely because of the power of delusion, but if one is free from thinking, then one no longer distinguishes the categories of perceptual objects.

Therefore each and every entity is from the very beginning free from the categories of spoken language, free from the categories of written words, freed from the categories of mental cognition. They are ultimately equal and cannot be changed into anything else, nor can they be destroyed. They are just this one mind, and this is why we call it *thusness*.[22]

It also says:

Ordinary people, hearers, solitary buddhas, bodhisattvas and buddhas all have thusness as their very essence. Nothing can be added to it, nor taken away. There was no point in time at which it came into being, nor will there be a point when it disappears. Always constant and consistent, from the beginning its nature is self-sufficient and complete, with each and every enlightened quality. Its essence is the clear light of great wisdom.[23] This is the nature of the pure mind.[24]

The *Laṅkāvatāra sūtra* says, 'The mind manifests the objects of perception', and later, 'It manifests them according to five dharmas.'[25] What are these five dharmas of which it speaks? They are (i) names, (ii) categories, (iii) delusion, (iv) perfect wisdom and (v) thusness. The great multitude of conditioned things are nameless; it is mind that makes names. The variety of categories have no categories; categories are made by the mind. But if you have no mind, then there can be no names or categories, and this is what we call perfect wisdom and thusness.[26]

The *Sutra of Dharma Verses on Reality* says:

The interweaved net of ten thousand images
Is stamped with the seal of the single dharma.[27]

* * *

After this, I devoted myself to solitude, and cultivated my nature deep in the mountains. In solitude, I maintained the purity of my mind; embraced by oneness, I left the valleys behind.[28] I will now commit this preface to words so that others, basing themselves in this realization, may traverse the path as I have done, with the sole aspiration of knowing their minds.

The true essence of reality is right here in the midst of samsara. The noble path is subtle and profound, but it is found within this physical body. The physical body is pure, even if it resides among the afflictions. The true nature of samsara is found in the same place as nirvana.[29]

So know this: living beings and the buddha nature are at root exactly the same. Consider water and ice – in essence, how do they differ? Ice creates a physical obstruction, which is like the ties that bind living beings. Water's nature is to be all-pervasive, which is like the complete purity of the buddha nature. There is no teaching to acquire, no qualities to be sought. Even good things should be discarded so that samsara remains far away.

The *Vimalakīrti-nirdeśa sūtra* says:

Those who want to reach the pure land,
Must purify their minds.
When they have purified their minds,
Then the buddha realm is pure.[30]

Though the body forms their foundation, consciousness and perception can be superficial or profound. Those with profound perception are the ones who have purified themselves for aeons through their practice, from the initial aspiration for enlightenment (bodhicitta) to the final accomplishment of buddhahood, never going back. Those with superficial consciousness are the modern students who appear nowadays. They are happy when they first go into solitude, but then the karma they have accumulated over lifetimes comes back to them. Because they have commited slander and held false views they do not have the strength to maintain genuine faith or practise the path. After a while they give up in defeat.

If we look closely at samsara, we can see that it is nothing more than repeated acts of grasping.[31] When one contemplates the mind that grasps, it is originally pure. In truth, mind does not exist. In this state of stillness there is no deluded thought. Where there is movement there is always stillness. Where there is stillness there is no striving.

Where there is thought, there is always thusness. In thusness there are no afflictions or attachment.[32] The absence of afflictions is purity. The absence of attachment is liberation. The afflictions are the cause of samsara, and purity is the result of awakening. The most profound teachings are actually empty. The end of the path is beyond language; language is contrary to the ultimate.[33]

Even if one considers the source in terms of emptiness of intrinsic nature, it is not a source that can be named. Emptiness itself is beyond language, and the mind cannot go there. The mind of a noble one is subtle and undefinable, having left knowledge and explanation far behind. Full enlightenment is what is truly real, beyond language and speech.[34]

The *Lotus Sutra* says: 'The quality of the stillness of the various entities cannot be described in words.'[35] There are no entities that can be spoken of, no mind that can be expressed. Intrinsic nature is empty and idle.[36] Return to the source, for the source is the path itself.

The nature of the path is empty yet boundless, liberating, vast, clear and subtle. It brings the entire universe to stillness. It pervades ancient and modern, yet is always pure by nature. It encompasses the highest and the lowest, is ever-present and pure. It is the pure buddha realm.

Know this – within a single hair there is the entire universe, and one mote of dust contains the limitless cosmos. These statements are true! Now, go and sit in meditation and verify them for yourself, rather than depending on what is expounded in the three vehicles.

As the sutras say:

The path to awakening
Is impossible to map.[37]
It is lofty but has no 'above';
Impossible to reach its limit.
Deep but has no 'below';
Impossible to measure its depth.
So large it encompasses heaven and earth,

So tiny it enters where there is no gap;[38]
This is why we call it the path.
This is why the dharmakaya is pure.

It is like emptiness.
Since emptiness has no emptiness.
How could existence attain existence?
Existence does not originally exist;
It is a label attached by people themselves.
Emptiness is not originally empty;
It is a label attached by people themselves.
So abandon both existence and emptiness.
Pure liberation
Is without action, without phenomena,
Without abiding, without attachment.
In this stillness,
Not a single thing arises.[39]

This, then, is the path to awakening. We can be sure that the path to nirvana is not located within existence or nonexistence, and does not go somewhere beyond existence and nonexistence. Accordingly, those who are now entering the path should not destroy existence or attack nonexistence. As we live in a time when there is merely the semblance of the dharma, these are provisional teachings.[40]

* * *

Essential emptiness is without categories.[41] It cannot be made existent, it just never stops functioning; nor can it be made nonexistent. So, though empty, it is always functioning, though functioning, it is always empty. Emptiness and function may be different, but there is no mind to distinguish them. Therefore thusness is pure by nature, ever present, never ending.[42]

If there are people under heaven who cannot know how to practise the path, it is because they are attached to existence and nonexistence. Existence is not inherently existent, because nothing cannot exist before its conditions have arisen.[43] Nonexistence is not inherently nonexistent, because it only happens after the conditions have dispersed.

If existence was the source of existence, then existence would itself always be, but things only exist after arising dependently. If nonexistence was the source of nonexistence, then nonexistence itself would always be, so why is there only nonexistence after the exhaustion of conditions?

Dependently arisen existence is not this kind of existence; in thusness there is no inherent existence. Dependently-arisen nonexistence is not this kind of nonexistence; in the pure mind that nonexistence does not exist. Existent and nonexistent entities are just the domain of conceptualization. How could one complete the noble path using these labels?

The *Radiant Light Sutra* says:

Is awakening attained through existence?
The Buddha answered 'no'.
Is it attained through nonexistence?
Again he answered 'no'.
Is it attained through both existence and nonexistence?
The Buddha answered 'no'.
Is it obtained through detachment from existence and
    nonexistence?
Again he answered 'no'.
What does it mean to say 'attain'?
The Buddha answered: 'There is nothing to be attained!
Attaining without attainment
Is how awakening is attained.'[44]

✦

CHAPTER EIGHT

GUṆABHADRA
Introducing the *Laṅkāvatāra*

The *Masters of the Lanka* begins the lineage of Zen with Guṇabhadra. Though this was not universally accepted at the time, it is not as odd as it might seem to us now. The *Masters of the Lanka* is describing, after all, a teaching lineage based on the *Laṅkāvatāra sūtra*, and it was Guṇabhadra who first translated this sutra into Chinese. Guṇabhadra was an important translator of Buddhist texts into Chinese, translating over fifty sutras and other texts during his time in China.[1]

Guṇabhadra travelled from India to China by sea, arriving in the port city of Guangzhou (also known as Canton) in the year 435. He travelled to the city of Danyang, capital of the Liu Song empire, and at the request of the emperor, led a translation team working on Buddhist sutras. This is all the biographical detail about Guṇabhadra that the *Masters of the Lanka* provides.

Other Chinese sources tell us a little more about Guṇabhadra. They all agree that he was a devotee of the bodhisattva of compassion, Avalokiteśvara. According to the *Further Biographies of Eminent Monks*, Guṇabhadra's ship was becalmed during his sea voyage to China. He instructed the other passengers to visualize the buddhas of the ten directions and recite the name of Avalokiteśvāra. Meanwhile, he 'secretly recited the sutra of spells, earnestly offered veneration, and performed confession'. After this, the wind began to blow, a fine rain fell, and the ship proceeded to Guangzhou.[2]

This story is typical of the accounts in the biographies of eminent monks, in which Indian masters are mainly celebrated for two things: their translation skills and their magical powers. More specifically, it gives us a picture of a Mahayana teacher, devoted to the bodhisattva of compassion, skilled in reciting spells (in Sanskrit, *dhāraṇī*) and in the rituals of veneration and confession. The picture in the *Masters of the Lanka* is a little different – we don't hear about devotion to bodhisattvas or about supernatural powers. Instead, we have a stern figure who lectures his Chinese audience about the inferiority of their country to India when it comes to practising the Buddhist path.

Apparently, Guṇabhadra observed that many Chinese Buddhist monks who claim to be practising meditation were actually practising forms of spirit worship, and making money by performing divination for their patrons. Practitioners of this kind of spirit magic may have been Buddhist or Daoist.[3] Guṇabhadra blames this corruption of meditation practice on the careless transmission of meditation teachings to those who are not ready for them:

> In the Central Land where I am from, we have the proper teaching, but it is kept secret instead of being carelessly transmitted. Only those for whom the conditions are ripe and who happen to meet a virtuous teacher on the road are accepted for this path.

Though the idea that teachings should be transmitted in secrecy is found in most tantric Buddhist traditions, it is less familiar in the context of Zen. Yet the reasons for doing so are the same here – concern that the teachings will be practised without proper training, leading to the abuse of the practice and the decline of the teachings.

So what teachings are attributed to Guṇabhadra here? One teaching bears a clear connection to the *Laṅkāvatāra* itself, and is presented in such a cryptic way that it might be intended to be secret:

> If you do not understand this, then the sixth will possess the seventh and eighth. If you do understand then the eighth will be free from the sixth and seventh.

This mysterious statement refers to the eight aspects of the mind, as detailed in the *Laṅkāvatāra*. This model of the mind, which has been hugely influential in many Buddhist traditions, is as follows:

1. Sight
2. Hearing
3. Smell
4. Taste
5. Touch
6. Mind
7. Ego
8. Basis

Thus we have the five sense perceptions of sight, sound, smell, taste and touch[4], followed by the sixth, mental perception. The sixth aspect of consciousness is what we use to distinguish and conceptualize the raw impressions coming from the five senses. The seventh level is the egoic aspect of consciousness: the neurotic clinging to our sense of being a self, and the emotional afflictions that come from that clinging. At the eighth level is the fundamental basis of consciousness. This is the basic fact of awareness, which is the same as the buddha nature itself.

In all sentient beings, the ego grasps the basic consciousness, mistaking it for a self, and this simple misapprehension causes all of our suffering. Under the influence of the ego, basic consciousness becomes conditioned by habitual clinging, and is the place where our habital negative patterns take root. Thus the basis is neutral, being neither essentially samsara or nirvana; when it is grasped by ego, sentient beings experience samsara, but when freed from the ego, sentient beings experience the state of awakening. This is called 'the transformation of the basis'.[5]

While many Buddhist texts emphasize the key role of the ego in this process, Guṇabhadra's teaching is more of a bottom-up approach. First one frees the five senses, and then mind will cease to activate the ego, which in turn will no longer grasp the basic consciousness. And how does one free the five senses? Guṇabhadra continues: 'Those who intend to become a buddha must first learn peace of mind.' But, he goes on to say, different practitioners understand 'peace of mind' in different ways. There are four levels, based on how people approach the nature of reality, which is referred to here as 'the principle' (a word closely associated with Bodhidharma's teachings, as we will see in the next chapter):

- ordinary people, who have no interest in the principle;
- practitioners of the hinayana, who seek the principle in nirvana, rejecting samsara and seeking tranquillity;
- practitioners of the mahayana, who clear away the things that obscure the principle, but have not gone beyond the duality of subject and object;
- practitioners who recognize that their own mind is the principle, or rather, mind is the luminosity of the principle shining forth. This is known as *buddha mind.*

The last and best kind of practitioner realizes that all dualities (not just the mind and the principle) are empty, including nirvana and samsara, good and bad, buddhas and ordinary beings. Thus true practice is free from ideas about getting better, becoming more pure, or approaching a goal. The sun is always there, even on a cloudy day, and reappears when the clouds drift away.[6]

What then of actual practice? There are few clues about how this should be done in Guṇabhadra's teaching, apart from these brief instructions towards the end:

Chase away the things that cause conceptualization. Do not allow contamination of consciousness. Be mindful of the Buddha with great devotion, continuously focused in every moment of thought without interruption.

This is a very brief description of the meditation practice of mindfulness of the Buddha, in which one concentrates on a real or visualized image of a buddha (which may be Śākyamuni or another buddha such as Amitabha). Often, though it is not mentioned here, one also recites the buddha's name.[7] The purpose of this meditative focus is to replace the ordinary mental processes with devotion to the Buddha. Ultimately, since the nature of the mind and the Buddha are one and the same, the duality of myself as a meditator and the object of my meditation disappears. This practice and its inherent non-duality are discussed in more detail in Daoxin's chapter later in the *Masters of the Lanka.*

✦

MASTERS AND STUDENTS OF THE LANKA, FIRST FASCICLE

Compiled by Jingjue, a Buddhist monk of the Eastern Capital, when he was staying at Taihang Shan.

Chapter One

The tripiṭaka master Guṇabhadra of the Song Dynasty was from the Central Land of India. Because he constantly trained in the Great Vehicle, he was given the name Mahayana.[8] During the Yuanjia period (424–53) he travelled by ship to Guangzhou. Emperor Taizu of the Song dynasty welcomed him to the prefecture of Danyang, where he produced a translation of the *Lankāvatāra sūtra*.

Princes and dukes, monks and laypeople all requested that Guṇabhadra bestow teachings on meditation, but he was uncomfortable about this because he was not yet able to speak Chinese properly.[9] Then he dreamed that a man cut off his head with a sword and replaced it with another one, and after that he began to bestow teachings on meditation.

The tripiṭaka master said –

This country, situated at the eastern end of the world, lacks the teachings on cultivating the path. Because these teachings are lacking, some fall into the teachings of the hinayana and the two vehicles.[10] Some fall into one of the ninety-five non-Buddhist paths. Some fall into the meditation practices of spirit worship – when they tell people's fortunes, they claim to be able to see this in the state of meditation.[11]

How sad! They have turned something wonderful into something harmful and ensnared others in the same trap they themselves are caught in. I feel compassion for such people – you have long had the misfortune to fall into the path of spirit worship, and for a long time you have just accepted samsara, never obtaining liberation.

Some other people fall into the forbidden techniques of enslaving spirits, predicting good or bad fortunes for other people's households, while claiming, 'I'm practising seated meditation and analysis.' Ordinary folk, blind and infatuated, who cannot see through these people, think that they have ascended the noble path when in fact they are all sorcerers.[12] They don't realize that this spirit worship is a false demonic teaching.

In the Central Land where I am from, we have the proper teaching, but it is kept secret instead of being carelessly transmitted. Only those for whom the conditions are ripe and who happen to meet a virtuous teacher on the road are accepted for this path. If they do not meet a virtuous teacher they will not obtain the father-to-son transmission.[13]

The *Laṅkāvatāra sūtra* says, 'The minds of the buddhas are supreme.'[14] I teach that the transmission of the dharma occurs only when the mind has no point of arising. This dharma exceeds the limits of the three vehicles. It goes further than the ten levels. It is the place of the final result, buddhahood.

> With a still mind, you will know it for yourself.
> Without mind, your spirit will rise up.
> Without thought, your body will be at peace.
> Living in a solitude, you will sit in purity.
> Guarding the source, you will return to the principle.

My dharma is secret and silent, and is not to be transmitted to foolish people with superficial consciousness. It is essential that only people of substantial merit and virtue are allowed to receive and practise this.

* * *

If you do not understand this, then the sixth will possess the seventh and eighth. If you do understand then the eighth will be free from the sixth and seventh.[15] Those who intend to become a buddha must first learn peace of mind. When the mind is not at peace, then even good is not good, never mind bad. When your mind has attained peace and tranquillity there is no distinction between good and bad to be made. As the *Avataṃsaka sūtra* says, 'entities cannot perceive entities'.[16]

Since I arrived in this country I have yet to see anyone cultivating the path, never mind anyone who has peace of mind. Occasionally, I see someone performing religious acts, but they have not yet devoted themselves to the path. Some want to get a name for themselves and make a profit. They are all practising with the belief in a personal self, and this creates an attitude of jealousy.

What is jealousy? When you see other people cultivating the path, good at reasoning, good at practising, with many people taking refuge and making offerings to them, then jealousy appears in your mind, along with hatred and disgust. You rely on your own cleverness and do not use it to overcome your self.

If you have this kind of attitude, and zealously cultivate various practices to stop the afflictions throughout the day and night, eliminating all obscurations and destroying each and every obstacle on the path, yet you do not attain peace and tranquillity, then you can only call this 'cultivation'. You cannot call it peace of mind.

If you engage in the practices of the six perfections, explaining the sutras, and progressing towards the second and third levels of meditation as you zealously engage in austerities, this might be called 'doing good', but it is not dharma practice.[17] Only those monks who do not irrigate the fields of karma with the water of attachment, planting the seeds of consciousness, can be said to be engaged in dharma practice.

Now in this case, when we are speaking of 'peace of mind', there are roughly four types:

- The first is the mind that turns away from the principle. This refers to someone whose mind is that of an ordinary person.
- The second is the mind that turns towards the principle, and therefore rejects samsara as evil, hurrying towards tranquillity in order to seek nirvana. This is known as having the mind of a hearer.

- The third is the mind that engages with the principle. This refers to someone who eliminates whatever obscures the manifestation of the principle, but has not yet done away with subject and object. Such a person has the mind of a bodhisattva.[18]
- The fourth is the mind that *is* principle. This means there is no principle other than the principle, and there is no mind other than mind. The principle is just this mind. When the mind is able to achieve equanimity, we call it *the principle.* When the principle's luminosity is allowed to shine, we call it *the mind.* When mind and the principle are identical, this what we call *buddha mind.*[19]

Those who have realized the true nature
See no difference between samsara and nirvana.
The ordinary person and the noble one are no different.[20]
Wisdom and its object are nondual.
The principle and phenomena interpenetrate.
Ultimate and conventional truth are the same view.
Defilement and purity are oneness.
Buddhas and sentient beings
Are one and the same from the very beginning.

The *Laṅkāvatāra sūtra* says:

In all of this, there is no nirvana,
No buddha endowed with nirvana,
No nirvana endowed with buddhas,
Beyond awareness and the objects of awareness.
Free from all dualities,
Such as existence and nonexistence.[21]

The great path is everywhere from the beginning.[22] It is completely pure, and has always existed. Consider the clouds beneath the sun – when the clouds fade away, the sunlight appears spontaneously. What then is the use of more and more learning about philosophical viewpoints? After you have passed through written and spoken words you will only come back to the path of samsara.[23] Those who take spoken or written transmission as equivalent to the path are filled with greed, seeking fame and profit. They ruin themselves and others as well. It is also like polishing a bronze mirror. Beneath the dust that rests on the mirror's surface, the mirror itself is always clean and luminous.

As the *Sarvadharmāpravṛtti-nirdeśa sūtra* says:

Buddhas do not become buddhas,
Nor do they save sentient beings.
It is sentient beings who impose the distinction
Between those who become buddhas,
And sentient beings who are saved.[24]

If you do not understand this attitude, then you cannot have concentration. If you do understand it, then the resulting illumination will bring about the beginning of great activity, all-pervading and unobstructed.[25] This is 'the great path of cultivation'.[26] Here there is no duality between self and other, all practices are practised simultaneously, without before and after, and without an inbetween.[27] This is what we call *the mahayana*:

- When there is no attachment to inner or outer things in the state of ultimate renunciation, this is *the perfection of giving.*
- When good and bad are equal so that neither can be achieved, this is *the perfection of morality.*
- When there is no clash between the mind and its objects, and animosity is extinguished for ever, this is *the perfection of patience.*[28]
- When great stillness is unmoving, yet all actions arise spontaneously, this is *the perfection of effort.*
- When one is deeply at peace through both trouble and prosperity, this is *the perfection of meditation.*[29]
- When luminosity arises from sublime stillness, this is *the perfection of wisdom.*

People like this are truly wonderful. They are all-embracing without obstruction, carrying out enlightened activities through both trouble and prosperity. They embody the mahayana. If those who seek the mahayana do not first learn peace of mind, then they will certainly go astray.

The *Mahāprajñāpāramitā sūtra* says:

> The Buddha's five kinds of sight
> Observe the minds of sentient beings
> As well as all entities;
> Ultimately they do not see.[30]

The *Avataṃsaka sūtra* says:

> When there is no seeing, then you can see.[31]

The *Sutra of the Questions of Viśeṣa-cinti-brahma* says:

> It is not what the eye sees, nor what the ears, nose, tongue, body and consciousness perceive. But if you are in tune with things as they truly are, seeing and the objects of sight, through to consciousness, the nature of these phenomena is just as it is. Being able to see in this way is called *true seeing*.[32]

The *Enquiry into Meditation* says:

> Bats and owls see nothing in the daylight, but they do see at night. This is because of the distortions of conceptualization. Why is this the case? Bats and owls see light where others see darkness. Ordinary people see darkness where others see light. Both of these are forms of conceptualization.[33]

Because of these distortions, because of their karmic hindrances, people do not see phenomena truly. Thus light is not fixed as light and darkness is not fixed as darkness. Those who understand this are free from distortion or confusion. They enter the state of a tathāgata, in permanence, bliss, self and purity.[34]

* * *

The great dharma teacher said – The *Laṅkāvatāra sūtra* asks how we purify our thoughts.[35] Chase away the things that cause conceptualization. Do not allow contamination of consciousness. Be mindful of the Buddha with great devotion, continuously focused in every moment of thought without interruption. Then you will be at peace, free from thoughts in the realization that everything is originally empty and pure.[36]

He also said – Once you accept this and do not go back, you will be in an unchanging state of peace. As the Buddha said, 'How could this be increased?'[37]

He also said – You should follow and learn from a teacher, but realization does not come from the teacher. An ordinary person teaching people about wisdom could never explain *this*.[38]

He used to go up to objects in order to clarify the situation; he would point to a leaf on a tree and ask, 'What is this?'[39]

He also said – You can enter the jar or the pillar.

And – You can enter the fire pit. Can't this staff explain the dharma?[40]

He also said – Your body enters your mind.[41]

He also said – In this room there is a jar. Isn't this jar outside the room as well? Isn't the water in the jar? Isn't the jar in the water? Indeed, from the greatest to the smallest of the various rivers and streams, aren't each and every one of them in this jar?

He also said – What is this water?

He also said – Things too, like the leaves on this tree, can teach the dharma. This pillar can teach the dharma. The roof can teach the dharma.[42] Earth, water, fire and wind can all teach the dharma. Earth, wood, tile and stone can also teach the dharma. How can this be?

✦

CHAPTER NINE

BODHIDHARMA

Sudden and Gradual

Bodhidharma is the Zen tradition personified. But like many founders of great movements, Bodhidharma was not well known in his own lifetime. His fame comes from those of later generations who traced their own traditions back to him. We do have one account of Bodhidharma by a contemporary, and while it only mentions him in passing, it is quite revealing. The author of these remarks was a monk called Yang Xuanze, who wrote a substantial book on the Buddhist monasteries of Luoyang. At the Yongning monastery he remembered meeting a foreign monk who praised the beauty of the building:

> At that time there was the monk called Bodhidharma from the western regions, a foreigner from Persia. When he came from that far country and was staying in China, he saw how the golden tiles sparkled in the sun, their light reflected in the clouds, and the precious bells rung by the wind whose voice rang beyond the heavens, he sang in praise: 'Truly how wonderful it all is!' He said that he was 150 years old and had travelled all countries in the world without exception, but that nothing in Jambudvīpa was comparable with the beauty of this monastery. 'I have gone to the edges of the world, but I have never seen anything like this!' With hands clasped, he chanted the name of the Buddha for several days.[1]

Clearly, for the author of this passage, the most interesting thing about Bodhidharma was that he was a well-travelled foreign monk who was deeply impressed by the monastery's architecture. But there are some other interesting features to the passage – for one, Bodhidharma is said to come from Persia, rather than India – though it is not clear what 'Persia' (Chinese *bosi*) referred to at this time; it may have been a general term for western Central Asia. The last line of the passage is intriguing as well, describing Bodhidharma's reciting the name of the Buddha. This practice, though not attributed to Bodhidharma in later accounts, and not found in the works attributed to him, was popular at the time, and was very much part of early Zen.

After this, the next account of Bodhidharma's life is in the preface to his work *The Two Entrances and Four Practices*, written by Tanlin, who may have been a disciple of Bodhidharma.[2] This account tells us that Bodhidharma was from south India, and was born into a royal family. This is a fairly conventional way of talking about revered teachers, so there seems no particular reason to believe that Bodhidharma was from India rather than Persia. Indeed, as Jeffrey Broughton has said: 'there is, however, nothing implausible about an early sixth-century Iranian Buddhist master who made his way to North China via the fabled Silk Road. This scenario is, in fact, more likely than a South Indian master who made his way by the sea route.'[3]

In any case, the *Masters of the Lanka* tells us that Bodhidharma travelled by sea to the eastern coast of China, possibly to the port city of Hangzhou – near modern Shanghai.[4] At that time, China was ruled by several different kingdoms, and the area where Bodhidharma first arrived was ruled by the Liang dynasty (502–87). Later, Bodhidharma travelled north to Luoyang, a great city of Buddhist monasteries and the capital of the Northern Wei dynasty (386–534). Bodhidharma then travelled on to Ye, which became the capital of the new Eastern Wei kingdom (535–50).[5] Here he met his closest students and passed on his teachings to them.

The *Masters of the Lanka* does not elaborate on the life of Bodhidharma, staying close to its sources. By contrast, the *Genealogy of the Dharma Jewel* adds more colour to the life of Bodhidharma with some – almost certainly fictional – stories about his activities in

China. For example, it is said that before he came to China, Bodhidharma sent two of his disciples to teach the path of immediate enlightenment. Speaking to a senior Chinese monk, they said, 'The hand changes into a fist, and the fist changes into a hand; does this happen quickly or not?' When the monk replies that it happens quickly, they disagree, saying, 'Defilement changing into enlightenment; *this* is quick!'[6]

Another story in the *Genealogy of the Dharma Jewel* became part of the legend of Bodhidharma: his meeting with Emperor Wu of the Liang dynasty. It is said that Emperor Wu came to meet Bodhidharma personally to ask him what teachings he had brought from his country. Bodhidharma replies, 'I have not brought a single word.' The emperor then asks about the merit gained through building monasteries, having scriptures copied and sculptures cast. Bodhidharma replies, 'None at all,' and goes on to say that this is a contrived form of virtue, not real merit. The emperor is discomfited, and Bodhidharma has to travel onwards.

The *Genealogy of the Dharma Jewel* paints a picture of Bodhidharma as an iconoclast who made enemies in China (something that is also mentioned in passing in the *Masters of the Lanka*). It tells several stories about how he survived poisoning attempts, before eventually passing away and being buried. However, after his burial, an emissary is said to have met him in the Pamir Mountains, on the Silk Route back to India, carrying one shoe in his hand.

* * *

The teachings of Bodhidharma are represented in the *Masters of the Lanka* by a single text, his *Two Entrances and Four Practices*. This accords with modern scholarship, which considers this text the most likely of all those attributed to Bodhidharma to represent his actual teachings. Also mentioned as being genuine, though not quoted here, are two compilations of texts known as the *Bodhidharma Treatise*. A third text, with the same name but longer, is mentioned as a fake.

The contents of these Bodhidharma treatises probably overlap to a great extent with the contents of a compendium known to modern scholars as The Long Scroll. This compendium is in fact derived from several scrolls from the Dunhuang cave. It begins with Bodhidharma's brief biography and the *Two Entrances and Four Practices*, much as we find it here, and continues with further teachings attributed to Bodhidharma, followed by quotations and dialogues involving Bodhidharma, Huike and other masters.[7]

In any case, in all of these early traditions, the *Two Entrances and Four Practices* was considered to be Bodhidharma's core teaching. This is not surprising – it is clear, well organized and explains how to integrate practice of the Buddhist path with realization that one's nature is already the same as a buddha's. At the beginning of the text, Bodhidharma presents his teaching not as something new, but as a distillation of a multitude of existing teachings. All of them, he says, can be summarized according to the two entrances: entrance by principle and entrance by practice.

The entrance by principle is based on the idea of the buddha nature, and requires 'a profound faith that sentient beings, whether ordinary people or noble ones, are the same in their true nature, yet due to adventitious and unreal obscuration this is not able to manifest clearly'.

If you want to abandon the unreal and turn to the real, sit steadily and gaze at a wall. Self and other, ordinary people and enlightened ones, are one and the same. Sit firmly without moving, no longer following spoken instructions. In this you are identical with the hidden form of the true principle, a stillness without name.

The first thing to notice here is that the entrance by principle is also a practice: sitting and gazing at a wall. Modern scholars often say that we cannot know what this 'wall gazing' (*bíguān* in Chinese) actually entailed. Based on other early sources, John McRae suggests that the 'wall' could be metaphorical, referring to the idea of keeping out the winds of distraction.[8] Thus the term would simply be a synonym for peaceful meditation (Skt 'śamatha').

On the other hand, it is interesting to see how the Tibetan translator rendered the term in the ninth century. Though the Chinese simply combines the characters for 'wall' and 'to see', the Tibetan translation clearly means 'gazing at the surface of a wall' (*rtsig ngos la bltas pa*). The Tibetan translator certainly did not see this as a synonym for peaceful meditation (which would be translated as *zhi gnas* in Tibetan). Though not a contemporary of Bodhidharma, the Tibetan translator was much closer to those who were transmitting his teaching tradition in its early stages than we are, and this translation is one good reason to think that 'wall gazing' did indeed involve sitting in front of a wall in meditation.

Taken literally in this way, wall gazing fits perfectly into the Buddhist tradition of peaceful meditation, in which the meditator usually has an object to focus on. The object may take many forms, and one of the classical lists of objects is the ten *kaṣina*, which are the four elements, the colours green, yellow, red and white, an open space or a bright light.[9] While kaṣina may be objects like a vase of flowers or a candle, contemplation of many of the kaṣina does involve actually gazing at a wall. For example, colours may take the form of coloured textiles or paper discs pasted to a wall; the light may be a circle of light cast from a lantern onto a wall; and the open space may be a hole in a wall. Thus many of these classic peaceful meditation practices could quite accurately be called 'gazing at a wall'.

Meditation on the ten kaṣina is best known from the Pali canon and the writings of the fifth-century commentator Buddhaghosa. Yet they were part of the *abhidharma* literature, and known in other Buddhist traditions as well.[10] The kaṣina objects were linked to the stages of experience in meditation (Skt 'dhyāna'). Thus the idea of gazing at a wall in meditation would be familiar to an Indian teacher well versed in dhyāna, as Bodhidharma is said to have been.

Since Bodhidharma's teaching does not mention the kaṣina object, perhaps the focus was meant to be the wall itself. Since his meditation is said to reveal the true principle, 'without form, beyond analysis, a stillness without name', this seems appropriate.[11] In any case, since this is a very common form of Buddhist meditation, it explains why Bodhidharma does not go into the details. Rather than explaining the basics of peaceful contemplation, the main point that Bodhidharma makes is that the meditator must be 'identical with the true principle'.

This phrase 'the principle' is a particularly Chinese way of referring to what is also called thusness, ultimate truth or the nature of things.[12] In a study of the meaning of this word (*lǐ* in Chinese), Brook Ziporyn writes that 'Li is the fact about things, in this case about all things without exception, hence the universal universal, attention to which will lead to liberation'. The term was used in this way from the early Tiantai writings of Zhiyi (538–97) onwards. We can't know whether Bodhidharma, as a foreign teacher, actually used the Chinese word *lǐ*, but his students did, and it soon became part of the transmission of his teachings.[13]

Bodhidharma's entrance by principle is in the background of meditation practice in many modern Zen traditions, including Japanese Soto. Yet it is striking that none of the successors to Bodhidharma in the *Masters of the Lanka* refer to the entrance by principle or the practice of gazing at a wall even once. Though their teachings often resemble Bodhidharma's in various ways, it is clear that they did not feel that they needed to frame their work in terms of the *Two Entrances and Four Practices*, or any of Bodhidharma's other works. This shows us clearly that early Zen did not develop as a one-to-one transmission from Bodhidharma onwards, but through the interaction of many different teachers and practices.

After the entrance by principle comes the entrance by practice, which is actually four practices. The first two of these form a pair: they are topics to contemplate when one is suffering and when one is happy and successful. Thus in the first practice, as an antidote to becoming angry or despondent when facing negative circumstances, one considers them to be karmic payback for one's own misdeeds in this and previous lives: 'For incalculable aeons in the past, I have abandoned the source to chase after trivialities, wandering aimlessly through all the realms of existence, incurring retributions for the wrongdoings and the unbounded harm I have done.' The point is not to blame others for one's suffering, but instead to turn it into something positive, i.e. the motivation to avoid doing harm to others in the future.

Similarly, the second practice is an antidote to the exultation or complacency that might come from experiencing good fortune. Here, one contemplates the fact of dependent arising – that every situation comes about through causes and conditions, and once those are no longer present, the situation changes. Again, present circumstances are considered to be the result of actions in past lifetimes: 'These circumstances are entirely due to my past lives. I am enjoying them at this moment, but when the conditions for them are gone, they will not remain either.' Bodhidharma states that if one does these two practices, one's mind will no longer be subject to ups and downs.

The third and fourth practices are more like general approaches to the Buddhist path. The third is 'not seeking', and is eloquently summarized by a quote from a sutra: 'Everyone who is seeking is suffering; only when you stop seeking will you be happy.' Seeking is the process of attachment, taught by the Buddha as the primary cause of suffering. To stop seeking, Bodhidharma writes, one should contemplate that all things are empty, so there is nothing to aim for. The fourth practice is to act in accord with the dharma; this comes about through realization of the principle: 'If wise people can develop confidence in the principle then their practice will be in accord with the dharma.'

Thus the fourth practice brings us back to the beginning of the text, the entrance by principle. The manifestation of acting in accordance with the dharma is the six perfections, beginning with the perfection of generosity. Bodhidharma explains that the practice of the perfections is an expression of the nature of mind itself. So generosity is not forced because mind is not stingy by nature. The perfection of generosity is a spontaneous act of giving which is not defined by the three aspects of the ordinary concept of giving: the person who gives, the one who receives, and that which is given. Since these aspects are all dependent on each other, they are empty.

The teachings in the *Two Entrances and Four Practices* are firmly grounded in the Indic Buddhist traditions that a teacher like Bodhidharma would have been familiar with, and apart from the unusual term 'wall gazing', they do not offer anything revolutionary. Yet taken as a whole, this is a concise and powerful text: the entrance by principle, practised through wall gazing, offers an immediate realization of one's own enlightened nature, while the four practices offer a graduated path culminating in the realization of the principle. Together they offer a way of bringing together immediate realization with graduated practice.

This chapter ends with a few miscellaneous fragments of teachings, which, as in the previous chapter, do not appear in the Tibetan translation. They are probably later additions, from the time of Shenxiu and his students. Still, even if we can't consider it a genuine description of Bodhidharma's teaching style, there is an interesting passage here describing how a teacher would question students about ordinary objects, challenging their conceptual framework:

> The great teacher would point his finger at something and ask about its significance. He would just point at a single object, and call upon someone and question them about that object. Then he would ask about all sorts of objects, swapping another name for the object and asking about it in a different way.

In this vivid picture of a teaching situation, we see the teacher asking the students to question their own basic assumptions about an object – that it is *x*, that it bears the name *x*. This draws on an important idea that runs through much of Buddhist philosophy – that language does not define reality, and that the connection between words and things is arbitrary. Buddhist philosophers developed this position in reaction to Vedic schools' belief that language (specifically, Sanskrit) exactly corresponded to reality.[14]

In China, there was less interest in the idea that language must correspond exactly to reality. Early discussions of language by the Mohists and Confucianists were more concerned with its practical application in ethics and politics, while in Daoism, language was considered misleading if used to define the true nature of things, as in the famous line from the *Daodejing*: 'The name that can be named is not the eternal name.' The teaching style attributed to Bodhidharma in the passage above seems to owe something to this Daoist heritage as well.

✦

Chapter Two

The dharma master Bodhidharma was the successor to the tripiṭaka master Guṇabhadra in the Wei dynasty. Bodhidharma was a meditation teacher who was determined to propagate the mahayana. So he crossed the sea to Wuyue and travelled from there to Luoyang before arriving in Ye. The monks Daoyu and Huike served him for five years before he taught them both the four practices.[15] Bodhidharma said to Huike: 'Here are the four scrolls of the *Laṅkāvatāra sūtra*. If your practice is based on this you will be spontaneously liberated.'[16]

The rest of Bodhidharma's life is told in the *Further Biographies of Eminent Monks*.[17] The following outline is from the preface to *Entering the Mahayana Path of the Four Practices* written by Bodhidharma's disciple Tanlin.[18]

This dharma master came from the western regions, specifically the south of India. He was the third son of a great Indian king.[19] His intelligence was piercing and bright, and he clearly understood everything he was taught. He was determined to follow the mahayana path, so he gave up the white clothes of a layman and adopted the black robes of a monk. He transmitted the noble lineage and helped it to flourish. His profound mind was empty and still, and saw right through worldly affairs, with a clear understanding of inner and outer matters.[20] His enlightened qualities went beyond all worldly conventions.

Bodhidharma greatly regretted that the true teachings were in decline at the borderlands. So he crossed distant seas and mountains, travelling to teach in the Wei kingdom of China.[21] Among the elite, whose minds were still and quiet, there was no one who lacked faith in him.[22] But the type who cling to categories and protect their own opinions went so far as to insult him.

At that time his only students were Daoyu and Huike. These two monks, though young in years, carried a lofty and profound resolve. They had the good fortune to meet the dharma teacher, and after serving him for many years they asked with great reverence if he would kindly bestow his thoughts upon them. The dharma teacher, recognizing their aptitude, taught them the true path.

> There is peace of mind,
> There is how you begin to practise,
> There is how you work with sentient beings,
> And there is skilful means.
> This is the mahayana dharma of peace of mind,
> Which allows you to be free from error.

Peace of mind means wall gazing.[23] Doing your practice means the four practices. Working with sentient beings means putting a stop to slander. And skilful means is abandoning whatever does not work.[24] This brief outline is based on Bodhidharma's own thoughts, which appear immediately below.[25]

* * *

For those who are yet to enter the path, there are many options. Ultimately, however, there are two basic types: first, entry by principle, and second, entry by practice.

Entry by principle means relying on the teachings and realizing their guiding principle: the deeply held faith that ordinary sentient beings and enlightened ones are the same in their true nature, yet due to adventitious and unreal obscuration this is not able to manifest clearly.[26] If you want to abandon the unreal and turn to the real, sit steadily and gaze at a wall.[27] Self and other, ordinary people and enlightened ones, are one and the same. Sit firmly without moving, no longer following spoken instructions. In this you are identical with the hidden form of the true principle, a stillness without name. This is the entrance by principle.

Entry by practice refers to four practices. All other practices are included within these four. What is the sequence of these four practices? The first is the practice of contemplating retribution for past wrongdoing.[28] The second is the practice of contemplating dependence.[29] The third is not seeking. The fourth is practising in accord with the dharma.[30]

1

What is the practice of contemplating retribution for past wrongdoings? When a person who is cultivating the path experiences suffering, they should think to themselves as follows: 'For incalculable aeons in the past, I have abandoned the source to chase after trivialities, wandering aimlessly through all the realms of existence, incurring retribution for the wrongdoings and the unbounded harm I have done. Even if I have done nothing wrong recently, this is the ripening of negative karma from my long past misdeeds. It is not sent by the gods or inflicted by other people.'

Those who bear suffering with willingness do not give rise to further wrongdoing. As the sutra says: 'When you meet with suffering, do not despair.'[31] How does this work? It works by recognizing the source. When you develop this attitude, you are in harmony with the principle. Understanding the nature of adversity, you progress on the path.[32] This is what I call the practice of contemplating retribution for past wrongdoings.

2

Second is the practice of contemplating dependence. Sentient beings have no self, but they continue to exist in dependence upon their past actions. The experiences of happiness and suffering are both based on dependent arising. If you become successful, prosperous, highly praised and the like, you should think: 'These circumstances are entirely due to my past lives. I am enjoying them at this moment, but when the conditions for them are gone, they will not remain either. How can I exult in having them when gaining and losing them depend on these conditions?'

Then your mind will not be subject to ups and downs, you will be unmoved by the winds of exultation, profoundly in accord with the path.[33] This is what I call the practice of contemplating dependence.

3

Third is the practice of not seeking. Worldly people are always deluded, developing attachment at every point.[34] This is called 'seeking'. Wise people understand how the true principle is applied to ordinary life.[35] Once peace of mind is unchanging, the body becomes adaptable to change.[36]

All existent things are empty, so there is nothing to aim for. Good and bad always follow one another.[37] The three realms in which we have lived for so long are like a house on fire. To have a body is to suffer. Who can find peace? When you fully understand this, you cease to think of the many forms of existence, and no longer seek anything.

The sutra says:

Everyone who is seeking is suffering;
Only when you stop seeking will you be happy.[38]

Thus to truly not seek anything is to genuinely practise the path.

4

Fourth, practising in accord with the dharma. It is thanks to the essential purity of the principle that it enacts the dharma. The many forms taken by the principle are empty, without defilement or attachment, without 'this' or 'that'.[39]

The sutra says:[40]

In the dharma there are no sentient beings,
Because it is free of the defilements of sentient beings.[41]

In the dharma there is no ego,
Because it is free from the defilements of ego.

If wise people can develop confidence in the principle then their practice will be in accord with the dharma.

Things in their essence are not parsimonious of body and life, so engage in the practice of giving.[42] The mind is not stingy; if you understand the three aspects of emptiness you will be without dependence or attachment.[43] So, once you have abandoned defilement, you will not grasp at categories when you are teaching sentient beings. Helping yourself in this way, you are also able to help others, and can be an ornament of the path to awakening.

This is what the perfection of giving is like, and the other five perfections as well. When you eliminate delusion and cultivate the practice of the six perfections, then there is nothing to be practised. This is practising in accord with the dharma.

* * *

These are the four practices that were personally taught by the meditation master Bodhidharma. His disciple Tanlin also recorded the master's other words and deeds and compiled them in a single scroll called 'the Bodhidharma Treatise'. Bodhidharma also wrote, for groups practising sitting meditation, a commentary on the key points of the *Laṅkāvatāra* in one scroll comprising twelve or thirteen sheets, which is also called 'the Bodhidharma Treatise'.[44]

These two books are perfect in both language and logic, and have spread across the world. Apart from these, there is a 'Bodhidharma Treatise' in three scrolls that someone has forged. Since the language is complicated and the logic is incoherent, it is not suitable to use for one's practice.[45]

* * *

The great teacher would point his finger at something and ask about its significance. He would just point at a single object, and call upon someone and question them about that object. Then he would ask about all sorts of objects, swapping another name for the object and asking about it in a different way.

He also said – Does this body exist? What kind of body is this body?

He also said – A haze of clouds in the sky is ultimately unable to stain the sky; nevertheless it can hide the sky so its clear light cannot be seen.[46]

The *Nirvana Sutra* says:

Internally, there are no six sense bases,
Externally, there are no six objects of the senses,
Because internal and external are combined;
This is called the middle path.[47]

✦

CHAPTER TEN

HUIKE
The Buddha Within

In Zen, Bodhidharma's student Huike is the great example of the devotion of a student to a teacher, and the determination required to follow the path. This is expressed in an extreme form in the story of Huike cutting off his own arm to show Bodhidharma his determination. In the *Masters of the Lanka*, this is reported in Huike's own words:

> When I first generated the aspiration for enlightenment, I cut off one of my arms, and stood up straight in the snow from dusk till the third watch of the night, not noticing as the snow piled up around my knees.[1]

The 'aspiration for enlightenment' is bodhicitta, an important concept in Mahayana Buddhism, meaning aspiring not just towards one's own enlightenment, but for the enlightenment of all sentient beings. Thus bodhicitta is the firmly held wish to enter the path of the bodhisattva. Huike's act of cutting off his arm is not intended as an example to be followed, but its extreme nature conveys the extreme seriousness of the bodhisattva vow: to personally undertake to liberate all living beings from samsara.

For a reader familiar with the world of Buddhism, Huike's sacrifice recalls the many self-sacrificing actions of the bodhisattva who eventually was born as Prince Gautama and became the Buddha Śākyamuni. In the stories known as *jātaka*, the previous lives of the Buddha include many accounts of sacrifice, some of them extreme, such as that of the Prince Sudana, who gave away everything, including his wife and children, or the unnamed bodhisattva who gave his body to a starving tigress and her cubs.

In Buddhist traditions around the world, these stories have elicited debates about the limits of self-sacrifice. Though rare, the cutting off of an extremity (usually fingers or toes) and self-immolation have been practised by Buddhist monks and nuns, yet these are not the way *jātaka* stories, or Huike's sacrifice, are usually understood. Rather than encouraging imitation, they are taken as the strongest possible way of communicating the seriousness of the bodhisattva's vow.

Much of the teaching contained in this chapter of the *Masters of the Lanka* is about the buddha nature (*tathāgatagarbha* in Sanskrit, *fóxìng* in Chinese). The common English translation 'buddha nature', which I am using here, is a direct translation of the Chinese. The Sanskrit 'tathāgatagarbha' is a little more difficult to translate: a 'tathāgata' is a buddha, which is straightforward enough, but 'garbha' means literally 'womb' and as an extension, anything interior. Thus it might equally be translated as 'the buddha within'. This is exactly how the buddha nature is often presented; a quotation from a sutra in this chapter states that, 'In the body of every sentient being there is a vajra buddha.'

Huike uses a series of metaphors to further illustrate the idea of the buddha nature. It is like a lamp placed in a vase – its light is undiminished, but cannot be seen in this state. Equally, the buddha nature can be compared to the sun temporarily obscured by clouds:

> The sun's light has not been diminished; it is just obscured by the hazy clouds and not seen by sentient beings. When the clouds part and are cleared away, the sunlight shines everywhere, its radiance pure and unobscured.

These metaphors for the buddha nature are drawn from the sutras, but Huike uses one further metaphor said to come from 'a secular book' –

meaning a non-Buddhist source. He quotes two brief sayings: 'Though ice appears in water, it is able to stop water', and 'When ice melts, water flows.' Though I have not found these exact words in Chinese literary sources, some very similar sayings are found in the *Anthology of Literary Texts*, a compendium of Chinese literary quotations taken from earlier works, which was compiled in the early seventh century.[2]

The analogy of ice and water continued through the centuries in both Buddhist and Daoist traditions.[3] It is central to the thinking of the neo-Confucian Zhang Zai (1020–77), who argued that the basis of all existence, called *qi*, is formless, but manifests as everything in the world through a transformation akin to water freezing into ice.[4] An eighteenth-century Daoist writer used the same analogy, with even more Buddhist leanings:

Water freezes into ice when it is cold, ice melts into water when it is warm. What I realize as I observe this is the Tao of becoming either a sage or an ordinary person. At first, human nature is basically good. There is originally no distinction between the sage and the ordinary person. It is because of the energy of accumulated habits that there comes to be a difference between sages and ordinary people.[5]

Back in the Buddhist tradition, the influential Japanese Zen reformer Hakuin Ekaku (1686–1768) began one of his most popular poems with the same analogy:

Sentient beings are in essence buddhas.
It is like water and ice.
There is no ice without water;
There are no buddhas outside of sentient beings.[6]

Here, the difference between ice and water is the difference between the ordinary person and the Buddha, much as in Huike's teaching. The analogy has also carried through to the present in Zen; in one of her talks the American Zen teacher Charlotte Joko Beck compared the nature of ordinary human beings to ice cubes, giving the metaphor a psychological reading:

> To protect ourselves we freeze as hard as we can and hope that when we collide with others, they will shatter before we do. We freeze because we're afraid. Our fear makes us rigid, fixed, and hard, and we create mayhem as we bump into others. Any obstacle or unexpected difficulty is likely to shatter us.

The positive side of this is that ice can melt, through the practice of meditation.

> Eventually what we are as ice cubes is destroyed. But if the ice cube has become a puddle, is it truly destroyed? We could say that it's no longer an ice cube, but its essential self is realized.[7]

The metaphor has continued outside Buddhism, in the way Bruce Lee described his system of martial arts, Jeet Kune Do. Here, while the aim might be different, the sense of the metaphor is very much akin to the way Charlotte Joko Beck uses it in her talk:

> When one has reached maturity in the art, one will have a formless form. It is like the dissolving or thawing of ice into water that can shape itself into any structure. When one has no form, one can be all forms; when one has no style, one can fit in with any style.[8]

Returning to Huike, we can see why the Daoist metaphor of ice and water is brought into dialogue with the idea of the buddha nature. It makes it clear that the buddha nature is not something separate from ourselves, or contained within ourselves, but something that is inseparable; it is what we are.[9]

* * *

In Huike's teachings, the idea that we are all buddhas as part of our very nature leads on to his insistence that we do not need to rely on other people's accounts of the path. Everything we need is here in our very nature. Huike presents his own experience as an example to follow: 'Once I had verified for myself the benefits of sitting meditation, I dispensed with the attitude of looking for the principle in books of written dharma, and strove to accomplish buddhahood.'

If we have the buddha nature – if we are ice that simply needs to melt – then reading about this will not get us very far. Huike advises his students to stay away from books, or at least not to spend too much time with them: 'those who read books should look into them for a while, then promptly set them aside'. And he quotes a verse from a sutra that stands as a sharp rebuke to those who spend most of their time reading or writing books:

> There is a story of a very poor person
> Who spent day and night counting the wealth of others
> Without a penny of his own.
> Scholarship is very much like this.

This is an uncomfortable message for scholars, both ancient and modern, but it is also addressed to anyone for whom the collecting and reading of texts takes the place of practice. Huike's chapter ends with a long quotation from the *Avataṃsaka sūtra*, with the message that realization about any aspect of reality is equivalent to total realization. This is because even the distinction between 'one' and 'many' is false, a theme that is continued in the next chapter, in the teachings of Sengcan.

Chapter Three

The monk Huike became the successor of the meditation master Bodhidharma in Ye, during the Qi dynasty.[10] The meditation master Huike's family name was Ji, and he came from Wulao.[11] He met Bodhidharma at the age of fourteen, when the master was travelling and teaching in Songshan and Luoyang. Huike served him for six years, mastering all aspects of the single vehicle while adhering to the profound principle.[12] He composed some brief teachings on the path of cultivation, the key dharma points regarding the luminous mind and completing the ascent to buddhahood.[13]

The *Laṅkāvatāra sūtra* says:

Observe the Sage in peace,
Beyond birth and death.
This is called 'not clinging'
Pure now and ever after.[14]

If there is a single one of all the buddhas of the ten directions who did not achieve this through sitting meditation, then there is no such thing as complete buddhahood.[15]

The *Daśabhūmika sūtra* says:

In the body of every sentient being
There is the vajra buddha.
This is just like the sun,

Luminous, perfect and complete.
It is vast and unlimited,
Yet covered by the dark clouds of the five aggregates,
So sentient beings cannot see it.[16]

When they meet with the winds of wisdom, the dark clouds of the five aggregates are blown away. Once they are gone, the buddha nature shines out, bright, luminous and pure.

The *Avataṃsaka sūtra* says:

Vast as the reality itself,
Endless as space.[17]

It is also like the light of a lamp inside a vase that cannot shine out. Or like when hazy clouds come across the land all at once from all directions, plunging the land into darkness. How can the sunlight be pure and clear? The sun's light has not been diminished; it is just obscured by the hazy clouds and not seen by sentient beings. When the clouds part and are cleared away, the sunlight shines everywhere, its radiance pure and unobscured.[18]

The pure nature of all sentient beings is like this; it is just that grasping, deluded thought, wrong views and dark clouds of the afflictions obscure the noble path so that it is unable to fully manifest.[19] On the other hand, if deluded thoughts do not arise, and you sit in pure stillness, then the pure luminosity of the sun of great nirvana arises spontaneously.[20]

A secular book says: 'Though ice comes from water, it is able to stop water', and 'When ice melts, water can flow again.'[21] Similarly, though delusion arises from reality, reality can get lost in delusion. But when delusion comes to an end, reality is revealed. The ocean of the mind becomes instantly and perfectly clear; this is the dharmakaya, empty and pure.[22]

Thus a student who takes written words and spoken teachings as the path is like a candle in the wind, unable to dispel the darkness when its flame blows out.[23] If they sit in purity, doing nothing, this is like a lamp kept inside a sealed house, which can thus dispel the darkness and illuminate objects so that they can be clearly seen. If they understand that the source of the mind is pure, then all desires will be satisfied, all activities accomplished. With absolutely everything achieved, they will not have to go through further rebirths.[24]

Among sentient beings as numerous as the sands on the banks of the Ganges, barely a single person exists who will attain this dharmakaya. In a billion aeons there may be no more than a single person who fulfils these criteria. If true sincerity has not arisen within you, then not even all the buddhas of the three times, who are as numerous as the sands on the banks of the Ganges, can help you.[25]

Know this: sentient beings who recognize the nature of mind liberate themselves. It is not buddhas who liberate sentient beings. If buddhas were able to liberate sentient beings, then since we have already met buddhas countless as the sand on the banks of the Ganges, why have we not accomplished buddhahood yet?[26] It is only because genuine sincerity has not arisen within us. We say we get it, but our minds do not get it.

As the dharma scriptures say, those who teach emptiness while keeping to worldly practices are imitating the ultimate path, and in the end they will not avoid being reborn in accord with their past actions.[27] Thus the buddha nature is like the sun and moon in the world or the potential for fire within wood.[28]

This buddha nature, which exists in everyone, is also known as 'the lamp of the buddha nature' and 'the mirror of nirvana'. This mirror of vast nirvana is brighter than the sun and moon, completely pure inside and out, unbound and unlimited. It is also like smelting gold: after the gold has taken shape and the fire has gone out, the nature of the gold remains unspoilt. Just so, after the succession of lives and deaths of sentient beings has come to an end, the dharmakaya remains unspoilt.

It is also like when a ball or lump of dirt is broken up – the individual particles are not destroyed.[29] When rough waves cease, the nature of the water is not affected; just so, after the succession of lives and deaths of sentient beings has come to an end, the dharmakaya remains unspoilt.[30]

Once I had verified for myself the benefits of sitting meditation, I dispensed with the attitude of looking for the principle in books of written dharma, and strove to accomplish buddhahood. There is not one person in ten thousand who does this.[31] As an old book says, drawing food does not make a meal.[32] If you just talk about food with people, how will you eat? When you try to remove a stopper, paradoxically, you often push it in more tightly.[33]

The *Avataṃsaka sūtra* says:

There is a story of a very poor person
Who spent day and night counting the wealth of others
Without a penny of his own.
Scholarship is very much like this.[34]

So those who read books should look into them briefly, then promptly set them aside. If they do not put them away again, how is this study of words different from looking for ice in hot water? Or boiling water but hoping to find snow? Thus the buddhas may teach the teachings, or teach the teachings by not teaching. In the true nature of things, there is neither teaching nor not teaching.[35] If you realize this, everything else follows.[36]

The *Lotus Sutra* says:

Not true, not false,
Not the same, not different.[37]

* * *

The great master said –

In this teaching of the real dharma, everything is in accord with
   the truth,

And is ultimately no different from the profound principle itself.
At first, deluded people see the precious stone and call it a rock;
Then they suddenly realize that it is a genuine jewel.
There is no difference between ignorance and wisdom;
Just know that all phenomena are like this.
Out of compassion for those who spend their lives seeing them as
    different,
I speak these words, and write them down with my brush.
When you see yourself as no different from the Buddha,
Why would you continue to search elsewhere?

* * *

He also said – When I first generated the aspiration for enlightenment, I cut off one of my arms, and stood up straight in the snow
from dusk till the third watch of the night, not noticing as the
snow piled up around my knees, in order to seek the unsurpassable
path.

As it is taught in the seventh volume of the *Avataṃsaka sūtra*:

When you enter a state of absorption in the east,
Samadhi arises in the west.[38]
When you enter a state of absorption in the west,
Samadhi arises in the east.
When you enter a state of absorption based on the eyes,
Samadhi arises in forms.[39]
Showing that the manifestation of forms is non-conceptual,
Something that gods and humans are unable to comprehend.
When you enter a state of absorption in forms,
Concentration arises in the eyes, and you are freed from
    confusion.[40]
The eye that sees is not produced, nor does it have an intrinsic
    nature;
I teach that emptiness is stillness which abides nowhere.

The ear, nose, tongue, body and intellect,
Are also like this.
When you enter the state of absorption in the body of a child,
Samadhi arises in the body of an adult.
When you enter the state of absorption in the body of an adult,
Samadhi arises in the body of an aged person.
When you enter samadhi in the body of an aged person,
Samadhi arises in the body of a virtuous woman.
When you enter the state of absorption in the body of a virtuous woman,
Samadhi appears in the body of a virtuous man.
When you enter the state of absorption in the body of a virtuous man,
Samadhi appears in the body of a nun.
When you enter the state of absorption in the body of a nun,
Samadhi appears in the body of a monk.
When you enter the state of absorption in the body of a monk,
Samadhi appears in the body of a hearer.[41]
When you enter the state of absorption in the body of a hearer,
Samadhi appears in the body of a solitary budda.[42]
When you enter the state of absorption in the body of a solitary buddha,
Samadhi appears in the body of a tathāgata.
When you enter the state of absorption in a single pore,
Samadhi appears in all of your pores.
When you enter the state of absorption in all of your pores,
Samadhi arises on the tip of a single hair.
When you enter the state of absorption on the tip of a single hair,
Samadhi arises in all of your hairs.
When you enter the state of absorption in all of your hairs,
Samadhi arises in a single mote of dust.
When you enter the state of absorption in a single mote of dust,
Samadhi arises in all motes of dust.
When you enter the state of absorption in a vast ocean of water,

Samadhi arises in a great blaze of fire.
One body can give rise to countless bodies,
And countless bodies can be one body.[43]

If you attain realization of this one thing, everything else follows.
Everything is just this – the dharmakaya, the guiding principle.[44]

✦

CHAPTER ELEVEN

SENGCAN

Heaven in a Grain of Sand

Sengcan is an obscure figure, whose main significance is as the link between Huike and Daoxin. Even the earliest Zen lineage histories, including the *Masters of the Lanka*, have little to say about his life, and what is added in later sources is suspect. Nevertheless, these later stories are also part of the Zen tradition. For example, the *Genealogy of the Dharma Jewel* tells us how Sengcan met his teacher Huike. The story is that they met in a crowded place, where Sengcan asked to study with Huike. Noticing that Sengcan was suffering from palsy, Huike asked him why he wanted to study with him. Sengcan answered that though his body was afflicted, his mind was identical to Huike's own mind.[1] The story is more elaborate in the *Further Biographies of Eminent Monks*:

> In the second year of the Tianping era of the Northern Qi dynasty [536], a layman whose name is not known came to Huike and said, 'My body has been wracked by a terrible illness. I ask that you help me absolve the transgression I've committed that has caused this.'
>
> Huike said, 'Bring to me the transgression you've committed and I'll absolve it.'
>
> The layman said, 'I look for the transgression but I can't find it.'
>
> Huike said, 'There, I've absolved your transgression. Now you should abide in Buddha, dharma, and sangha.'[2]

If this conversation seems familiar, it is because it echoes the story of Huike's conversation with Bodhidharma, in which Bodhidharma challenges Huike to show his mind so that it can be made calm, and Huike cannot do so.[3] Thus mind is shown to be an empty concept. In this version of the story, it is karma, the cause and effect of actions, that is shown to be empty. The conversation continues:

> The layman said, 'Seeing you here, I know what is meant by "sangha," but I still don't know what are called Buddha and dharma.'
>
> Huike said, 'Mind is Buddha. Mind is dharma. Buddha and dharma are not two different things. Along with sangha they comprise the three jewels.'
>
> The layman said, 'Today, for the first time, I realize that my transgression was not internal, was not external, and was not in between these two states. It was entirely within mind. Buddha and dharma are not two things.'[4]

After this exchange, Huike gives the layman the name Sengcan, meaning 'Jewel of the Sangha'. The three jewels – Buddha, dharma and sangha – represent the Buddha, his teachings and the community of practitioners. To say the Buddha is the same as the dharma is to say that the Buddha is what he taught. To say that both are the mind is to affirm that they are not external things to be sought or worshipped, but are to be realized as one's own mind.

Despite the success of this meeting, the *Genealogy of the Dharma Jewel* states that the two had little chance to spend time together, because Buddhism was being suppressed at the time and Sengcan had to spend a decade in hiding on Mount Huangong. His late adoption of Zen and this remote and solitary existence might explain Sengcan's obscurity. The story of Sengcan's death is told in the same way in the *Masters of the Lanka* and the *Genealogy of the Dharma Jewel* – how he died in a standing position, showing his mastery of body and mind.[5]

Though the *Masters of the Lanka* tells us that Sengcan never wrote a book, it does quote his words. These are from a commentary on a teaching called *Explaining the Hidden*. The original text was written by Huiming (531–68), a contemporary of Sengcan.[6] The teaching of

Explaining the Hidden may be summarized as the sameness of all things, due to the redundancy of all our categories. The essence of this teaching is expressed in this verse:

> We do not get stuck on whether things are self or other;
> We do not judge situations to be right or wrong.
> A single atom contains all the phenomena of the universe;
> A single moment contains all time, past, present and future.

For a Western reader, these words may be reminiscent of the opening lines of William Blake's *Auguries of Innocence*:

> To see a World in a Grain of Sand
> And a Heaven in a Wild Flower,
> Hold Infinity in the palm of your hand
> And Eternity in an hour.

An educated Buddhist, on the other hand, would be reminded of similar statements in the sutras about the nature of enlightened awareness. In the *Gaṇḍavyūha sūtra*, for example, the Tower of Vairocana is a visionary abode of those who have attained enlightenment; in a hymn of praise to these enlightened beings, it is said that:

> Here they enter infinite aeons
> In a single thought.

And:

> In a single atom they see
> Congregations, lands, beings, and ages,
> As numerous as all atoms,
> All there without obstruction.[7]

And Jingjue, in the preface to the *Masters of the Lanka*, says something similar: 'Within a single hair there is the entire universe, and one mote of dust contains the limitless cosmos.' Statements like these may seem mystical and impossible to justify, but in Buddhism they do have a philosophical basis. As we have already seen, Madhyamaka philosophy argues that everything exists in dependence on other things. In Sengcan's brief text, this is expressed in metaphors:

> Like a precious palace decorated with jewels,
> Or a crystal tower hung with mirrors,
> This and that are separate but enter into each other.

The image of a network of jewels or mirrors, all reflecting each other, is a poetic expression of the network of dependence. A Buddhist of Sengcan's time would also recognize the reference to the Tower of Vairocana. When the hero of the *Gaṇḍavyūha sūtra*, Sudhana, enters the tower, he sees:

> Hundreds of thousands of other towers similarly arrayed; he saw those towers as infinitely vast as space, evenly arrayed in all directions, yet those towers were not mixed up with one another, being each mutually distinct, while appearing reflected in each and every object of all the other towers.[8]

This is a metaphor for the nature of things: while any thing may be distinguished from another, it cannot exist independently because its existence depends on a variety of causes and conditions. Like jewels or mirrors that all reflect each other without losing their specific existence, all things – including ourselves – are ultimately linked to all other things. Yet Buddhists do not believe that everything merges into an amorphous Oneness. As Sengcan says:

> Though large and small are different, they blend with each other like images in mirrors, each one distinct, like different forms intersecting in a single shape. The one is the same as the all, and the all is the same as the one.

The most well-known image of this interdependence is Indra's net, a network of jewels, all reflecting each other, which had become popular in China due to the success of the Huayan school.[9] The realization of the network of dependence is at the core of Sengcan's text, and indeed of much Zen discourse. Little is said here on how this translates into practice, but it does seem that the understanding of the dependent and relative nature of all categories, including right and wrong, does not mean that Buddhist practices are abandoned:

> Just as a monkey put in chains stops jumping around,
> Or a snake entering a bamboo tube stops being crooked,
> Cross the wide sea in the vessel of the precepts,
> Illuminate the darkness with the flame of insight.

In other words, even if right and wrong are relative, it is necessary to follow the Buddhist moral precepts. And even if the state of confusion and enlightenment are fundamentally the same, it is important to practise meditation to achieve wisdom. Otherwise the mind is like the monkey jumping around, never staying still long enough to recognize its own nature. Apparently Sengcan never put into writing any instructions on how to practise meditation, but that was to be remedied by his student, Daoxin.

✦

Chapter Four

In the Sui dynasty, the successor to Huike was meditation master Sengcan, from Sikong Mountain in Shuzhou. The name and status of meditation master Sengcan's family are unknown, and his place of birth cannot be found. The *Further Biographies of Eminent Monks* simply says, 'after Huike came the meditation master Sengcan'.

He lived in seclusion on Sikong Mountain, sitting in pure solitude, and never wrote down his teachings. His secret dharma was only transmitted to the monk Daoxin, who served him for twelve years. Like water poured from one vessel to another or the passing of the flame from one lamp to another, Daoxin received everything.[10] Once Daoxin had seen the buddha nature in himself, Sengcan gave his seal of approval in the genuine path.

Sengcan said to Daoxin –

The *Lotus Sutra* says:
There is only this one true way,[11]
    No second or third.[12]

Know then that this noble path is profound, and cannot be grasped by explaining it in words. The dharmakaya is empty and still, and cannot be reached through seeing and hearing. So written words and oral explanations are just efforts wasted in speculation. The *Laṅkāvatāra*, the sutra that embodies the principle of peace of mind in the special greater vehicle, and distinguishes truth from error, says 'the dharma path of the saints is silence, never taught in words'.[13]

Then the great master said, 'Everyone else regards sitting at the moment of death as something exceptionally rare. I will now leave this life while I stand, liberating myself from samsara.'[14] As soon as he had finished speaking, he held on to a branch, and in this posture he breathed his last breath. After his death an image of him was placed in the temple of Yugong Mountain monastery, where it can still be seen.[15]

* * *

From The Commentary on Explaining the Hidden:[16]

There is only one true way, profound and expansive,
But oh, the difficulties caused by our many categories!
Ultimate and conventional appear to be different,[17]
But they are the same in essence.
Ordinary people and sages may seem far apart,
But they are on the same path.
Look for a limit and you find
That in this openness there are no borders.
No end at the furthest point,
No beginning at the source,
No stopping at the edges.
This permeates understanding and confusion;
This blends together purity and defilement,
Combining existence and emptiness in tranquillity,
Embracing space and time so they are one and the same,
Just as gold is inseparable from rings and bracelets,
And a lake is unspoiled by the ripples on its surface.

The commentary says:[18]

The discussion of limits and borders shows that the principle is without interruption or adulteration. The discussion of beginnings and ends is because the buddha nature is not something that can be created. This way of teaching the nonduality of light and dark brings together good and evil in the path of equality.

It is without movement, but does not rest; without difference, but does not conform. The similes for this are the way the water makes waves, and the way gold is used to make objects.[19] The gold of which these objects are made is their very substance, so there can be no objects without the gold. The waves which the water makes are its own activity, so likewise there are no waves separate from the water.

See how dependent arising is without obstruction!
Be confident that the nature of things is beyond comprehension!
Like a precious palace decorated with pearls,
Or a jade tower hung with mirrors,[20]
This and that are separate but blend with each other,
Red and purple are different but merge in the reflected light.
Things do not get stuck on self or other;
Events do not judge about right or wrong.
A single atom contains all the phenomena of the universe;
A single moment contains all time, past, present and future.
Since those of little faith may be afraid of statements like these,
We borrow the image of Indra's net to remove their doubts.
This is hidden so that only true vision can observe it;[21]
How could it be known by a deluded consciousness?

The commentary says:

> This is an explanation of the secret of dependent arising. Indra's net is the phenomenal world. The one is the same as the all – they intermingle yet they are not the same. Why? Categories lack a reality of their own, yet they must be based on what is real. Since categories are always an aspect of the true principle, they cannot obstruct it.[22]

Though large and small are different, they blend with each other like images in mirrors, each one distinct, like different forms intersecting in a single shape. The one is the same as the all, and the all is the same as the one. Dependent arising does not obscure the principle; it is actually the same as the principle. Thus we know that the entire expanse of the universe is held within a tiny particle, without being confined. The whole extent of past, present and future times is contained in the briefest of moments.

Wise people who have grasped the principle can clearly see what is on the other side of a metal screen without obstruction, and pass through a stone wall without the slightest hindrance.[23] On the other hand, those who are not able to grasp the principle in this way may be wise, but do not have such powers. If you understand that the principle permeates everything then you will no longer be hindered by the pressure of thoughts and emotions, and with the wisdom of universal vision you will be able to recognize the ultimate truth.

Just as a monkey put in chains stops jumping around,
Or a snake entering a bamboo tube stops being crooked,
Cross the wide sea in the vessel of the precepts,
Illuminate the darkness with the flame of insight.[24]

The commentary says:

The monkey in chains is a metaphor for the way the precepts regulate the mind, and the snake entering a bamboo tube is a metaphor for how concentration settles confusion.[25] The *Mahāprajñāpāramitā-śāstra* says, 'The snake's gait is normally crooked, but when it enters a bamboo tube, it immediately straightens out.'[26] This is like the way that concentration regulates the mind. In the chapter on the three bodies in the *Suvarṇaprabhāsa sūtra* it says, 'Though the Buddha has three names, he does not have a threefold essence.'[27]

✦

CHAPTER TWELVE

DAOXIN I
How to Sit

Daoxin was the first Zen teacher who left clear and specific instructions on how to practise sitting meditation. These instructions survive thanks to their inclusion in the *Masters of the Lanka*. The way that the *Masters of the Lanka* includes only the bare minimum of Daoxin's biography but the whole of his teachings on meditation shows how much this text differs from the other Zen lineage histories from around the same time – both the *Transmission of the Dharma Jewel* and the *Genealogy of the Dharma Jewel* give more details from Daoxin's life, but nothing of his teachings.

The *Transmission of the Dharma Jewel* tells a story that is repeated in various forms in most later biographies. In the year 607, Daoxin travelled to a town near China's eastern coast. When he arrived a group of bandits had surrounded the town and were laying siege to it. The town's wells had run dry and the people were desperate. The town magistrate asked Daoxin for help, and he advised the local monks and laypeople to recite the *Perfection of Wisdom Sutra*. They did, and this caused the bandits to see giant soldiers advancing on them; the soldiers fled and the city was saved.[1]

Apart from stories such as this, about events which may or may not have happened, we know little about the activities of Daoxin. We do know that from 624 onwards, Daoxin settled on Shuangfeng Mountain (in English, Twin Peaks) where he built a monastery, the first teacher in this early Zen lineage to do so. In building his monastery, Daoxin established the model followed even more successfully by Hongren in the next generation, and with huge and lasting impact by Shenxiu in the generation after that.

In any case, this chapter of the *Masters of the Lanka* is dedicated to Daoxin's teachings. The way the text introduces these teachings has previously been translated as a single long title.[2] However, the text does actually indicate two things, the first of which is a volume with the title *Methods for the Bodhisattva Precepts*. The text then goes on to state that Daoxin 'also composed' teachings for novices on methods for attaining peace of mind.[3] I believe this should be read as a phrase rather than a title because of the previous statement that only a single book of Daoxin's survives. Then the teachings for beginners would refer to scattered records of Daoxin's teachings without specific titles.

Therefore what we appear to have here in *Masters of the Lanka* is the complete text of *Methods for the Bodhisattva Precepts* followed by some of his shorter teachings. The *Methods for the Bodhisattva Precepts* itself looks like a record of a sermon, along with several questions from students that are answered by Daoxin. If so, the text belongs to the genre of sermons given during the ceremony of bestowing the bodhisattva precepts, which would make it the first Zen text in this genre, later examples being Shenhui's sermon and the famous *Platform Sutra* of Huineng.

I suggest that the teachings for beginners that follow the *Methods for the Bodhisattva Precepts* start with the sentence, 'When you are beginning the practice of sitting meditation, you should stay in a quiet place and closely observe your own body and mind.' The instructions on meditation that follow overlap considerably with what came before, which suggests that this is another text. Furthermore, these instructions end with the words, 'the above are the skilful means for novices'. Following this, the Daoxin chapter contains a few more miscellaneous teachings, including instructions on how to die, and critical comments on the Daoist classics *Daodejing* and *Zhuangzi*.

In this chapter I include the translation of the whole text of Daoxin's *Methods for the Bodhisattva Precepts*. The translations of the instructions for novices and other supplementary material, including Daoxin's criticism of Daoist classics, are in the following chapter. As a sermon given at the ceremony for bestowing the bodhisattva vows, the *Methods for the Bodhisattva Precepts* could be intended for a lay audience, or at least a mixed audience. At the beginning of the text, Daoxin says that his teachings are for those 'who possess the appropriate conditions and fully ripened capabilities', a description that encompasses both monastics and laypeople.

The sermon covers several different meditation techniques, three of which are described in detail. Since I discussed these thoroughly in chapter 5 above, I will only mention them briefly here. The first is mindfulness of the Buddha, that is, visualization of a buddha and recitation of his name, leading to a state of nondual awareness. This is also called 'the single practice concentration'. The second is simply becoming aware of and residing in mind's nature, which is clear and luminous. The third is the practice of analysing physical forms, particularly one's own body, in order to establish that they are empty, followed by resting in a state of oneness.

✦

Chapter Five

The meditation master Daoxin became the successor to the meditation master Sengcan in the early Tang, at Shuangfeng Mountain in Jizhou.[4] He was a true master of meditation who reopened the gates to meditation practice, disseminating it widely across the land. One book of his, titled *Methods for the Bodhisattva Precepts*, is extant, and he also composed teachings for beginners on methods for attaining peace of mind.

Methods for the Bodhisattva Precepts

I shall explain these key methods to you who possess the appropriate conditions and fully ripened capabilities. This will be in accord with the *Laṅkāvatāra sūtra*, which says, 'for all buddhas, the mind is supreme'.[5] It also accords with the *Wisdom Sutra Taught by Mañjuśrī*, which says that when you are mindful of the buddha in the single practice concentration, your mind *is* the buddha, but if you have deluded thoughts then you remain an unenlightened person.[6]

The *Wisdom Sutra Taught by Mañjuśrī* says:

Mañjuśrī asked the Buddha: 'Oh you whom the world honours, what is the single practice concentration?'

The Buddha replied, 'The nature of reality exists in equality. Being connected to the nature of reality is called "the single practice concentration". If you, sons and daughters of the noble ones, want to enter the single practice concentration, you must first study the perfection of wisdom, learning what the Buddha taught. Only after that will you be capable of the single practice concentration.[7] Stay connected in this way to the nature of reality. Without stepping away from it, or changing it at all, for it is beyond conceptualization, free from obstructions and categories.

'Sons and daughters of the noble ones, if you want to enter the single practice concentration, you should remain quiet and unmoving, and let go of the multitude of confused thoughts. Do not grasp at appearances, focus your mind on a single buddha and only recite his name. Then, with an upright posture, facing towards the place where the buddha resides, stay constantly mindful of this single buddha. In this state of mind, you will be able to see every buddha of the past and future clearly manifest.

'Why is this? The merits of mindfulness of a single buddha are immeasurable and unbounded, and no different from the benefits of all innumerable buddhas. This is one and the same as the nonconceptual buddhadharma itself, bringing all the vehicles together as one, the ultimate state of enlightenment to completion, replete with uncountable merit and immeasurable discernment. So, if you enter the single practice concentration then you will know for certain that all buddhas, as numerous as the grains of sand in the Ganges, are no different from the nature of reality itself.'[8]

And so this very body and mind are always the site of awakening, in every step you take.[9] Whatever you do, wherever you go, it is all awakening.

The *Samantabhadra-dhayana sūtra* says:

The whole ocean of karmic obstacles
Originates from conceptualization.
Anyone who wants to repent
Should begin by sitting in mindfulness of the nature of
    things.[10]

This is what we call supreme repentance, which is being mindful of the Buddha to eliminate the mentality of the three poisons, the mentality of grasping, the mentality of making judgements.[11] When you are mindful of the Buddha continuously through every state of mind, it will simply become clear and calm, and mindfulness will no longer be based on perceptual objects.

It says in the *Mahāprajñāpāramitā sūtra*:

When you have mindfulness without an object,
This is called mindfulness of the Buddha.[12]

What does 'mindfulness without an object' mean? Mindfulness of the Buddha is the same state of mind as that which we call 'mindfulness without an object'. There is no separate buddha distinct from the mind, nor a separate mind distinct from the Buddha. So mindfulness of the Buddha is the same as mindfulness of the mind, and seeking the Buddha is the same as seeking the mind.

Why is this? Consciousness has no shape, and the Buddha has no qualities.[13] If you comprehend this principle, then you have peace of mind. In constant mindfulness of the Buddha, grasping does not arise. Then there is nondiscrimination free from categories, sameness free from duality. When you reach this stage the mentality of recalling the Buddha fades away, as it is no longer needed.

When we observe this state of mind, it is identical to the tathāgata's ultimate dharmakaya. It is also called the true dharma, the buddha nature, the ultimate truth that is the nature of all phenomena, the pure land. It is also called awakening, the vajra concentration, intrinsic enlightenment, and so on. It has been given names like the realm of nirvana, *prajñā*, and so on. Though these names are innumerable, they all refer to the same thing. There is no object which is observed or mind which observes. This state of mind needs to be kept clear, so that it is always apparent and you cannot be distracted from it by the variety of situations that arise.[14]

Why is this? The variety of situations are just the single dharmakaya of the tathāgata. Through this oneness of mind all the knots of anxiety and irritation untangle themselves. A single particle contains worlds beyond measure. And worlds beyond measure are assembled on the tip of a single hair. Because all things have always been this way, they never obstruct each other. As the *Avataṃsaka sūtra* says: 'In a tiny particle you can see everything in the universe.'[15]

Peace of mind
Cannot be summed up in words;
True understanding of it
Comes from your own heart.

* * *

For the sake of the younger ones who might be harbouring doubts, Daoxin then took a question: 'If the tathāgata's dharmakaya is like this, how is it that their bodies, endowed with all the excellent qualities of a buddha, can appear in the world to teach the dharma?'[16]

Daoxin said –

It is precisely because the tathāgata's dharmakaya is pure that it is all-encompassing and manifests in everything. Yet the dharmakaya is not guided by thought.[17] Like a mirror made of *sphaṭika* crystal hung in a high hall, everything is visible within it.[18] The mirror has no mind either, but is still capable of making a multitude of things visible.

The sutra says: 'Tathāgatas appear in the world to preach the dharma due to the conceptualization of sentient beings.'[19] If you modern practitioners cultivate the mind until it is completely pure, then you will know that tathāgatas never teach the dharma. This is the real meaning of learning – for those who truly learn, there are no categories at all.

As the sutra says:

The faculties of sentient beings are grasping by nature.
Because the types of grasping are innumerable,

I teach innumerable dharmas.
Because I teach innumerable dharmas,
There are also innumerable meanings.
Yet these innumerable meanings
Arise from a single teaching.
This single teaching
Is freedom from qualities.
This complete lack of qualities
Is what I call True Quality.[20]

Thus everything disappears into purity.

The truth of these words
Must be experienced directly.
When you sit, you will become aware of it.
Recognize the first movement of your mind,
Then follow its constantly evolving flow,
Its comings and goings,
Being aware of everything as a whole,
Examining it with vajra wisdom.

This is similar to the way grass and trees do not distinguish between objects. Knowing the absence of knowing is what we call 'being all knowing'.[21] This is how bodhisattvas teach sameness.[22]

Another question was asked: 'What is a meditation master?'

Daoxin replied –

One who is unconcerned by either serenity or disturbance. That is to say, a person who is good at applying the mind in meditation. If you always stay in calmness (śamatha), your mind will become drowsy. If you spend a long time practising insight meditation (vipaśyanā) your mind will become distracted.

The *Lotus Sutra* says:

The buddhas themselves abide in the great vehicle,
As their attainment of the dharma:

Arrayed with the power of concentration and wisdom,
Dedicated to the liberation of sentient beings.[23]

Others asked: 'How can we truly understand the nature of things so that the mind becomes luminous and clear?'

Daoxin said –

Don't be mindful of the Buddha;
Don't control the mind;
Don't examine the mind;
Don't speculate about the mind;
Don't deliberate;
Don't practise analysis;
Don't become distracted;
Just let it be.
Don't try to get rid of it,
Don't try to make it stay.

In solitude and peace, the mind will of itself become luminous and clear. If you can carefully observe the mind in this way, the mind will become luminous and clear, like a bright mirror. If you do this for one year, the mind will be even more luminous and clear. If you do this for three to five years, the mind will be yet more luminous and clear. This can be brought about by somebody teaching you, or you may attain liberation without ever having to be taught.

It is taught in the sutras that for sentient beings, the nature of mind is like a precious pearl sunk beneath the water. When the water is dirty the pearl is hidden; when the water is clear, the pearl can be seen.[24] Because sentient beings have slandered the three jewels and disrupted the harmony of the sangha, everything they see is tainted with irritation and distorted by desire, hatred and ignorance. They do not realize that the nature of mind has always been pure from the beginning.[25]

Thus the way students attain this realization is not always the same, and these differences are due to the fact that currently their inner faculties and outer conditions are not the same. A person who wants to be a teacher must be capable of recognizing these differences. Among students there are four types of people:

- Those who practise and have understanding and experience are the best.
- Those who don't practise, yet do have understanding and experience are the upper middling type.
- Those who practise and have understanding, yet lack experience are the lower middling type.
- Those who practise, yet lack understanding and experience are the lowest type.

Another question was asked: 'At this stage, should we practise analytical meditation?'

Daoxin said – The only thing you need to do is let it be.[26]

And: 'Should we practise facing the direction of the pure land in the west?'

Daoxin said –
Once you know that mind, from the start, has never arisen or ceased to be and is perfectly pure, and that it is identical with the pure lands of the buddhas, there is no longer any need to face the pure land in the west.
The *Avataṃsaka sūtra* says:

Immeasurable aeons exist in a single moment of thought,
And one thought lasts for immeasurable aeons.[27]

Know that in any one direction there are immeasurable directions, and immeasurable directions are really one direction. When they spoke of facing the pure land in the west it was for the sake of sentient beings with dull faculties, and not for people with sharp faculties.

The *Avataṃsaka sūtra* says:

> The physical qualities of Samantabhadra
> Are like space.
> Their location is in thusness,
> Not in a buddha realm.[28]

This means that the buddha realm is completely present right now; it is exactly the same as this realm but entirely free from clinging.[29] The *Nirvāṇa sūtra* says, 'Limitless is the body of the bodhisattva, a body immeasurable as space', and 'Because their bodies shine with virtue, they are like the summer sun.' It also says, 'Because their bodies are limitless, this is called *great nirvana*', and 'This is the greatest kind of nirvana because its nature is vast and wide.'[30]

* * *

Bodhisattvas at the stages of further progress engage with samsara in order to transform and liberate sentient beings.[31] Yet they do this without clinging to intellectual views. If I hold the view that sentient beings exist in samsara – that I am the one who can liberate them, while they are powerless – I should not be called a bodhisattva. Liberating sentient beings is like liberating emptiness: how could emptiness be liberated when it has already come and gone?

The *Vajracchedikā sūtra* says: 'As for the liberation of innummerable sentient beings – in truth, there are no sentient beings who achieve liberation.'[32] A bodhisattva of the first level begins with the realization that everything is empty; later they come to the realization that nothing is empty. This is the wisdom of nondiscrimination. It is the same with form: form is emptiness, and it is not that form eliminates emptiness; rather, the inherent nature of form is emptiness.

A bodhisattva's cultivation of emptiness turns into realization. New students have only an intellectual view of emptiness. This intellectual view of emptiness is not true emptiness. Those who realize true emptiness on the path of practice do not hold views about emptiness or the lack of emptiness, or any other kind of view.[33] Thus it is important to understand exactly what 'forms are empty' really means.[34]

For those who are studying how to apply the mind, the key point is that the mind's flow should be clear and luminous. They should be aware of the qualities of phenomena in utter clarity and distinction. Only then will they be qualified to teach others. In addition, their outer behaviour should correspond with their inner state, and their practice should not contradict their principles. They absolutely must give up written and spoken words, which are the conditioned phenomena of the noble path. Instead, staying in solitude, they should realize for themselves the fruits of the path.[35]

There are also people who have yet to comprehend the ultimate dharma, yet guide sentient beings for the sake of wealth and fame. Failing to recognize the sharp and dull faculties of students and make appropriate distinctions, they give their seal of approval far too easily. This is very distressing![36] Some observe their students' minds, and if they seem to be luminous and clear, immediately give them the seal of approval. These people are ruining the Buddha's dharma, deceiving themselves and others.

People who apply the mind all have their similarities and differences. Everyone has their own personality, but all of them have yet to realize the mind. Those who have truly realized the mind have recognized it clearly for themselves. In the future, they will open the eyes of the dharma themselves and be able to see how their own good students are different from the empty counterfeits.[37]

Some people believe that the body is empty in the sense of not existing and that the nature of mind is mere nothingness. These people are nihilists, no different from those who follow non-Buddhist paths. They are not followers of the Buddha. Some people believe that the mind exists in the sense of never coming to an end. These people are eternalists who are also just like the followers of non-Buddhist paths. Now, the intelligent disciples of the Buddha do not believe that the nature of mind is existent or nonexistent.[38]

Always liberating sentient beings,
Without clinging to views.
Always acquiring wisdom,
In the sameness of wisdom and ignorance.
Always in the state of meditation,
Without the duality of stillness and wildness.
Always perceiving sentient beings,
Without reifying their existence.[39]
Manifesting their bodies everywhere,
Yet showing that they have never truly existed.
Not seeing or hearing anything,
Yet aware of everything,
Without grasping or rejecting.
Never dividing their bodies,
Yet pervading the nature of reality.

Furthermore, wise and compassionate meditation masters of earlier times taught that when we are learning the dharma path, understanding and practice need to support each other.[40] First you recognize the mind's source, its essential nature and manifold activities, seeing appearances clearly and without confusion.[41] After this, you will be able to accomplish great things. If this one thing is understood, a thousand others will follow. But if you are mistaken about this one thing, ten thousand delusions will follow. Lose it by a hair's breadth, and you will go astray by a mile. These are not empty words!

The *Larger Sukhāvatīvyūha sūtra* says:

The dharmakaya of all buddhas
Is present in the mental activities
Of all sentient beings;
This mind makes the buddha.[42]

Know then that 'buddha' is identical with 'mind'. Aside from the mind, there is no buddha.

* * *

Briefly, there are five general types of meditation:[43]

- The first is to recognize mind's essence. This essence is naturally clear and pure, and this essence is the same as the buddha.
- The second is to recognize mind's activity. This activity gives birth to the jewel of the dharma, and is the manifest aspect of constant stillness, found within all the myriad delusions.
- The third is to be always aware without interruption. Awareness manifests as the mind, yet the phenomena of awareness cannot be categorized.[44]
- The fourth is to see the physical body as empty. Inner and outer are interdependent, and the body is at the very centre of the phenomenal realm, without the least obstruction.
- The fifth is to maintain oneness without wavering, throughout both stillness and movement.[45] This allows the practitioner to see the buddha nature clearly and enter the gate of concentration quickly.

The sutras contain all of these types of meditation. Fu Dashi's teachings recommend just maintaining oneness without wavering, but one should begin with practice and close observation, taking the body as the basis for analysis, as follows.[46]

This body is composed of four elements and five aggregates. In the end, it is impermanent, and it cannot be autonomous. Even while it has not yet perished it is ultimately empty. The *Vimalakīrti-nirdeśa sūtra* says: 'This body is like drifting clouds that change and disappear in moments.'[47]

Next, constantly perceive your own body in this way: it is empty and clear like a reflection; it can be seen, but not grasped. Wisdom is born in the midst of reflections; ultimately it has no location. It never moves, yet it responds to the needs of beings, manifesting without limitation.[48] The six senses come into being within emptiness. They are completely empty themselves, facing the six kinds of object, which should be understood as dreams and illusions. When the eye sees an object, that object is not located in the eye.

Just as a mirror reflects the image of a face with the greatest clarity, forms manifest within emptiness like reflections. There is not a single object in the mirror itself; we know that a person's actual face does not go into the mirror, nor does the mirror enter a person's face. Analysing in detail like this, we can see that the face in the mirror has never entered or departed, never come or gone. This is the meaning of tathāgata.[49]

This kind of analysis shows that the eye, like the mirror, is and has always been empty. The reflection in the mirror and the reflection in the eye are the same. So, using this as a point of comparison, smell, taste and all the other faculties are the same. If you know that the eye is fundamentally empty, then for all forms the eye sees, you will know them to be the objectification of form. When your ears hear sounds, you will know them to be the objectification of sound. When your nose detects smells, you will know them to be the objectification of smell. When the tongue distinguishes tastes, you will know them to be the objectification of taste. When the intellect responds to phenomena, you will know them to be the objectification of phenomena. When the body receives sensations, you will know them to be the objectification of sensation.[50]

To examine knowledge in this way is to meditate on emptiness and stillness:

- When you see forms, you know that those forms cannot be grasped.
- The forms that cannot be grasped are just emptiness.
- Emptiness is the nonexistence of categories.
- This nonexistence of categories is not something contrived.

Seeing this is the gate to liberation. When students attain liberation, all of their sense faculties are like this. To put it another way, they are always mindful of the emptiness of the six faculties. In this sense there is no hearing or seeing. As the *Sutra of the Deathbed Injunction* says: 'At the hour of midnight, silence is undisturbed.'[51] This means that the tathāgatas teach the dharma by means of emptiness, and to be constantly mindful of the emptiness of the six faculties is to be always like the night. What you see and hear in the daytime are things external to your body.

That was the emptiness and purity of the body. Now for maintaining oneness without wavering.[52] With this pure and empty vision, concentrate your attention on a single object without concern for the passing of time. Continue to focus your energy without moving. If your mind wants to wander off, quickly take it in hand and gather it back, again and again, like using a string attached to a bird's foot to pull it back and catch it when it wants to fly away. Finally, after spending a day in uninterrupted attentiveness, you can stop and the mind will settle on its own.

As the *Vimalakīrti-nirdeśa sūtra* says:

Gathering the mind is the site of enlightenment itself;
This is the dharma of gathering the mind.[53]

And the *Lotus Sutra* says:

For incalculable aeons he tirelessly and continually gathered his mind. Because of this achievement he could generate all the levels of meditative concentration.[54]

The *Sutra of the Deathbed Injunction* says:

The mind is the master of the five faculties. Once you capture this territory, there is nothing else to do, no more to be accomplished.[55]

This is exactly it. These teachings on the five types of meditation are also the true principle of the great vehicle. They are all based on what is said in the sutras, not on mistaken non-Buddhist teachings. This is uncontaminated activity, the ultimate truth itself.[56] Going beyond the stage of a hearer, this is the real destination of the bodhisattva's path.

* * *

Listeners, do your practice properly and without even a moment of doubt![57] Be like a person learning to shoot an arrow. They begin with a large target, then aim at a small target, then aim at a large circle, then aim at a small circle, then aim at a single piece of twine, then split the piece of twine into a hundred threads and aim at one of the hundred threads. Then they shoot their arrow into the previous one so that the arrow is fixed in the nock, preventing both arrows from falling.

This is a metaphor for a person learning the path. As the stream of consciousness flows through the mind, every moment of mind is continuous, without the briefest interval. True mindfulness is uninterrupted – true mindfulness is always there.[58] As it says in the sutras: 'Using the arrows of wisdom, shoot at the nocks of the arrows that are the three gates of liberation, so that each arrow is fixed in the nock of the other without falling to the ground.'[59]

It is also like rubbing sticks together to make a fire; there will be no heat if you stop, and however much you want to make a fire it will be difficult to achieve. It is also like the family that possessed a wish-fulfilling jewel and received whatever they wanted from it. One day they lost it, and after that there was never a moment when they didn't remember what it was like before they lost it. It is also like a person with a poison arrow in their flesh. When the shaft has been pulled out but the arrowhead remains embedded, they undergo agonizing pain. They cannot forget about it even for a moment; recollection is constantly in their mind. The way you practise should be like this.

The secret essence of the dharma is not transmitted to those who are not meant to hear it. It is not that we are stingy with the transmission of the dharma. We are just apprehensive that such people will have no conviction and will fall into the trap of slandering the dharma.

We must choose people who will not teach the dharma as soon as they have got hold of it.

Take heed! Though the ocean of dharma may be immeasurable, it can be crossed with a single teaching.[60] Once you have grasped the intention, the teaching can be forgotten, for even a single teaching is of no use any more.[61] Attaining final realization is the same thing as grasping the Buddha's intention.

✦

CHAPTER THIRTEEN

DAOXIN II

Teachings for Beginners

There is a colourful story about Daoxin that gives us the sense that he was known for just sitting, without engaging in other practices that would take him from place to place. The story is from the *Genealogy of the Dharma Jewel* and occurs late in Daoxin's life, in the year 643 when he had been living at his monastery on Shuangfeng Mountain for many years. The emperor Wenwu sent a messenger to the mountain to invite Daoxin for an audience at court. Daoxin refused, pleading old age, but the emperor sent the messenger back to insist on Daoxin travelling to the court. Daoxin refused again, sending a message back to the emperor: 'If you want my head, you are welcome to behead me and take it, but I will not go.'

Undeterred, the emperor sent his messenger back with the sword, telling him to threaten Daoxin but not to hurt him. Upon seeing the sword, Daoxin still refused to obey the emperor's summons, and extended his neck to the messenger, saying, 'Chop it off and take it!' The messenger then had to admit that he had been told not to harm Daoxin, who laughed and replied, 'I've taught you to recognize someone who stays put!'[1] In this story 'someone who stays put' suggests more than mere stubbornness; it implies the resolve and stability of someone who spends their time in meditation.[2]

As we have seen, most of Daoxin's teachings in the *Masters of the Lanka* are from a text called *Methods for the Bodhisattva Precepts*, which was translated in the previous chapter. The rest of the Daoxin section, which is translated here, contains his instructions for novices and other miscellaneous teachings. The word 'novices' – literally 'those who have entered the path' (*rùdào*) – indicates that these are teachings for newly ordained monastics.

While Daoxin's *Methods for the Bodhisattva Precepts* is presented as a sermon given in the context of the ceremony for bestowing the vows of a bodhisattva, which may have been attended by lay Buddhists as well as monastics, the teachings for novices may have been written down in his monastery on Shuangfeng Mountain, and circulated among his students.

The teachings for novices are followed by advice on meditating during the process of death, some critical comments on the Daoist classics *Daodejing* and *Zhuangzi*, and a few lines on the idea that nonliving things have a buddha nature. As we have seen, other chapters in the *Masters of the Lanka* seem to have grown with additional material added at the end of the chapter in the process of manuscript transmission. We do not have the earlier, Tibetan translation to compare here, because that version does not extend this far into the text; however, it seems plausible that some of this material, particularly the comments on Daoism and the lines on the buddha nature, are similarly later additions.

The meditation instructions for novices begin with the phrase, 'When you are beginning the practice of sitting meditation . . .' and end with, 'the above are the skilful means for novices'. In this text, Daoxin outlines two meditation methods, both of which he has already taught in the *Dharma Teachings for the Bodhisattva Precepts.* The first meditation technique is the classic twofold Buddhist meditation practice of insight meditation (vipaśyanā) and calmness (śamatha). This begins with sitting and thinking about the nature of one's body and sensations. The resulting realization is that 'upon examination, they are simply stillness, pure and free from the very beginning'.

Daoxin teaches that the realization of the emptiness of the body is the true form of repentance:

Then you will realize that your own body, for past immeasurable aeons, has ultimately never been born, and in the future there is

ultimately no person who dies. To be able to carry out this observation at all times is the true practice of repentance.

This echoes his earlier statement in *Methods for the Bodhisattva
Precepts* that mindfulness is 'the supreme repentance'. Fortnightly
repentance ceremonies, for alleviating the negative karmic effects of
one's past actions, are a part of life in most Buddhist monasteries
and nunneries. As I discussed in chapter 3 above, these ceremonies
often involved meditation, and the visions that arose in meditation
could be taken as indications of the nature of one's past karma. In
Daoxin's teaching, rather than meditation being part of the repentance
ritual, the realization that comes from meditation is the true form of
repentance.

The second meditation technique that Daoxin explains in his
instructions for novices is 'observing the mind'. Again, this is a
condensed version of the teachings on the same practice in the
Methods for the Bodhisattva Precepts. One thing that Daoxin explains
in more detail is how to actually assume the meditation posture
and breathing – indeed, these are the most detailed instructions in
early Zen:

> To begin, sit with your body upright, in comfortable clothes
> without a belt. Relax your body and loosen your arms and legs by
> rubbing them seven or eight times. Allow your mind to come to
> rest in your abdomen, and let your breath out completely.

This is clearly an instruction on breathing from the abdomen, in
which one's concentration is moved down to that point in the body
(called *fú* in Chinese, *hara* in Japanese). Breathing in and out of the
abdomen, and allowing one's consciousness to descend to that point
in the body, is taught by modern Zen teachers, as well as in other
contemplative, martial arts and medical traditions.[3] In one of the most
popular twentieth-century books on Zen meditation, *Zen Mind,
Beginner's Mind*, Shunryu Suzuki gives this instruction:

Also to gain strength in your posture, press your diaphragm down towards your *hara*, or lower abdomen. This will help you maintain your physical and mental balance. When you try to keep this posture, at first you may find some difficulty breathing naturally, but when you get accustomed to it you will be able to breathe naturally and deeply.[4]

Examples are to be found in the earlier Japanese tradition as well; for example, the influential masters Dogen and Hakuin both gave instructions on breathing from the abdomen.[5] However, the fact that this practice was also taught much earlier, here in the *Masters of the Lanka*, seems to have been missed. In Daoxin's teaching abdominal breathing leads to a calm and and lucid state, 'with body and mind in harmony'. Once they have achieved this peace, the meditator is able to 'turn the mind within', meaning to turn the mind away from external objects to rest in awareness of itself.[6]

Similar instructions on observing the mind are found in a work by another early Zen teacher, Wolun. His *Dharma of Observing the Mind* has been studied by Carmen Meinert, who describes the technique taught there:

> The inner, the nature of mind, is described as clear like empty space and without arising and ceasing, whereas mind is discursive on the outside. Whenever thoughts arise in the mind, the practitioner is asked to immediately turn to the inside of mind.[7]

We can see this as an instruction to observe thoughts themselves, rather than be guided by thoughts towards their objects, which is the usual mental process leading to distraction and submergence in the constant production of thoughts. The result of this is that 'the spiritual path will become clear and sharp, the mind's ground pure and luminous'. The mind's ground is the fundamental level of mind, known in Indian Yogācāra texts as the *ālaya-vijñāna*.[8] In Yogācāra, meditation practice leads to a transformation of the basis, from its usual function as the source of deluded awareness to its proper function as the source of enlightened awareness. Thus the practice is to realize that the external world consists of the manifestations of mind through the senses, and to trace these manifestations back to their source, the pure and luminous basic consciousness.

After the instructions for novices, there is another brief text of meditation instructions, this time for the process of dying. The practice for this process is to settle the mind, to become 'absorbed in the pure sky-like mind'. At the moment of death, the meditator will 'abide in the clarity of the dharmakaya and will not undergo another lifetime'. However, if this mindfulness is lost at any point, the process of rebirth and new life will start again.

Buddhist discussions of the process of death are best known from Tibetan literature, especially the 'Tibetan Book of the Dead'. These works describe the whole process in much greater detail, but they do share a significant feature with Daoxin's description: the vision of a clear light that is equivalent to the dharmakaya as the first manifestation of entering the state between death and the next rebirth, and the idea that if the consciousness of the dying person becomes distracted from nondual absorption in this clarity, they will go on to the next process of the intermediate state, leading to rebirth.

The Tibetan meditation teachings of Dzogchen, 'the great perfection', put particular emphasis on recognizing this light at the moment of death; as Bryan Cuevas has written, in Dzogchen 'emphasis was on the clear light as equivalent to the primordial ground's original pure radiance'.[9] Furthermore, in Dzogchen, meditators are taught to recognize this light as the dharmakaya at the moment of death. These similarities between Daoxin's brief instructions on dying and those in the later Tibetan tradition are intriguing.

The idea of an intermediate state between death and rebirth was discussed in the abhidharma literature of the Sarvāstivādins, and descriptions of the experience of dying appear in some sutras. However, as Stephen Eskilden has pointed out, techniques for actively directing one's experience of death seem to be found only in the

Chinese and Tibetan traditions.[10] Perhaps they both grew from Indian Buddhist oral teachings on meditation techniques for the dying. In any case, Daoxin's instructions on dying are one of the earliest examples of this practice in Chinese Buddhism, though there are also Daoist texts containing instructions for dying which may be just as early. Later, the techniques for navigating the process of dying continued to be developed by Daoists, who often attributed the origins of the practice to Bodhidharma.[11]

The instructions on dying for meditators conclude Daoxin's meditation teachings in this chapter. They are followed by some comments on Daoist texts. Daoxin does occasionally borrow phrases from Daoist literature, and seems to have been especially fond of the *Zhuangzi*, a book of teachings attributed to the sage of the same name, who lived in the third century BC. The *Zhuangzi* is a complex text, probably formed over centuries. It is difficult to sum up, but many chapters (including the one quoted here by Daoxin) present us with arguments suggesting that our concepts and judgements are merely conventions, relative and not absolute.

At times, the *Zhuangzi* sounds very like a Zen teaching. Perhaps the greatest difference is that in *Zhuangzi* the ultimate truth is oneness, whereas for many Zen teachers, the ultimate truth is emptiness. It is this idea of oneness that Daoxin criticizes here, quoting the cryptic lines:

Heaven and earth are one finger.
All things are one horse.

Here is the full passage from the *Zhuangzi*:

To use this finger to show how a finger is not a finger is no match for using not-this finger to show how a finger is not a finger. To use this horse to show that a horse is not a horse is no match for using not-this-horse to show that a horse is not a horse. Heaven and earth are one finger. All things are one horse.[12]

This doesn't help much, but the following passage makes it clearer:

> Something is affirmative because someone affirms it. Something is negative because someone negates it. Courses are formed by someone walking them. Things are so by being called so.[13]

In other words, our logic is merely conventional; even the linguistic distinctions between a horse and what is not a horse only apply because we apply them. Ultimately horse and not-horse depend on each other and are one and the same thing. Daoxin then quotes from a Buddhist sutra to show the limitations of *Zhuangzi*, picking up on the idea of oneness:

> 'One' does not just mean the number one;
> It implies a refutation of phenomena being many.

To be honest, it is hard to see how this passage can be used to criticize the *Zhuangzi*; the oneness of the *Zhuangzi* is very much 'a refutation of phenomena being many'. Nevertheless, Daoxin's criticism that Zhuangzi gets 'stuck' at the idea of oneness does have a point, as his text does not deconstruct the concept of oneness itself, which a Buddhist would.

Daoxin then turns to the *Daodejing*, the early Daoist classic attributed to the sage Laozi, which needs no introduction here. Daoxin quotes these lines:

> So subtle! So profound!
> Its essence is within.

In criticizing these words, Daoxin quotes from two sutras stating that the duality between internal and external is false. He accuses Laozi of doing away with the category of the external but keeping the idea of an internal essence. This criticism comes from the point of view of the classic Indian Yogācāra texts, such as those of Vasubandhu, in which it is often said that the true nature of consciousness is nondual, without internal or external elements.[14]

Whether these criticisms are fair or not, they position Daoxin as a true Mahayana Buddhist by rejecting the emphasis in the *Zhuangzi* on oneness, and the privileging of the internal in the *Daodejing*. The final lines of the chapter seem to have little bearing on this, and go off on another tangent instead – the idea that the buddha nature resides in all things, not just sentient beings. This ties in with the teachings of Hongren in the next chapter, so we will consider it there.

Chapter Five
(Continued)

Instructions for Novices

When you are beginning the practice of sitting meditation, you should stay in a quiet place and closely observe your own body and mind. Observe and examine the four elements and five aggregates, the senses of sight, smell, taste, touch and intellect, up to greed, anger and ignorance – whether bad or good, hated or loved, ordinary or sacred – through to each and every aspect of existence. They are empty from the very beginning, neither coming into being nor passing away. In their sameness and nonduality, they have never had a defining feature. Upon examination, they are simply stillness, pure and free from the very beginning.

Don't ask whether it is day or night – just continue with this observation, whether you are walking, standing, sitting or lying down. You will come to realize that your own body is like the reflection of the moon in water, like the image in a mirror, like the heat of a fire, like an echo in an empty valley. If you say it is existent, why do you not see it when you search for it everywhere? If you say it is nonexistent, why does it appear with constant clarity before your eyes? The dharmakaya of all the buddhas is also like this.

Then you will realize that your own body, for past immeasurable aeons, has ultimately never been born, and in the future there is ultimately no person who dies. To be able to carry out this observation at all times is the true practice of repentance.[15] Millions of aeons' accumulation of the most serious karma soon vanishes on its own. This practice is only to remove doubt and confusion; it cannot give rise to conviction in people who are unable to truly grasp it. On the other hand, those sentient beings who do have the conviction to rely on this practice will always be able to enter into the uncreated true principle.

Next, when mental apprehension of external objects arises, observe it at the point of arising.[16] Ultimately it does not arise, for when this mental apprehension appears, it does not come from any direction, or arrive anywhere. Constantly observe how objects are apprehended, using your awareness to observe deluded consciousness, perception and distracted thoughts.[17] When mental disturbance ceases you will have attained basic stability. If you attain mental stability you will no longer anxiously dwell upon objects.

Then, depending on your ability in calmness meditation, you will attain the cessation of all emotional afflictions, and not create any new ones. This is known as liberation through observation. The mental shackles of unhappiness, turmoil and depression will then disappear by themselves, slowly, slowly, settling into peacefulness. When you give it the opportunity mind becomes peaceful and clear all by itself. Yet one must have a sense of urgency, as if saving someone whose hair is on fire. Don't become complacent – keep striving!

* * *

When you begin sitting in meditation to observe the mind, sit on your own in a single place. To begin, sit with your body upright, in comfortable clothes without a belt. Relax your body and loosen your arms and legs by rubbing them seven or eight times. Allow your mind to come to rest in your abdomen, and let your breath out completely.[18] You will suddenly realize your nature to be pure and lucid, calm and clear, with body and mind in harmony.

Then as you pacify mind and spirit, subtle and profound, with calm, refreshing breathing, gradually turn the mind within.[19] The spiritual path will become clear and sharp, the mind's ground pure and luminous. When you examine this luminosity, you find that both internal and external are empty and pure. This is mind's natural stillness.

This stillness is the manifestation of the Buddha's mind itself. Though it is formless in nature, it always has purity of intention. This spiritual energy is never exhausted; it is always present in its bright clarity.[20] This is what we call the buddha nature. Those who can see the buddha nature are for ever free from samsara, and their fame transcends that of worldly people. So when the *Vimalakīrti-nirdeśa sūtra* speaks of 'suddenly re-acquiring your original mind', it speaks the truth.[21]

A person who has realized the buddha nature is known as a bodhisattva. He or she is also called a person who has realized the path, a person with understanding, and a person who has actualized the buddha nature. So, as it says in the sutra: 'This single phrase has a profound energy which is not depleted over an aeon.'[22] Novices who practise these skilful means should remember that all the skilful means taught on the path are joined in the mind of the Noble Ones.

Instructions on dying

Now, a summary of the dharma of giving up the body.[23] First settle the mind in complete emptiness. Let your mind and its objects become tranquil. Let your perceptions melt into deep quietude. Don't let your mind move about, and settle into the tranquillity of mind's nature, without the apprehension of objects, subtle and profound, absorbed in the pure sky-like mind, in peaceful, settled equanimity. When you pass away, at your last breath, you should abide in the clarity of the dharmakaya and will not undergo another lifetime. But if you give rise to thought and lose your mindfulness, you will not avoid undergoing rebirth, as previously determined by your mental attitude.[24]

'The dharma should be like this' – that is how the dharma is created.[25] Yet the dharma is originally non-dharma. Only dharma that is not dharma can be called 'dharma'. Thus the dharma cannot be created. The true dharma jewel is the dharma which has never been created. That is why the sutra says: 'Empty without formulation, without aspiration, without qualities.'[26] This is true liberation, and this is the reason that the real dharma cannot be created. What I call 'the dharma of giving up the body' is a metaphor for the observation of the mind and its objects based on the body.[27] The level of illumination means using your luminous energy to decide your own fate.[28]

Miscellaneous teachings

The great master said –

Zhuangzi taught:

> Heaven and earth are one finger.
> All things are one horse.

But the *Dharmapada sūtra* says:

> 'One' does not just mean the number one;
> The intention is the refutation of all numbers.
> Only students of shallow intellect
> Mean the number one when they say 'one'.[29]

Thus Zhuangzi seems to be stuck at the idea of 'one'.

Laozi said:

> So subtle! So profound!
> Its essence is within.

Here, even though there are no categories outside, the mind is still preserved within. The *Avataṃsaka sūtra* says:[30]

> Do not be attached to dualistic entities,
> As there is neither singularity nor duality.

And the *Vimalakīrti-nirdeśa sūtra* corroborates this by saying:

> Mind does not exist internally or externally,
> Nor anywhere in between.[31]

When we understand this, we can see that Laozi is stuck at the idea of the existence of an essential awareness.

* * *

The *Mahāparinirvāṇa sūtra* says: 'All sentient beings have the buddha nature.'[32] How could we teach that walls, tiles and stones do not lack the buddha nature? How could they teach the dharma? Moreover, Vasubandhu writes in his commentary: 'The physical manifestation of the buddha is not the true buddha and does not teach the dharma.'

✦

CHAPTER FOURTEEN

HONGREN

The Buddha in Everything

With Hongren, Zen comes of age. Many of his students went on to become famous meditation teachers in their own right, and his meditation centre on East Mountain gave its name to a whole tradition of teaching. According to all the early histories, Hongren first travelled to study with Daoxin on Shuangfeng Mountain. After he had been authorized by Daoxin to teach meditation, he moved to Mount Fengmao, which was to the east of Shuangfeng, and therefore known as East Mountain. There he established his residence, and over the years attracted many students who travelled to East Mountain to receive his teachings.

After Hongren's death, his residence on East Mountain was turned into a monastery. However, his most famous students did not stay on the mountain – they travelled, taking the 'East Mountain tradition' of teaching meditation across China. In the *Masters of the Lanka*, Hongren is a quintessential meditation teacher. He lives in a secluded retreat, where he teaches orally, but never commits words to writing. His teaching style is pithy, sometimes puzzling, sometimes approaching the style of the koan.

According to the *Masters of the Lanka*, Hongren never wrote a book, yet there is a text attributed to him in some Dunhuang manuscripts: *Treatise on the Essentials of Cultivating the Mind*.[1] John McRae argues that this is a genuine record of Hongren's teachings by his students. He also shows that while the *Treatise on the Essentials of Cultivating the Mind* is not quoted in the Hongren section of the *Masters of the Lanka*, parts of it do appear in the chapters on

Guṇabhadra and Huike. Therefore he believes that Hongren's work was plagiarized for these earlier sections.[2]

I would agree with McRae that Jingjue (or whoever compiled the *Masters of the Lanka*) probably did struggle to find meditation teachings firmly attributed to these two figures. However, to state, as McRae did, that Jingjue plagiarized Hongren's work (while at the same time denying that Hongren ever wrote anything) is odd. As I have argued earlier, plagiarism is a very modern idea, entirely out of place in a pre-modern manuscript culture (whether in China or anywhere else in the world).

What's more, just because one manuscript attributes the *Treatise on the Essentials of Cultivating the Mind* to Hongren does not mean that this was generally accepted. When we work directly with the manuscripts, we see how often attribution of a text can change. This is a well-known feature of Chinese bibliography, as Endymion Wilkinson has written: 'A problem encountered throughout Chinese history is the use of more than one title for the same book, caused in the early days by the fact that books circulated as manuscripts in different versions with no fixed title or author.'[3] We are lucky enough to have access to one group of local manuscripts, preserved by chance in the Dunhuang cave; in other communities, now lost to us, some of the same texts will undoubtedly have been attributed to different authors.

In any case, it is worth looking at the *Treatise on the Essentials of Cultivating the Mind* as a compendium of teachings that some at least considered to be by Hongren. The text is a series of questions and answers between an unnamed teacher and student. It is quite long, but has a simple message: the true nature of mind is present in all living beings, but temporarily obscured, like the sun when it is hidden by the clouds. It is always present, but we are not aware of it. There is no buddha apart from one's own mind, and to be a buddha is just to be always aware of the true nature of mind.

The practice taught in the *Treatise on the Essentials of Cultivating the Mind* is to recognize the inherent purity of one's own mind, and then to maintain that awareness. This is the essence of meditation, but it is an advanced practice; the text also teaches a preliminary practice for beginners, to calm the mind by sitting and visualizing the sun in the distance:

> Sit properly with the body erect, closing the eyes and mouth. Look straight ahead with the mind, visualizing a sun at an appropriate distance away. Maintain this image continuously without stopping.[4]

Here we have a classic Buddhist meditation technique, in which the focus of concentration is a visualized image of light. Once beginners have learned to calm their minds through this practice, they can do the main practice, which is described thus:

> Make your body and mind pure and peaceful, without any discriminative thinking at all. Sit properly with the body erect. Regulate the breath and concentrate the mind so it is not within you, not outside you, and not in any intermediate location. Do this carefully and naturally. View your own consciousness tranquilly and attentively, so that you can see how it is always moving, like flowing water or a glittering mirage. After you have perceived this consciousness, simply continue to view it gently and naturally.[5]

These instructions for meditation fit the third type of meditation in Daoxin's fivefold scheme, 'to be always aware'. They also look very much like his practice of 'observing the mind'. A practice like this could well have been taught by Hongren, or indeed many other meditation teachers of his generation and later.

* * *

Turning to Hongren's meditation teachings as presented in the *Masters of the Lanka*, there are two main types: a visualization practice taking the syllable 'a' as the focus of meditation, and the use of difficult questions, especially 'What is this?'

The visualization instruction is as follows:

> When you sit, let your face relax and sit with your head and body
> straight. Calmly let go of your body and mind. Resting in empti-
> ness, visualize the single syllable.

The 'single syllable' is a term most commonly found in tantric practice
literature, occurring in a number of esoteric texts in the Chinese canon.
It is not common elsewhere, though in later Zen texts, the 'key phrase'
of koan practice is sometimes spoken of in similar terms. In Hongren's
meditation teachings this is not a koan practice; it is a visualization
practice. In the esoteric tradition, the syllable that is visualized is
usually the syllable *a*, the first letter of the Sanskrit alphabet.[6]

The visualization of the single syllable is only the first part of the
practice, which expands into a vast and spacious visualization in
which the meditator imagines him or herself on top of a mountain:

> After you have mastered this, when you are sitting, imagine that you
> are in the wilderness. In the middle there is a solitary mountain. You
> are sitting on the barren ground on top of the mountain, looking in
> the four directions, seeing far into the distance, without barriers or
> boundaries. As you sit, you fill the whole world, completely relaxing
> your body and mind, abiding in the realm of the buddhas.

This striking visualization is not just intended to generate a sense of
spaciousness and clarity; as Hongren says, in this imagined state of
'filling the whole world' one is already in the realm of the buddhas.
There is an echo of this practice in Hongren's last words, as recorded
in the *Masters of the Lanka*: 'The great master then raised his hand and
gestured towards the ten directions, each time stating that the realized
mind was already there.'

This practice can be seen as exemplifying the Yogācāra position
that the distinction between internal senses and external objects is a
false one; one's mind always reaches as far as one can see. There is also

a similarity between Hongren's teaching here and Daoxin's instructions on seeing one's own body as that of a buddha:

> It is empty and clear like a reflection; it can be seen, but not grasped. Wisdom is born in the midst of reflections; ultimately it has no location. It never moves, yet it responds to the needs of beings, manifesting without limitation.

We can also compare Daoxin's teachings on dying, during which one should be 'absorbed in the pure sky-like mind'.

* * *

This chapter on Hongren ends with a series of questions. Though they may seem unrelated, a theme emerges from them: the presence of the buddha nature in everything. The classic idea of the buddha nature is that the potential for enlightenment exists in all sentient beings, whether human or otherwise. In China, this idea was extended to nonsentient living things such as grass and trees, and even inanimate objects such as rocks. Discussions about this were common in the eighth century.[7]

In the *Masters of the Lanka*, the idea first comes up in the teachings of Guṇabhadra, who almost certainly did not teach the buddha nature of things, and here in the teachings of Hongren, who might have. But whoever originally gave these teachings, they come together in a consistent message: ordinary things have the buddha nature, and they can be our teachers.

> Aren't earth, wood, tile and stone also able to sit in meditation? Can't wood, tile and stone also see forms and hear sounds, wear a robe and carry a bowl? When the *Laṅkāvatāra sūtra* talks about 'the dharmakaya of the realm of objects', this is what it means.

This passage approaches the idea of the buddha nature in inanimate objects in a different way. With a series of questions which are not meant to be answered in any conventional way, Hongren asks why we consider inanimate objects to be nonsentient. Can't they also wear a robe and sit in meditation?

The key is the quote from the *Laṅkāvatāra*: 'The objects of perception are the dharmakaya.' This means that, in the state of meditative awareness, one does not see the objects of perception as external. Everything one sees is merely one's own mind, and this mind is inherently luminous and pure: the dharmakaya itself. From this perspective there is absolutely no difference between any ordinary thing and a buddha, as Hongren tells his students:

> A buddha possesses thirty-two qualities. Doesn't a jug also have these thirty-two qualities? Doesn't a pillar also have these thirty-two qualities? And how about earth, wood, tile and stone: don't they also have these thirty-two qualities?

So things have a buddha nature, and the nature of a buddha is to liberate sentient beings from suffering. Can this be true of things as well? According to statements attributed to Guṇabhadra, things definitely can teach the dharma:

> Things too, like the leaves on this tree, can teach the dharma. This pillar can teach the dharma. The roof can teach the dharma. Earth, water, fire and wind can all teach the dharma. Earth, wood, tile and stone can also teach the dharma.

The idea of things teaching the dharma did not come out of nowhere. In the sutras of Amitabha, the sources of the pure land visualization practices taught by Daoxin and others, it is said that in Amitabha's pure land, the songs of birds teach the dharma and the sounds of trees bring about mindfulness of the Buddha.[8] As we have seen in Daoxin's teachings, the pure land is present here and now when we realize the true nature of our mind.

At the end of Daoxin's chapter, there is a specific argument for how things teach the dharma. He quotes from Vasubandhu's commentary on the *Diamond Sutra*: 'The physical manifestation of the buddha is not the true buddha and does not teach the dharma.'⁹ The second part of Vasubandhu's answer, which is not quoted, is: 'Teach the dharma without clinging to subject and object; do not teach the linguistic distinction of categories.'

So what is the argument here? Rather than trying to intellectually justify the idea of things teaching the dharma, the very idea of teaching the dharma is challenged. How? Because the true sense of 'teaching the dharma' is not a dualistic activity carried out by the physical manifestation of the buddha. It is the communication of nonduality, the absence of subject and object. Therefore 'teaching the dharma' is no more applicable to buddhas than it is to walls, tiles and stones. But when nonduality is understood, everything has the potential to teach the dharma.¹⁰

✦

Chapter Six

In the Tang dynasty, at the Youju Monastery on Shuangfeng Mountain, Jizhou, the great master whose personal name was Hongren, became the successor to the meditation master Daoxin.[11] He was patient in his work of transmitting the dharma and his sublime dharma became famous, known at the time as the pure tradition of East Mountain.[12] It was praised by both monastics and laypeople in the capital city of Luoyang, due to the abundance of people who attained the result at East Mountain in Jizhou thanks to the East Mountain teaching tradition.

People asked Hongren, 'Why don't your students gather in cities or towns? Do you really need to be mountain dwellers?'

He replied: 'The timber for large buildings is sourced from secluded valleys, not from inhabited places. It is only because the trees are far from human beings that they have not been carved with knives or chopped down with axes. Left alone, they are able to reach their full growth over a long time till they are suitable for use as ridgepoles and rafters.[13] That's the reason we live in secluded valleys far from the noise and pollution, cultivating ourselves among the mountains, always staying far away from worldly business. With no objects before the eyes, mind becomes steady and peaceful on its own. As we follow this path, the blossoms bloom on the trees and the forest of meditation bursts into fruit.'

This great master, Hongren, sat quietly in meditation and did not produce any books, only giving people oral teachings on the profound

principle and bestowing upon them his silent transmission.[14] There is
a book on meditation methods in circulation which is claimed to
contain the teachings of the meditation master Hongren, but this is
wrong.[15]

According to the master of Shoushan in Anzhou whose personal
name was Xuanze, and who wrote the *Record of the People and Dharma
of the Lanka*, the great master's secular name was Zhou.[16] His family
were from Xunyang and he was born in the county of Huangmei.
Because his father left when he was young, he took care of his mother,
showing great filial piety.[17] At the age of seven, he entered the service
of the meditation master Daoxin, and after leaving home he lived in
Youju Monastery.

He dwelt in the perfection of vast compassion, holding integrity
and purity close to his heart. He kept his lips sealed in the arena of
claims to truth and falsehood, while merging his mind within the
realm of empty forms. Thanks to his efforts in expanding the practice
of offering rituals, his dharma community were able to support him.[18]
They tamed their own minds while applying themselves exclusively to
all of the ritual practices.[19]

This teacher alone had the clear understanding that the four
postures are the site of enlightenment, and three kinds of activity are
all the work of the buddha.[20] He transcended the two extremes of
peacefulness and disruption, and thus for him speech and silence were
ever one.[21]

All the time, people came from the four directions to request
instruction. All nine types of disciple asked him to be their master,
going to him empty and returning full.[22] Every month there were over
a thousand disciples. He never wrote a book in his life, yet his teachings always tallied with the profound intention.

* * *

At one time, a meditation master from Jingzhou called Shenxiu pros-
trated himself before Hongren's eminent example, and personally
received the entrustment of his transmission. In the first year of the

Xianheng era (670), Xuanze arrived at Shuangfeng Mountain and received instruction from Hongren with reverence. He respectfully offered his services, and over the next five years he returned three times for audiences.

When monks and laypeople assembled together to reverently perform the offering ritual, upon accepting the offerings Hongren gave a sermon on the meaning of the *Lankāvatāra*, saying, 'This sutra can only be fully understood by verifying it with your own mind; written commentaries cannot explain it.'

In the second month of the fifth year of the Xianheng era (674) Hongren ordered Xuanze and the others to begin work on a stupa.[23] Together, the disciples transported uncut stone and built a beautiful structure. On the fourteenth day of the same month, Hongren asked if the stupa had been completed yet, and they respectfully answered that they had finished. He then said: 'It should not happen on the day of the Buddha's *parinirvāṇa*, but from that time onwards, you should use my residence as a monastery.'[24]

He went on to say: 'I cannot count the number of people I have taught in this lifetime. All of the most excellent have died and now there are only ten who might be able to transmit my methods in the future.[25] When I discussed the *Lankāvatāra sūtra* with Shenxiu, he swiftly got to the profound principle, and I am sure he will be of the greatest benefit. Zhishen from Zizhou and Registrar Liu from Baisong Mountain are both educated people.[26] Huizang from Huazhou and Xuanyue from Suizhou, I remember, though I no longer see them. Laoan of Songshan has progressed far along the profound path.[27] Faru from Luzhou,[28] Huineng from Shaozhou,[29] and the Korean monk Zhide from Yangzhou are all equally capable of being teachers, though only to people of their local regions. Yifang from Yuezhou will continue to give sermons.'

He also spoke to Xuanze, saying: 'You should take great care of your simultaneous practice yourself.[30] After I pass into nirvana, you and Shenxiu will make the sun of the buddha shine again, and the lamp of the mind light up again.'

On the sixteenth day of the same month, Hongren asked, 'Do you now know my mind?'[31] Xuanze respectfully answered that he did not know. The great master then raised his hand and gestured towards the ten directions, each time stating that the realized mind was already there. At noon on the sixteenth day he sat at ease, facing south, closed his eyes and died. He had seen seventy-four springs and autumns.[32]

Hongren's body was ritually interred in a stupa on Mount Fengmao. Up to the present day, the stupa is just as it was back then.[33] Lu Zichan of Fanyang painted Hongren's portrait on a wall in Anzhou monastery. Li Jiongxiu of Longxi, a former head of the Ministry of Defence, eulogized Hongren in the following words:[34]

Oh excellent man,
With a deep connection to the truth of the way!
Concentrating his mind, he came to the end of wisdom,[35]
And high realization pervaded his spirit.
Free from birth, he brought about the result,
Demonstrating extinction, he became one with the dust.
Now that he has transformed himself,
How many years before we see his like again?

* * *

The great master said – There is a room that is completely full of excrement, earth and hay. What is this?

And he said – We sweep and clean away the excrement, earth and hay until it is all gone and not a thing remains. What is this?

* * *

When you sit, let your face relax and sit with your head and body straight. Calmly let go of your body and mind. Resting in emptiness, visualize the single syllable from afar. These are the stages of practice: if you are a beginner who grasps at every object, visualize the single syllable in your mind. After you have mastered this, when you are sitting, imagine that you are in the wilderness. In the distance there is a solitary mountain. You are sitting on the barren ground on top of the mountain, looking in the four directions, seeing far into the distance, without barriers or boundaries. As you sit, you fill the whole world, completely relaxing your body and mind, abiding in the realm of the buddhas. This is akin to the experience of the pure dharmakaya without barriers or boundaries.

He also said – At the point when you truly realize the vast dharmakaya, who is there to experience this realization?

* * *

He also said – A buddha possesses thirty-two qualities. Doesn't a jug also have these thirty-two qualities? Doesn't a pillar also have these thirty-two qualities? And how about earth, wood, tile and stone: don't they also have these thirty-two qualities?

Once he picked up two fire tongs, one long and one short, held them up side by side and asked: 'Which one is long? Which one is short?'

Once, Hongren saw someone lighting a lamp, bringing a myriad things into being with one touch, and he said to everyone, 'That person is a maker of dreams, a creator of illusions.'[36]

Sometimes he used to say, 'Nothing is created, nothing is made; everything, of every sort, is the great nirvana.'

* * *

He also said – Ultimate arising is the lack of arising as an entity.[37] It is not that there is a lack of arising independent of arising as an entity. As Nāgārjuna wrote:

> Entities do not arise from themselves,
> Nor do they arise from other,
> Nor from both, nor without any cause;
> Therefore we know that there is no arising.[38]

If entities arise from conditions, then they lack an inherent nature. If they lack an intrinsic nature how can they be said to exist? Furthermore:

> Space has no centre or periphery;
> All of the buddhas' bodies are like this too.[39]

When I give you my seal of approval because I can clearly see the buddha nature in you, it is this that I see.

* * *

He also said – When you are sitting in meditation in the monastery, aren't you also sitting in meditation under a tree in a mountain forest? Aren't earth, wood, tile and stone also able to sit in meditation? Can't earth, wood, tile and stone also see forms and hear sounds, wear a robe and carry a bowl? When the *Laṅkāvatāra sūtra* talks about 'the dharmakaya of the realm of objects', this is what it means.

✦

CHAPTER FIFTEEN

SHENXIU

Zen in the World

The balance of the *Masters of the Lanka* changes in the chapter on Hongren, which gives as much space to his life as to his teachings. And then in the chapter on Shenxiu, the focus is almost entirely on his life. Certainly, much more was known about his life than that of his predecessors, but his teachings were also much more widely circulated. The *Masters of the Lanka* gives us his oral teaching style, but says nothing of the many written texts attributed to Shenxiu. This may be due to the number and length of his works, which would have been in general circulation anyway. These works, which survive in the Dunhuang manuscripts, include his *Treatise on Original Luminosity* and *Treatise on Contemplating the Mind*.[1]

In this chapter we see Shenxiu's progress from being a student of Hongren on East Mountain, to being a court teacher, highly in demand, constantly travelling between the two capital cities of Luoyang and Chang'an. His favour with the empress Wu Zetian led to him being given the title of Imperial Preceptor. In fact, the chapter implies that Shenxiu was also the National Preceptor, a post that was subsequently held by Hongren's other students, Xuanze and Laoan. Perhaps Shenxiu was appointed Imperial Preceptor to Empress Wu, and later National Preceptor to her successor, Zhongzong.[2]

In any case, the *Masters of the Lanka* reports a conversation between Empress Wu and Shenxiu, in which the empress asks for the essence of his teaching. Shenxiu replies that it is the single practice concentration, as taught in the 700-verse *Perfection of Wisdom Sutra*. This is the practice that is taught at length in Daoxin's teachings in the

Masters of the Lanka, which involves visualization and repetition of the name of a buddha. Of course we cannot know whether this conversation really took place, but it does play a key role in one of Shenxiu's most important works.

Shenxiu's *Five Skilful Means* is a liturgy and sermon for the ceremony of receiving the vows of a bodhisattva – like the *Platform Sutra* and Daoxin's *Dharma Teachings for the Bodhisattva Precepts.*[3] It begins with a verse that is to be recited by all participants, making the four great vows:

> I vow to save the innumerable sentient beings.
> I vow to eradicate the limitless afflictions.
> I vow to master the infinite teachings.
> I vow to realize the unsurpassable enlightenment of buddhahood.

This aspirational prayer, the expression of the bodhisattva's awakening mind (bodhicitta), is followed by five commitments: to stay away from harmful associations, to stay close to spiritual companions, to maintain the bodhisattva vows at all times, to read and contemplate Mahayana sutras, and to strive to liberate sentient beings from suffering. After this the participants recite a prayer of repentance for all of their past actions that have transgressed the ten virtues of Buddhism.

After these conventional preliminaries, the teacher explains 'the precepts of purity', which is the understanding that the true nature of the precepts is the buddha nature. This is, in principle, an immediate and instantaneous method for realization: 'In one instant you can purify your mind and suddenly transcend to the stage of buddhahood.'[4] After explaining this, the preceptor strikes a wooden sounding board, and everyone sits in mindfulness of the buddha.

This is followed by a ritualized question and answer session. The preceptor begins by quoting a passage from the *Diamond Sutra* to the effect that all categories are unreal. The participants in the ceremony then do the meditation practice that we have seen in Daoxin's and

Hongren's chapters, letting go of the distinction between internal senses and external objects and letting the mind and body fill the world in a sense of 'sameness'. The preceptor then asks, 'What do you see?' and the participants all reply, 'I do not see a single thing.'

Similar ritualized questions and answers feature in later parts of the ceremony as well. The similarity of the questions to those that appear in the *Masters of the Lanka* is intriguing. As John McRae has suggested, it may be these kinds of ritualized exchanges that formed the basis for the later question and answer dialogues of koan practice. That is to say, they came out of a new kind of organized monastic practice, rather than spontaneous encounters between teachers and students.[5]

When we look at Shenxiu's career, this makes sense. During his time, Zen teachings became established in monasteries, and with Shenxiu we see the first examples of what Zen monastic rituals looked like. And it is with him, or at the earliest with his teacher Hongren, that the teaching method of breaking through ordinary conceptual thinking with questions first appears. Shenxiu's teachings in the *Masters of the Lanka* do not come directly from the *Five Skilful Means* or his other known works, but they do overlap. For example, at one point in the latter, the preceptor strikes his wooden sounding board and asks the participants, 'Do you hear the sound?'[6] And in the *Masters of the Lanka*, Shenxiu is said to have asked his students:

When you hear a bell being struck, does the sound exist when it is struck? Does it exist before it is struck? Is sound really sound?

I think we can be fairly confident in crediting Shenxiu with playing a significant part in popularizing this particular kind of question and answer teaching style, which seems to have developed into the koan tradition. It is also interesting to read the *Five Skilful Means* next to the *Platform Sutra* and see how much they have in common. Since both are intended for the bodhisattva precepts ceremony, they share a similar structure, but there is more to it than that. Shenxiu's 'precepts of purity' are akin to Huineng's 'formless precepts': both use the perfection of wisdom sutras as their authority for a nonconceptual realization, and both extol an immediate access to one's own buddha nature, the nature of mind.

This undercuts the characterization of Shenxiu's teachings in the *Platform Sutra* as conventional, gradual and indirect. Criticism of Shenxiu does not feature in Huineng's sermon itself, but in the material before and after, which was added later. For instance, before the sermon in *Platform Sutra*, in the biography of Huineng, there is the famous 'poetry battle' in which Huineng is said to have bested Shenxiu – though this can never have happened, as the two were not studying with Hongren at the same time. And after the sermon, there is a story of Shenxiu dispatching one of his students to spy on Huineng: the student goes to see Huineng, receives instruction, and becomes convinced of the latter's superiority.

In words attributed to Huineng, the text directly explains why his teachings are better than Shenxiu's:

> The Master continued, 'The morality, meditation, and wisdom of your master are intended for small-minded people. My morality, meditation, and wisdom are intended for people of bigger minds. Once people realize their own nature, they don't differentiate between morality, meditation, and wisdom.'[7]

This is hardly a fair characterization of Shenxiu, the author of the treatises *Original Luminosity* and *Contemplating the Mind*, but as those works faded into obscurity, and the *Platform Sutra* did not, this is the picture of Shenxiu that endured. Still, we might wonder why the authors of the *Platform Sutra*, which was dedicated to communicating the nature of Huineng's teachings and the story of his life, also had to denigrate his contemporary.

The answer is surely found in Shenxiu's fame and success in gaining the support of Empress Wu, which brought Zen into the realm of politics. In the next generation his students, especially Puji, benefited from his fame, and became influential in their own right. And while Shenxiu had never, as far as we know, claimed to be the only legitimate successor to Hongren, the fact that he had been given the role of Imperial Preceptor gave him a great deal of legitimacy.

Zen teachers whose lineages did not come via Shenxiu were not always happy with this situation, and this resulted in the promotion of the relatively obscure figure of Huineng as the true successor to Hongren. And Huineng's promotion had to be at the expense of Shenxiu. So we can see Shenxiu as a victim of his own success, at least posthumously – in the end, known to later generations only through the story in the *Platform Sutra* in which his poem was beaten by Huineng's, and the characterization of his teaching as gradualist, rather than immediate.

However, this is only one part of the story. What the Dunhuang manuscripts tell us is that by the tenth century the teachings of Shenxiu and his lineage were being transmitted right alongside those of Huineng and his lineage. If not forgotten, the disputes of the eighth century were at least no longer relevant. The so-called 'Northern School' of Shenxiu had not died out in the meantime, as people often assume; its texts and practices were still being transmitted and copied. Some two centuries after the original controversies, the distinction between the 'Northern' and 'Southern' schools was irrelevant in the context of teaching and practising meditation.

For Buddhist practitioners, lineage is always important, and differences do exist between one teaching lineage and another; but a teacher may belong to more than one lineage, and often the most important principle in Buddhism is: use what works. The teachings are, after all, only a means to an end. Splits between religious schools, which scholars like to trace to doctrinal distinctions, are usually caused by local political situations. The distinction between the Northern and Southern schools of Zen was largely made by a single influential monk, Shenhui, who took his polemical sermons across the country when he went on tours in which he gave the bodhisattva precepts ceremony to large audiences.

The differences between Shenxiu and Huineng's teaching are minor, and the *Platform Sutra* simply preserves a particular point in time when some students of the latter were attempting to differentiate their own doctrines from those of the more dominant students of Shenxiu. Afterwards, there was little interest in continuing to insist on a distinction that didn't make any difference. There is a passage in the *Platform Sutra* itself that expresses this view, going in the opposite direction from some of the other polemical passages in the text. Here, the text explains that the names 'Northern' and 'Southern' are only used because Shenxiu was at Yuquan monastery, and Huineng lived some twelve miles to the south. In this passage, the *Platform Sutra* is equally dismissive of the idea that the teachings of the Southern School are 'direct', and those of the Northern School 'indirect'.[8]

> And what is the origin of 'direct' and 'indirect'? Although there is only one kind of dharma, understanding can be fast or slow. When understanding is slow, we say it's 'indirect'. And when understanding is fast, we say it's 'direct'. The dharma isn't direct or indirect, it's people who are sharp or dull. This is why we have the terms 'direct' and 'indirect'.[9]

* * *

One mysterious and pithy teaching attributed to Shenxiu appears only in the *Masters of the Lanka* – his last words. I have translated these as 'Bend with the crooked and the straight'. However, this enigmatic three-character phrase *qū qū zhí* has been interpreted in many other ways as well. For example, J.C. Cleary has 'bend the crooked and make it straight', and John McRae suggests in a similar vein 'the vagaries of the world are now straightened'. He also cites with approval the interpretation of Yanagida, which takes the first and second characters as a reference to the indirect teachings of the Buddha: 'the teachings of the expedient means have been made direct'.[10] Bernard Faure has simply 'plié, courbé, redressé' ('bent, curved, straightened').[11]

So, why 'Bend with the crooked and the straight'? The first character (*qū*) has several meanings, usually as a verb, around the concept of bending; one of these is 'submit to, yield to'. The second and third characters (*qū zhí*) are conventional antonyms, 'crooked and straight', which appear together in Chinese Confucian classics such as the *Liji*: 'The round and the deflected, the crooked and the straight, each has its own category.' And in the *Shangshu*: 'The nature of water is to soak and descend; of fire, to blaze and ascend; of wood, to be crooked and straight; of metal, to yield and change.'[12]

Thus I would suggest that Shenxiu was using a phrase that would be familiar to an educated audience at the court. What does it mean? Roughly, the sense is be flexible, not rigid; one might say, go with the flow. This interpetation is also reminiscent of a later statement by Dogen about the most important thing he learned from his Zen teacher in China: 'a soft and flexible mind'.[13]

* * *

The *Masters of the Lanka* concludes with a very brief chapter on four of Shenxiu's students. Really, almost nothing is said about them or their teachings, and they are not differentiated from each other. The chapter only serves to let us know who were considered to be the foremost inheritors of Shenxiu's teachings. From other historical sources we know that one of these four, Puji, took Shenxiu's place at the imperial court, and was very successful there, with hundreds of monastic students as well as his royal patrons.[14]

It is interesting to see, in these last two chapters, that the model of a single teacher to student transmission is dropped. The beginning of Shenxiu's chapter mentions him alongside two other students of Hongren, and repeats Hongren's statement that ten of his students are authorized to carry on his teachings. In the concluding chapter, four teachers representing the next generation of the Lanka lineage are mentioned.

Thus the *Masters of the Lanka* does not take part in the arguments that arose in the generation after Hongren's students about which one of those students was the true inheritor of his authority. Instead the model of one master per generation ends with Hongren. This is different from both the slightly earlier *Transmission of the Dharma Jewel*, which has Shenxiu as the sole representative of Hongren's authority, and the somewhat later *Genealogy of the Dharma Jewel*, which has Huineng in the same role. Instead, the *Masters of the Lanka* has the Zen teachings spreading outwards, like the branches of a tree moving away from the trunk, reaching towards the sky.

✦

Chapter Seven

In the Tang dynasty, the three great teachers, Master Shenxiu of Yuquan monastery in Jingzhou, Master Xuanze of Shoushan monastery in Anzhou, and Master Laoan of Huishan monastery on Mount Song in Luozhou, were appointed by the noble Empress Wu Zetian, Emperor Yingtian Shenlong and Emperor Taishang in succession to the post of National Preceptor.[15] The great master Hongren made a prediction about them when he said, 'Only ten of my disciples will be capable of passing on my methods'.[16] Together, they were the successors to meditation master Hongren.

According to the master of Shoushan in Anzhou, who compiled the *Record of the People and Dharma of the Lanka*, the meditation master Shenxiu had the family name Li. His family were from Weishi in Bianzhou.[17] He left home and crossed the upper Yangtse river to seek the path that he yearned for, travelling till he reached the home of the meditation teacher Hongren at Shuangfeng Mountain in Qizhou.

> And he was accepted by this meditation master,
> Who was silently illuminated by the lamp of meditation,
> Who had abandoned the methods of verbal expression,[18]
> Who had put an end to the operation of his mental functions,[19]
> Who never produced any written records.[20]

Later, when Shenxiu was living at Yuquan monastery in Jingzhou, in the first year of the Dazu era (701), he was summoned to the

Eastern Capital (Luoyang). He accompanied the imperial carriages back and forth between the two capitals, giving teachings, and was personally appointed by the empress as her Imperial Preceptor.[21]

The noble Empress Wu Zetian asked the meditation master Shenxiu, 'Which school of thought does the dharma that you transmit belong to?'[22]

He answered, 'I belong to the teaching tradition of East Mountain in Jingzhou.'

She asked him to tell her what their scriptural authority was, and he answered, 'Our authority is the the *Saptaśatikā-prajñāpāramitā sūtra*'s teaching on the single practice concentration.'

Zetian said, 'If we were to assess the practice of the path, no other teaching tradition surpasses that of the East Mountain. Since Shenxiu is a follower of Hongren, he is somebody who speaks the truth.'[23]

* * *

On the thirteenth day of the third month of the first year of the Shenlong era (705), Emperor Yingtian Shenlong issued the following decree:[24]

> This meditation teacher's footprints are free from the dust of the world, and his spirit roams free of worldly concerns. In accord with the subtle principle free from categories, he guides those who have lost their way in the bonds of existence. Inside, the waters of concentration are still and pure. Outside, the pearls of morality are bright and clear. His disciples turn their minds to Buddhism, setting off towards fords and bridges to ask for an explanation of his teaching tradition, hoping to take the first steps on the path.[25] Recently the meditation teacher has been wishing to return to his homeland. You must act without delay to assist him in his heart's desire. Do not get in the way of his yearning for the elm trees![26] I have granted him this letter to make my intentions known. Now I have pointed my finger, no more words need be said.[27]

Thus the meditation teacher gained the respect of two emperors.[28] Teaching in both capitals, he brought benefit to both court and countryside, bringing innumerable people to liberation.[29] By imperial decree, Baoen Monastery was established in his birthplace, the great village of Li.[30]

On the twenty-eighth day of the second month of the second year of the Shenlong era (15 March 706), he sat in meditation posture without discomfort and spoke three words as his last testament: 'Bend with the crooked and the straight.'[31] He passed away peacefully at Tiangong Monastery in the Eastern Capital, having seen over a hundred springs and autumns. Monastic and lay devotees from across the city came together and hung the temples with banners.[32] The funeral was carried out on Longmen Mountain, with the imperial princesses and sons-in-law all providing memorial statements.[33] The emperor issued the following decree:

> The late meditation teacher Shenxiu,
> His immaculate awareness in harmony with the world,
> His spiritual energy permeating his inner being,
> Has reached the inner core of nonduality.
> He alone has won the topknot jewel,[34]
> While defending the gate of true oneness.
> The mirror of his mind, hanging alone,
> In perfect clarity responds to the needs of beings.[35]
> All appearances come together in his luminous spirit,
> Unconditioned and spontaneously present,
> Clear of dust, free of entanglements.[36]
> Even as he moved towards the sunset of his life,
> His spirit became brighter day by day.
> The moment that he pierced the depths of subtle and profound
>   awareness,[37]
> He became a guide for the eyes and ears of a multitude of beings.
> In the sameness of non-conceptualization and vast compassion,
> He devoted himself to guiding those who came under his influence,

Setting his heart on nirvana for everyone.[38]
He thought long and hard about the transmission of the teachings,
Even though the principle is free from name and form.
He never needed or pursued respect,
Yet he was an ideal teacher of students.
So, with the aspiration that he should always be covered in glory,
I hereby confer on him the title *Meditation Teacher Datong*.[39]

The emperor decreed: 'It would be fitting to dispatch the frontrider
to the heir apparent, Lu Zhengquan, to escort Shenxiu's remains to
Jingzhou, and to establish a stele at Dumen Monastery. Zhengquan
should also make a report about the condition of the monastery on
the day of his return.'[40]

One of the monks at the monastery wrote the following eulogy:

Our incomparable teacher
Has traversed the path to the ultimate truth,
Pure liberation,
Reality itself, perfectly luminous.
He explained the unsurpassed path,
Opened the path to unsurpassed insight.
His karmic imprints dissolved in the sameness
Of a mind that is free of the three times.
He used conventional language to demonstrate the principle,
In accordance with the way of the principle.
He always acted as a ship of the dharma,
Taking people across the river.

* * *

The great teacher said – The *Nirvana Sutra* teaches that, 'If you understand a single word of this properly, then you are worthy of the title of
Preceptor.'[41] The words come from the sutra, but the realization is within.

He also said – Does this mind have a mind? What kind of mind is
your mind?

He also said – When you see forms do they have form? What kind of form are forms?

He also said – When you hear a bell being struck, does the sound exist when it is struck? Does it exist before it is struck? What kind of sound are sounds?

He also said – Does the sound of a bell being struck only exist inside the monastery, or does the sound of the bell pervade the whole universe as well?[42]

He also said – The body disappears but the reflection remains.[43] The bridge flows but the water does not. My path is based on the unity of two words, 'essence' and 'activity'.[44] It is also called 'the gate to the twofold mystery'.[45] It is also called 'turning the wheel of the dharma'. It is also called 'the path and its result'.

He also said – First no seeing, then seeing. Seeing is always the cessation of seeing, and the return of seeing again.[46]

He also said – The *Jewel Garland Sutra* says: 'Bodhisattvas illuminate stillness; buddhas make luminosity still.'

He also said – A mustard seed may enter Mount Meru, and Mount Meru may enter a mustard seed.

Also, seeing a bird fly past, he would ask – What is this?

He also said – Can you spend the time sitting in meditation at the end of a branch?

He also said – Can you walk straight through a wall?

He also said – It is taught in the *Nirvana Sutra* that the bodhisattva's body has no limits, yet he came from the east.[47] Since the bodhisattva's body has no limits or boundaries, then how did he come from the east? Why could he not come from the west, or from the south or north? Are they not equally possible?

Conclusion

In the Tang dynasty, meditation teacher Puji from Songgao Mountain in Luozhou, meditation teacher Jingxian from Song Mountain, meditation teacher Yifu from Lan Mountain near Chang'an, and meditation teacher Huifu from Yu Mountain in Lantian, all studied as dharma companions at the same time with a single master. They were all successors to Master Datong.[48]

They left home when they were young, kept their precepts pure, and sought a teacher to ask about the path. Travelling far to find a tradition of meditation, they arrived at Yuquan monastery in Jingzhou where they met Master Datong, whose personal name was Shenxiu, and received the transmission of his meditation teachings.

All of these teachers served the great teacher together for more than ten years. They each attained clear realization. The jewel of meditation was the only thing that shone for them. The great teacher entrusted Puji, Jingxian, Yifu and Huifu together with the blazing lamp that lights up the world, and transmitted to them the great crystal mirror.[49]

All people under heaven who sit in meditation admired these four meditation teachers, saying:

The mountain of dharma is pure,
The sea of dharma is clear,
The mirror of dharma is bright,
The lamp of dharma shines out.

They sat at ease atop famous mountains and cleared their minds in deep valleys. Their virtue merged with the ocean of the original nature. Their practice bloomed on the branches of meditation. In unconditioned purity, they walked alone and unhampered. They illuminated the dark with the lamp of meditation, and all who learned from them realized the buddha mind.

* * *

Ever since the Song dynasty (420–77), there have been eminent meditation teachers of great virtue, coming one generation after another.[50] Beginning with the tripiṭaka master Guṇabhadra in the Song, the flame has been passed on through the generations down to the Tang dynasty; altogether eight generations have accomplished the path and attained the result, comprising twenty-four people.[51]

   Record of the Teachers and Students of the Lanka

   — one volume

NOTES

PREFACE

1. Ford 2012: 75.

CHAPTER 1. THE PRACTICE OF ZEN

1. Here, 'peace of mind' is a translation of the Chinese *ānxīn* 安心.
2. Monier-Williams 1998: 483.II.
3. See chapter 9 above for a discussion of this metaphor in Zen and beyond.
4. In Bodhidharma's *Two Entrances and Four Practices*, the fourth practice is to perform giving and the other six perfections informed by the three aspects of emptiness (*sānkōng* 三空), i.e. emptiness of agent, object and action (see chapter 8 above). Elsewhere in Buddhist literature, this classification of all interpersonal events into agent, object and action is usually known as 'the three spheres' (Chinese *sānlún* 三輪, Sanskrit *trimaṇḍala*). To be governed by this categorization is an obstruction to the truly selfless behaviour of a bodhisattva. The *Tiansheng Extensive Record (Tiansheng guangdeng lu)* states that the followers of the Buddha's Zen teaching were not attached to these three spheres; see Foulk 1999: 255.
5. This statement is from Daoxin's teachings in *The Masters of the Lanka*; see chapter 12 above.
6. Translation in Ferguson 2011: 22.
7. An early Zen text, which survives in translation on the same manuscript as the Tibetan translation of the *Masters of the Lanka*, uses this image when discussing the relationship between teachers and students; see van Schaik 2015: 65.
8. On the early texts on mindfulness of breathing, and their introduction to China, see Deleanu 1992. The quote from Robert Aitken is in *Taking the Path of Zen* (Aitken 1982: 11–12). This book provides a detailed and practical guide to beginning Zen meditation, though it should be noted that Aitken belonged to a specific Japanese teaching lineage, the twentieth-century reformist Sanbo Kyodan school.
9. The Japanese word 'shikantaza' can also mean to concentrate on sitting alone (i.e. not on other practices). It comes from the Soto Zen school, where it is attributed to Dogen (1200–53), though some form of this kind of meditation is practised in almost all Zen traditions.
10. The word 'satori' is Japanese, based on the Chinese *wù* 悟, which can be translated as 'enlightenment'. The word 'kenshō' is Chinese *jiànxìng* 見性, meaning 'to see the nature'; this term appears in early Zen works including the *Platform Sutra* of Huineng. See for example Yampolsky (2012: 149), where the term is translated

as 'see into your own nature', and Red Pine (2006: 22), where it is translated as 'see your nature'.

11. As an example of the use of the English word 'enlightenment' for a glimpse or temporary breakthrough, see the American Zen teacher Setsuan Gaelyn Godwin: 'In our tradition, enlightenment is not a permanent state. [The Zen monk] Ikkyu had a taste or a glimpse that was verified' (*Buddhadharma* magazine, Spring 2016, p. 48). Sheng Yen's definition is from Sheng 2008: 29.

12. Welch 1967: 84.

13. From the Keisei Sanshoku chapter of Dogen's *Shōbōgenzō*. Translation from Tanahashi 2010: 92. See also Nearman 2007: 75; Nishijima and Cross 2006: I.78.

14. From the preface of *Masters of the Lanka* – see chapter 7 above.

15. One short-lived early school of Zen did apparently take the radical step of abandoning all formal practices; see Adamek 2007: 218–26.

16. Translation from Tanahashi 2015: 60.

17. Translation from Tanahashi 2015: 35.

18. This version of the ten precepts comes from the *Brahmajāla sūtra*. Slightly different versions are chanted in different traditions of Zen and other schools of Mahayana Buddhism.

19. Translation from Tanahashi 2015: 57.

20. *Laṅkāvatāra* XIII; translation from Red Pine 2013: 83.

21. *Laṅkāvatāra* XXVII; translation from Red Pine 2013: 109.

22. Giving is the first of the six perfections (Skt *pāramitā*) practised by the bodhisattva. The others are: morality, patience, effort, meditation and insight.

23. *Laṅkāvatāra* III; translation from Red Pine 2013: 63.

24. Dogen's commentary on the story of killing the Buddha is in the 'Zazen Shin' chapter of *Shōbōgenzō*, trans. Nishijima and Cross 2006: 2.82–3; Tanahashi 2010: 308; Nearman 2007: 343.

25. Thich Nhat Hanh 1995: 53–4.

26. This story appears in many Zen collections, including the *Anthology of the Patriarchal Hall*. For a more literal rendering, see McRae 2003: 81.

27. In English translation, see for example Chang 1983: 68, from Taisho 310, no. 36: *Shanzhuyi tianzi hui* (Skt *Susthitamati-devaputra-paripṛcchā*).

28. From Zongmi's *Chan Prolegomenon* translated in Broughton 2009: 154.

29. The relationship between sudden realization and gradual practice was discussed insightfully by the seventh-century scholar Zongmi, in his *Chan Prolegomenon* (see Broughton 2009: 152–5). The question is alluded to poetically in the *Laṅkāvatāra sūtra*, which gives four examples of gradual progress and four of sudden realization (see Broughton 2009: 277, n.269). The tension between sudden and gradual is also at the heart of the spiritual quest of Dogen, as described in his biography (see Ford 2006: 45).

30. For a discussion, see Dumoulin 1988: 85.

31. This has been the interpretation offered by most Zen teachers who have addressed the issue. See the discussion in Foulk 1999, esp. p. 260.

32. The first image is quoted from an unnamed 'ancient book' while the second is from the *Avataṃsaka sūtra*.

33. This is my own translation from the Chinese. The poem is popularly attributed to Layman Pang, also known as Pangyun (740–808). The phrase 'carry water and haul firewood' appears in many other Zen texts, including Dogen's *Eihei Kōroku*; see Leighton and Okumura 2010: 203–4, 215, 221, 232.

CHAPTER 2. ZEN AND THE WEST

1. Watts 1991: 15.
2. Watts 1991: 42
3. Kapleau 1989: 31.
4. McMahan 2008: 186–7.
5. Harris 2014: 10.
6. The significant figures in this mindfulness movement are usually explicit about its origin in Buddhism, though further down the line the technique is often presented as a purely secular one. See for example 'This is not McMindfulness by any Stretch of the Imagination', an interview with Jon Kabat-Zinn in *The Psychologist*, 18 May 2015. For an academic critique of 'mindfulness' in relation to Zen Buddhism, see Sharf 2014 and the papers in Rosenbaum and Magid 2016.
7. The arguments of the above two paragraphs are based on Foulk 2006.
8. For the involvement of some of these teachers in the Second World War, see Victoria 2006.
9. Sharf 1993: 39.
10. 'Jargon File' (Version 4.4.7, 29 Dec. 2003), ed. Eric Raymond, is to be found at www.catb.org/jargon/html/. It is also archived at: http://jargon-file.org/archive/ jargon-4.4.7.dos.txt. See also: http://www.catb.org/jargon/html/koans.html
11. Raymond 2015.
12. Pirsig 1974: 6.
13. Eugen Herrigel (1884–1955) was a German philosopher and, later in life, a nationalist and Nazi. His presentation of Zen has been critiqued in Yamada 2001.
14. On Samurai Zen, see Victoria 2006: 215–55.
15. It has been argued, by Batchelor and others, that rebirth is not as significant in Zen teaching as in many other Buddhist traditions. While this may be true for some contemporary teachers, karma and rebirth are certainly present in the works of many of the most revered teachers of the tradition. For example, in Bodhidharma's *Two Entrances and Four Practices*, the first and second practices are based on the contemplation of the results of one's actions in past lives. And for a classic discussion of karma and rebirth in the Japanese Zen tradition, see the two chapters 'Sanji No Go' and 'Shinjin Inga' from Dogen's *Shōbōgenzō* (Nishijima and Cross 2006: 4.101–9, 165–71; Tanahashi 2010: 779–91, 851–7; Nearman 2007: 1019–43).
16. For Sam Harris, rebirth is one of the superstitions of Buddhist traditions that can and should be ignored; see Harris 2014: 137.
17. Midgley 1996: 80. The moral problems that arise from this view of humanity have been explored by Alastair MacIntyre in his influential *After Virtue*. MacIntyre identifies modern moral discourse as emotivism, 'the doctrine that all evaluative judgements and more specifically all moral judgements are *nothing but* expressions of preference, expressions of attitude or feeling' (MacIntyre 2011: 11–12).
18. See Baier 2009, especially chapter 1, 'The Rights of Past and Future Persons' – the phrase she uses is 'the temporal continuity of the moral community' (p. 9).
19. On the discussions about the possible applications of Buddhist concepts to environmentalism, see Ives 2009.
20. See Ford 2006: 66–71.
21. From the website of the San Francisco Zen Center: http://sfzc.org/about-zen-center/principles-governance/vision.
22. On the nature and history of Zen centres in the USA, see Ford 2006.

23. Satō and Nishimura 1973: 12.
24. From the Kankin chapter of *Shōbōgenzō*, translation in Tanahashi 2010: 229; Nearman 2007: 238–9; Nishijima and Cross 2006: 1.232.
25. This popular saying is attributed to Baizhang Huaihai (749–814); see Poceski 2010: 16.
26. Satō and Nishimura 1973: 35.
27. On the shukushin ceremony and its sources in Chinese Chan, see Mohr 2008.

CHAPTER 3. THE HISTORY OF ZEN

1. The story and its earliest appearances are discussed in Welter 2000. He writes that 'the textual record indicates that the story was fabricated in China as part of an effort by Ch'an monks to create an independent identity within the Chinese Buddhist context' (p. 76).
2. On the evolution of the stories of Bodhidharma, see McRae 2003: 22–8.
3. For an exhaustive study of Huineng, see Jorgensen 2012.
4. Shibayama 1974: 60.
5. McRae 2003: 27–8.
6. See Greene 2012: 17–28.
7. Zürcher 2007: 33.
8. *Meditation Essentials* (*Chan miyao fa jing*) 1.9; translation based on Greene 2012: 349.
9. *Meditation Essentials* 3.33; translation based on Greene 2012: 473.
10. There is discussion of this in the Mūlasarvāstivāda vinaya section on poṣadha (MSV 1,02: *Poṣadhavastu*); this is in the first part, on *niṣadyā*, i.e. 'sitting', which is also called *yoga*. This meditation practice is exclusively a consideration of the impurity of the body, going through all its physical elements.
11. This is the point made by Eric Greene (2012: 11): 'In fifth- and sixth-century China, *chan* seems to have been valued in large measure as a means of divining the efficacy of such rites.' Similar points have been made about a Sanskrit meditation book found in the Central Asian city of Kucha, dating from the same period, which gives vivid details of visualizations and visions; see Schlingloff 2006.
12. In Daoxin's instructions for novices in the *Masters of the Lanka* (see chapter 13 above), the meditation practice of analysing the body and establishing its emptiness is said to be 'the true practice of repentance'.
13. On early Tiantai and Pure Land in relation to early Chan, see Poceski 2015; for a critical history of Pure Land practice in China, see Yu 2006. Yu points out that the idea that there was a 'Pure Land school' separate from other currents of Buddhism (such as Zen) is a later construction.
14. Zongmi, 'Chan Prolegomenon', translated in Broughton 2009: 110 (square brackets in original translation removed).
15. On the importance of the bodhisattva precepts ceremony to the transmission of Zen, see Adamek 2007: 67–88.
16. Morten Schlütter (2008: 36–9) has shown that Zen monks benefited from a Song practice of converting hereditary monasteries, with a family succession of abbots, to public monasteries, where the abbots were chosen from outside, often by local rulers. However, as John McRae has pointed out, the presence of an abbot from a Zen lineage did not make these public monasteries into 'Zen monasteries' as has often been imagined; see McRae 2003: 116.

17. From *Hongzhi chanshi guanglu* (T.48, no. 2001, p. 74b25), translated in Leighton 2000: 10, and discussed in McRae 2003: 137–8.

18. From *Dahui yulu*, translated in Buswell (1987: 349) and discussed in McRae (2003: 127).

19. There are many books on koans, but one of the best is still *Zen Dust* (Fuller Sasaki and Miura 1965).

20. See McRae 2003: 122: 'There never was any such thing as an institutionally separate Chan "school" at any time in Chinese Buddhist history.'

21. See Foulk 2006: 151–2.

22. There are now several English translations of the *Shōbōgenzō* available, in print and online. In this book, I have primarily consulted the translation by Gudō Nishijima and Chodo Cross which tends to follow the Japanese closely and is well footnoted; however, some consider it to be rather idiosyncratic. The four volumes of the first edition were published in 1994–99; a second edition, also in four volumes, was published in 2006; and there is also a 2009 electronic edition available online at www.thezensite.com, which unfortunately omits the Chinese and Japanese characters of the print edition. Here, my page references are to the print 2006 edition. Additionally, I used the collaborative translation edited by Kazuaki Tanahashi (2010), which tends to fluency rather than literal translation, for quotations. Another good translation, comparable in approach to the Tanahashi edition, was done by Hubert Nearman (2007) for the Shasta Abbey; this version is free and appears to be available only in an electronic edition, from shastaabbey.org/pdf/shoboAll.pdf. I have also used the first volume of the translation by Kōsen Nishiyama and John Stevens (1975–83), which contains a good account of Dogen's life.

23. See Welter 2008; quote from p. 114.

24. Foulk 2006: 150.

25. Foulk 2006: 150.

26. Jaffe 2001: 2. For a discussion by a Japanese Zen priest see Okumura 2012: 54–5.

27. This issue is discussed at some length in Ford 2006: 50–5.

28. Reverend Kim and his teachings are discussed at various points in Adamek 2007. For his role in Tibetan Zen, see van Schaik 2015: 147–9.

29. For a much more detailed discussion of Zongmi's thought in the context of Korean Buddhism, see the introduction to Buswell 1983.

30. Ford 2006: 96; Batchelor 2008.

31. For a detailed account of Zen in Vietnam, see Thich Thien-An 1975.

32. Thich Nhat Hanh 1995: 23.

33. Thich Nhat Hanh 1995: 25.

CHAPTER 4. THE LOST TEXTS OF ZEN

1. Robson 2011: 311.

2. Stein 1921: 820.

3. Salomon 2011: 30.

4. This account of Hongbian and the cave at Dunhuang is informed by Yoshiro Imaeda's excellent article 'The Provenance and Character of the Dunhuang Documents' (2008). Another recent attempt to explain the contents of the cave by

Rong Xinjiang (2000) focuses on the evidence in manuscript colophons for the role of a monk who was collecting manuscripts to repair the contents of the Sanjie monastery's library. Then in the early eleventh century, Rong argues, the entire library of the Sanjie monastery was moved over to the Dunhuang cave and sealed, probably for its own safety, for fear of the Islamic armies who were threatening the Silk Route cities to the west. Thus for Rong, the contents of the Dunhuang cave represent a complete monastic library, rather than a variety of libraries and personal collections. Imaeda's article offers various points of criticism of Rong's theory.

5. The idea of the fear of invasion motivating the closing of the cave was first suggested by Paul Pelliot, and more recently in Rong (2000: 272–5). The more prosaic reason that I suggest here has also been suggested by Yoshiro Imaeda (2008: 98), and in van Schaik and Galambos (2011: 27–8).

6. For a good summary of the Zen texts found in the Dunhuang manuscripts, see Sørenson 1989.

7. Cole 2009: 7.

8. On these early lineage texts, see Wendi Adamek 2007: 161–9. Timothy Barrett (1991) has argued that the *Masters of the Lanka* must have been composed before 716 (though his argument refers to the preface, so the main part of the text may be earlier).

9. Red Pine 2013: 3.

10. The three levels of reality are: (i) the imagined level of reality, which is completely false; (ii) the dependent level of reality, which is a correct conceptual understanding; and (iii) the perfected level of reality, which is nonconceptual thusness. The eight aspects of consciousness are the five senses, mental consciousness (Skt *mano-vijñāna*), ego (Skt *manas*) and basic consciousness (Skt *ālaya-vijñāna*). This model of consciousness is discussed in chapter 8 above.

11. The inclusive nature of the *Masters of the Lanka* is discussed in Adamek 2007: 168–9.

12. In S.2054 the character is *jí* 集. In Pelliot chinois 3436, it is *huì* 會. Both mean to collect or gather together.

13. These issues have been discussed by Bernard Faure (1997: 167–73). Faure argues that there are four 'editorial layers' to the *Masters of the Lanka*: the fundamental text; Jingjue's preface; the entries on Daoxin (second section), Hongren and Shenxiu; and the final entry, dedicated to Shenxiu's four disciples.

14. See Jorgensen 2012 for an account of Shenhui's activities.

15. See, for example, Faure 1998: 25–6.

16. Schlütter 2012: 10.

17. Zongmi, 'Chan Prolegomenon', translated in Broughton 2009: 110.

18. The process by which the idea of transmission and lineage became so important in Chinese Zen is discussed in depth in Adamek 2007.

19. A comparable situation to the Dunhuang manuscripts in China is the more recent discovery of Qin dynasty bamboo slips, which has challenged the traditional historical account of discrete philosophical schools; see Allen 2015.

20. Cole's (2009) discussion of Jingjue is in his chapter 5. In other chapters he critiques other Chan figures, including Shenhui and the author of the *Transmission of the Dharma Jewel*, Du Fei.

21. Robson 2011: 338.

22. Robson 2011: 335–6.

23. Adamek 2011: 6.

CHAPTER 5. EARLY ZEN MEDITATION

1. This has been pointed out by Sharf (2014: 934).
2. While Daoxin does not explicitly recommend the practice of reciting the Buddha's name, it is quite clear in the passage that he quotes from the *Saptaśatikā-prajñāpāramitā sūtra*; the Chinese translated here as 'only recite his name' is *zhuānchēng míngzì* 專稱名字.
3. I have translated *niànfó* 念佛 here as 'mindfulness of the Buddha'. The Buddha (*fó*) is the object of the verb (*niàn*), so this must be understood as the practitioner keeping the Buddha in mind. It is important to understand how this differs from the way the word 'mindfulness' is used currently, as Robert Sharf has shown (Sharf 2014).
4. Ferguson 2011: 30.
5. According to Charles Muller (Digital Dictionary of Buddhism, http://www.buddhism.dict.net [hereafter DDB]), *rènyùn* 任運 can also mean: 'That which is arisen spontaneously, and is not directly initiated by one's present discrimination or volition.'
6. See van Schaik 2015: 134–5, 141.
7. See the discussion on the metaphor of the mirror in this text and other early Zen texts in McRae 1986: 144–7.
8. In this case I disagree with John McRae's opinion (1986: 138–9) that the term was adopted from Daoism because it denoted 'a general technique that was applicable in all situations and far superior to the myriad other techniques of more specific use and elaborate description'.
9. McRae 2003: 85–6.
10. McRae 2003: 86–8.
11. According to DDB (Muller), *héwù* 何物 is equivalent to Skt *yad idam*.
12. In the context of contemporary Zen, the phrase *shì shénme* 是什麼, also meaning 'what is this?', is also commonly used.
13. This story is in Dogen's *Extensive Record*, translation from Leighton and Okumura 2010: 435.
14. Batchelor 2008: 1.
15. Shōji Yamada (2001) has shown in detail how Herrigel created a myth of Zen archery. In his research into Japanese Zen writing on archery, he located only one reference to archery with a Buddhist interpretation, and this was based on the doctrines of the Shingon school, rather than Zen (Yamada 2001: 27).
16. *Tractatus Logico-Philosophicus* 6.54, in Wittgenstein 1922: 90.
17. *Zhuangzi*, chapter 6, translation in Ziporyn 2009: 114. The last sentence is also quoted in the *Transmission of the Dharma Jewel* (see McRae 1986: 267).

CHAPTER 6. MANUSCRIPTS AND TRANSLATION

1. Manuscripts with numbers beginning Or.8210/S. and IOL Tib J are from the British Library (London). The Pelliot chinois manuscripts are from the Bibliothèque nationale de France (Paris). Manuscripts beginning with BD are from the National Library of China (Beijing), and those beginning with Dh are from the Institute of Oriental Manuscripts (St Petersburg). Digital images of many of the manuscripts are available at the website of the International Dunhuang Project (http://idp.bl.uk). Editions of all the manuscripts have been made avail-

able at the website of the Dunhuang Manuscript Full Text Digitization Project: http://dev.ddbc.edu.tw/Dunhuang_Manuscripts/. Printed and facsimile editions are also available in Bingenheimer and Chang 2018.

2. Pelliot tibétain 3294 (including Pelliot chinois 3294 Pièce) has not previously been considered part of the same original scroll as these other two manuscripts. However, despite some differences in the way the paper has been treated, and perhaps the use of a different brush by the scribe, the handwriting, layout and size strongly suggest that it is part of the same scroll. I would like to thank Nathalie Monnet at the Bibliothèque nationale de France for examining the original manuscripts there and confirming this.

3. It is possible that some of the fragments from the Bodhidharma section may not be from the *Masters of the Lanka*, as Bodhidharma's text circulated on its own and in other collections as well.

4. For an edition of the Tibetan text see Drikung Kyabgön Chetsang 2010. For a translation of the text, see van Schaik 2015: 79–97. There are also manuscript fragments of a Sogadian translation of the *Masters of the Lanka*, from the preface and the Bodhidharma chapter; see Yoshida 2015.

5. See for example Faure 1997: 168–9.

6. Robson 2011: 334.

CHAPTER 7. JINGJUE: STUDENT OF EMPTINESS

1. The lack of any explicit statement in the *Masters of the Lanka* itself – in the preface or at the end – that Jingjue was the primary successor to Shenxiu and Xuanze makes Alan Cole's claim that this was the sole purpose of the text questionable.

2. Empress Wu has also been linked to the spread of print technology in China, long before its emergence in the West. See Barrett 2008.

3. This passage is from Wang Wei's account translated in Faure 1997: 135.

4. The manuscripts containing the preface are:

   • the large scrolls Pelliot chinois 3436 and Or.8210/S.2054, which are missing the beginning of the preface (the former missing more);
   • the scroll fragment Pelliot chinois 4564, the only manuscript containing the very beginning of the preface;
   • other fragments overlapping with the above: Pelliot chinois 3294 and Dh 5654.

5. See for example the meditation teachings of the eighth-century monk Moheyan – from Tibetan texts – in van Schaik 2015: 134–7. Shenxiu's meditation teachings are discussed in my introduction to his chapter in the *Masters of the Lanka*.

6. Here, 'delusion' translates *wàngxiǎng* 妄想, literally 'false thought'. In the Buddhist context, this term is often translated as 'conceptualization' or 'discrimination'. The Sanskrit equivalent is *vikalpa*.

7. In Or.8210/S.382, the last two characters of this line are *zìyòng* 自用, meaning 'autonomous' or perhaps 'spontaneous' rather than 'still or active'.

8. The two vehicles are the hinayana paths of the hearers and solitary buddhas. Or.8210/S.382 has 'three vehicles'.

9. This first part of the text survives only in the manuscript fragment Pelliot chinois 4654. The prayer itself is found independently elsewhere in the Dunhuang

manuscripts; see Or.8210/S.382; it is also included in the Taisho as T.85, no. 2828, p. 1266b7–11. There are a few differences in the Or.8210/S.382 version of the prayer.

10. There are gaps in the only manuscript containing this part of the text (Pelliot chinois 3436), so we only have fragments of the next few lines. With the lacuna, they read: 'Imprints . . . [I,] Jingjue had only a hazy and limited understanding, the imprints of not having heard . . . rare . . .'

11. Datong was the posthumous name given by the emperor to Shenxiu – see chapter 15 above.

12. The phrase 'possessed the seal of approval' refers to Xuanze being an authorized student of Hongren, as Shenxiu was.

13. The characters *chuán dēng* 傳燈 are usually translated as 'transmission of the lamp' but the image is more accurately the passing on of the flame from one oil lamp or candle to another. It is not meant to be the passing of a lamp from one person to another; therefore 'passing on the flame' is a less misleading translation.

14. This is where the text in Or.8210/S.2054, and the Taisho edition based on it, begin. This is also where Cleary's translation begins. The reference in this passage to 'entering the state of purity' and to relics implies the death of Xuanze; this is not in chronological order, as the following passages (which are written in the third person and may have been interpolated here) discuss how Jingjue and Xuanze met.

15. Zhongzong, fourth ruler of the Tang dynasty, ruled in 684 and again in 705–10. Zhongzhong's wife was the Empress Wei, Jingjue's sister. The Jinglong era is 707–10, so this passage describes events after the death of Shenxiu in 706.

16. While *guīyī* 歸依 usually means 'to take refuge', here it makes more sense to read *guī* in its basic meaning 'to return (something)'. The second character may be a scribal hypercorrection.

17. Faure's translation (1989: 91) is somewhat different here: 'Il répandit alors sa méthode de dhyana dans la capitale de l'est. Sur-le-champ, j'allai prendre refuge auprès de lui, et le servis avec zèle. Voilà bien dix ans que je fis va-et-vient entre les deux capitales pour le consulter. Depuis lors, la terre de mon esprit, que je lui soumettais, a été soudain définitivement aplanie.'

18. This part of the preface is written in the third person, and somewhat overlaps with the previous (first-person) account. I have inserted the name of Xuanze in the second and third paragraphs as his name is not repeated in the Chinese text.

19. Here, 'categories' translates *xiàng* 相, which renders the Sanskrit Buddhist term *lakṣaṇa*. These are the characteristics that we attribute to reality, which have no existence in and of themselves. In Buddhist translations, *xiàng* / *lakṣaṇa* is variously translated as 'characteristics', 'marks', 'qualities' and 'names'. In addition, here 'knowing' translates *zhī* 知, which could also be translated as 'perceiving'.

20. Thusness is a translation of the Chinese *zhēnrú* 真如, which renders the Sanskrit Buddhist term *tathātā*. In the *Masters of the Lanka*, it is sometimes shortened to *rú* 如, especially in metrical passages.

21. 'Nature of reality' is a loose translation of *fǎjiè* 法界, the Sanskrit equivalent being *dharmadhātu*.

22. *The Arising of Faith in the Mahayana*, attributed to Aśvaghoṣa. The quotation is from T.32, no. 1666, p. 576a8–13 (also no. 1668, p. 605b3–9). The beginning of the same passage is in no. 1667, p. 584c7–8. This quote is from the beginning of the first chapter of *Arising of Faith in the Mahayana*, which explains mind in its ultimate aspect.

23. Here and in most cases elsewhere, I have translated *zhì* 智 as 'wisdom', the Sanskrit equivalent being *jñāna*.

24. This passage is also from *Arising of Faith in the Mahayana*: T.32, no. 1666, p. 579a12–13.

25. From T.17, no. 670, p. 497a22 and a23 (with some intervening lines omitted).

26. In this passage following the list of the five dharmas, 'mind' is clearly being used as a synonym for the third dharma, 'delusion'. This passage draws on the discussion of the five dharmas in the *Laṅkāvatāra* LXXXIII; they are a way of categorizing how the mind functions, moving from its ordinary functioning in samsara to its awakened state. See the translation in Red Pine 2006: 247.

27. Source not found. The same quote appears in Xuzangjing 63, no. 1231, as 'an ancient saying': *gù yún* 故云 . It also appears (unattributed) in a lecture of Mazu; see Ferguson 2011: 75. The 'seal of the single dharma' is related to the concept of the 'seals of three dharmas', which are impermanence, nonself and nirvana. The 'single dharma', which includes and transcends these three, is ultimate reality, mind's true nature, emptiness.

28. Here Jingjue seems to be saying that he chose the life of solitude and contemplation in the mountains over the life of society and politics in the valleys.

29. Instead of 'found' (*huò* 獲), Taisho and S.2054 have *quán* 權, 'temporarily'.

30. From T.14, no. 475, p. 538c4–5. In the first line, the the canonical sutra has *jìngtǔ* 淨土, 'pure land'. The manuscripts of the *Masters of the Lanka* actually have *jìngdù* 淨度, 'pure salvation/perfection'. This near-homonym is probably a scribal variant or error.

31. 'Grasping' here translates *pānyuán* 攀緣, literally 'to grasp at conditions'. Elsewhere in the *Masters of the Lanka*, the Tibetan translator chose the Tibetan word *yan lag*, which refers only to the conditions, not the grasping. In Tibetan translations of Chinese scriptures, such as the *Gangottara-paripṛcchā sūtra*, the Tibetan term used is *dmigs*, meaning 'to fixate' or 'objectify'; my thanks to Jonathan Silk for this information.

32. The passage from 'in truth, mind does not exist' to 'In thusness there are no . . .' is missing from Or.8210/S.2054 and Taisho.

33. 'The end of the path' here is a translation of *zhì dào* 至道, which is a synonym for enlightenment and the ultimate truth.

34. 'Truly real' is *shí shí* 寔寔 which appears in S.3436. The character is mistranscribed in Taisho as *hán* 寒 'cold'.

35. From T.9, no. 262, p. 10a4–5 (verse section).

36. 'Intrinsic nature' (*zìxìng* 自性, Skt *svabhāva*) refers to things having an essential nature that is not dependent on anything else; this is what is refuted by the argments for emptiness, and is considered to be completely nonexistent ('empty') and useless as a concept ('idle').

37. The path to awakening (*pútí dào* 菩提道) can be translated simply as 'awakening'. Sanskrit equivalents are *bodhi-mārga* and *bodhi-patha*.

38. The phrase 'enters where there is no gap' is from chapter 3 of the *Daodejing*.

39. Compare the line from the famous verse attributed to Huineng in the *Platform Sutra*: 'Originally there is not a single thing', *běnlái wú yī wù* 本來無一物.

40. This is a reference to the general belief in the gradual decline of the Buddha's teachings. In Tang dynasty China many believed that they were in an era in which what remained of the Buddha's teachings was a mere semblance.

41. 'Essential emptiness' (*tǐkōng* 體空) is distinguished from 'analytical emptiness' (*xīkōng* 析空). The former is emptiness as the essential nature of all things, while the latter is emptiness as the result of intellectual analysis. This is similar to the twofold distinction of the ultimate truth in the works of Bhāvavikeka and the Tibetan Madhyāmikas who followed him; see van Schaik 2016: 83. The term 'essence' (*tǐ*) is important in Chinese Buddhist and non-Buddhist philosophy. The Tibetan translator renders it with *ngo bo nyid*, which is also usually translated into English as 'essence'.

42. 'Emptiness and function' translates *kōngyòng* 空用. This dyad is similar to the more common *tǐyòng* 體用, 'essence and function', which describes the relationship between the true nature of things and phenomenal reality, and is found in many important early Chinese philosophical texts, including the *Yijing*, *Liji* and *Mencius*.

43. 'Inherently existent' is Chinese *zìyǒu* 自有. Like *zixing* this translates the Sanskrit Buddhist term *svabhāva*, which means to exist independent of any cause or condition. In Mahayana Buddhist thought, nothing can exist in this way, therefore nothing has a *svabhāva*.

44. The title used here, *Fangguang jing*, usually refers to the *Perfection of Wisdom in 25,000 Verses* (*Pañcaviṃśati-sāhasrikā-prajñāpāramitā sūtra*). However, this passage is not found in the canonical texts.

CHAPTER 8. GUṆABHADRA: INTRODUCING THE *LAṄKĀVATĀRA*

1. In a study of the *Saṃyuktāgama sūtra*, which was translated by Guṇabhadra, the authors note that the translation was actually a collaborative effort, in which Guṇabhadra recited the text while three Chinese monks interpreted it. This was soon after his arrival in China, so he may have played a more active role in translation in later efforts, such as the *Laṅkāvatāra*. See Glass and Allon 2007: 38–9. As the authors point out, it is interesting to consider whether a manuscript was used as the basis for this translation (and others), or Guṇabhadra's recitation of his memorized version was the primary source.

2. This account and translation are from Stevenson 1987: 224.

3. See Mollier 2008 for a discussion of these practices, shared across Buddhist and Daoist traditions.

4. Here, 'senses' translates *chù* 處, which means 'location', but in Buddhist (especially Yogācāra) texts it is also used to translate the Sanskrit *āyatana*, a technical term for the site of perception (i.e. the eyes, ears and so on). The Sanskrit terms for the sixth, seventh and eighth level of consciousness are *mano-vijñāna, manas* (or *kliṣṭa-manas*) and *ālaya* (or *ālaya-vijñāna*).

5. For a detailed study of these processes as described in the scriptures and treatises of Yogācāra, see Brown 1991.

6. In another metaphor that strikingly resembles Huineng's criticism of Shenxiu's teaching in the *Platform Sermon*, Guṇabhadra compares taking the idea of a path and goal literally to polishing a mirror, not realizing that it is reflective by nature: 'beneath the dust that rests on the mirror's surface, the mirror itself is always clean and bright'.

7. It is interesting to see that the Tibetan translator rendered the Chinese *niànfó* 念佛 here straightforwardly with *sangs rgyas bsam pa*, meaning 'to think of (or perhaps visualize) the Buddha'.

8. A tripiṭaka master (Skt *trepiṭaka*) is a title given to Buddhist scholars in honour of their mastery of the three baskets (Skt *tripiṭaka*) of sutra, vinaya and abhidharma. Guṇabhadra's other honorary name Mahayana (Ch. Moheyan) was later the name of the eighth-century Chinese Zen monk who was influential at the Tibetan court.

9. Literally, 'the language of the Song'.

10. The two vehicles are usually the vehicles of the hearers (Skt *śrāvaka*) and solitary buddhas (Skt *pratyekabuddha*), considered lower than the vehicle of the bodhisattvas; together they form the hinayana. Therefore it would make more sense for this sentence to read 'the hinayana, that is, the two vehicles'. However, the Chinese reads 'the hinayana *and* the two vehicles' and the Tibetan translation supports this.

11. In the second half of this sentence, I have followed the version in the Tibetan translation (van Schaik 2015: 79). The Chinese is 'to gain visions of all things, to divine good and bad fortunes of other people's households'. This reference to other people's households is repeated below, and therefore may have resulted from a scribal error at some point in the transmission of the Chinese text.

12. 'Sorcerers' translates *xiángfú* 降伏; W.E. Soothill's *Dictionary of Chinese Buddhist Terms* defines this as '*abhicāraka*, exorciser; magic; subjugator (of demons)'.

13. In the Tibetan translation, the first half of the sentence is 'If their faculties are not ripe' (*dbang po ma smyin na*). The Tibetan adds at the end of the sentence: 'So what need is there even to speak of those whose minds are full of doubt?' (van Schaik 2015: 80).

14. T.16, no. 670, p. 481c2.

15. This is a reference to the levels of consciousness – see my discussion in the introduction to this chapter. Cleary's translation (1986: 27) is aware of this but Faure's (1989: 106) is not and thus misinterprets the sentence. The Tibetan translation is significantly different here: 'When there is ignorance about the hundred, then there are a hundred. When there is knowledge about the hundred, there is only one' (see van Schaik 2015: 80–1, where my previous translation somewhat misinterprets the Tibetan).

16. There is a similar line in the canonical *Avataṃsaka*: 'Therefore, of all the dharmas no two perceive each other' (T.9, no. 278, p. 427a09). Thanks to Imre Galambos for this reference. See also T.8, no. 221, p. 105c2–3, and no. 223, p. 363c13.

17. The context here is probably the four levels of meditation in the *Laṅkāvatāra*:

    1. the meditation of ordinary people – meditation on the nonself of persons, suffering, impermanence and impurity;
    2. meditation that investigates the nature of things – meditation on the nonself of dharmas;
    3. meditation on thusness;
    4. the tathāgata meditation.

18. The Tibetan translation (see van Schaik 2015: 82) has a different caveat: 'but since this is a way of being (*sattva*) that is skilled in ordinary mental states, it is not the mind of enlightenment (bodhicitta)'.

19. Mind as luminosity (Skt *prabhā/prabhāsvarā*) is a recurring theme in several Mahayana sutras, including the *Aṣṭasāhasrikā Prajñāpāramitā* – see Kapstein 2004: 124. Note that the references to light in the *Masters of the Lanka* do not

appear to be in scholastic, metaphorical mode. The sense here is that the mind is manifest and active, yet not material, and therefore it is unobstructed.

20. The text in fact has 'The ordinary person and the noble one are different', which does not make sense in this context. Therefore I am reading *wéi yì* 為異 as *wú yì* 無異.

21. T.16, no. 670, p. 480b6–8.

22. The 'great path' is *dàdào* 大道, which appears in Confucian and Daoist literature. In Buddhist sources it can translate the Sanskrit *mahāpatha,* meaning 'great road' or 'high road', found in *Udānavarga, Ratnāvali, Abhisamayalaṅkara* and other Buddhist sources.

23. The Tibetan translation has: 'If one sees or hears written letters or spoken words as manifold as atoms or grains of sand, one will turn back toward the path of samsara' (see van Schaik 2015: 82).

24. The text here is similar to Kumarajiva's translation: T.15, no. 650, p. 760b1–2. The sutra exists in both Sanskrit and Tibetan. The Sanskrit is from a Central Asian manuscript (incomplete) dating from around the fifth century; see Braarvig 2000.

25. The term *dàyòng* 大用, meaning 'great activity' (or 'great functioning'), is seen in early Chinese literature including the *Shiji* and *Zhuangzi* – see Sharf 2002: 207–8. According to DDB (Muller), the term continues in later Zen biographical literature:

> Commonly seen in Chan records when referring to the words and deeds of a greatly enlightened master ... Thus, in this Chan application, the term often refers to the carrying out of such mundane activities as chopping firewood and carrying water.

26. This is a reference to the fourth of the five paths, the path of cultivation (*bhāvanā-patha*). The Tibetan translation appears to miss this reference and has 'cultivation of the dharma path' instead.

27. This is a variation on the common Buddhist phrase *yīxíng yīqiè xíng* 一行一切行, 'one practice that includes all practices'. It is probably also a reference to the single practice concentration discussed in Daoxin's chapter above.

28. Instead of 'animosity is extinguished forever', the Tibetan has: 'equanimity towards enemies and friends' (van Schaik 2015: 83).

29. This is a difficult line; I interpret the character *fán* 繁 to have the rare meaning of 'difficult, vexatious' (Kroll 2015: 106), and the character *yǔ* 與 to be a mistake for the similar-looking *xīng* 興, which can mean 'prosper' (with thanks to Imre Galambos for the latter). This reading is close to the Tibetan translation, which reads 'no difference between flourishing (*gso ba*) and not flourishing'. The same interpretation applies to the line immediately below: 'When one is deeply at peace through both trouble and prosperity'.

30. The title of this sutra refers to various canonical translations known as the *Mahāprajñāpāramitā sūtra.* The first line occurs several times in Xuanzang's translation (T.7, no. 220, p. 569a4, c6, p. 570b2 and p. 571a3). However, the quote in general seems to be a paraphrase or alternative translation of the *Avataṃsaka*, T.10, no. 279, p. 9b29–c2. See also T.8, no. 223, p. 324b18–20.

31. T.9, no. 278, p. 443a6.

32. T.15, no. 586, p. 56a13–15. Faure (1989: 110, n.40) states that this sutra is frequently cited in Chan texts, including Shenxiu's *Five Skilful Means.*

33. This text was not identified by Faure or, before him, Yanagida (Faure 1989: 110, n.41). Yanagida suggested that it could be an oral transmission related to Guṇabhadra. The end of the quotation is not marked in the text itself; however, there is a column break in Pelliot chinois 3436 that suggests it may be at the point I have chosen here.

34. These are the four attributes of the dharmakaya, as propounded in Mahayana sources which discuss the *tathāgatagarbha,* including the *Śrīmālā Sūtra,* the *Nirvana Sutra* and the *Ratnagotravibhāga.* The four attributes are the positive complements of the features of samsara: impermanence, suffering, nonself and impurity. On the role of the four attributes in Zen and particularly Zongmi's writings, see Gregory 2002: 218–23.

35. S.2054 and the Taisho version have: 'The *Laṅkāvatāra sūtra* of the Great Teacher'. However, Pelliot chinois has *yún* 云 instead of *zhī* 之, which gives the reading I use here.

36. Compare the instructions on mindfulness of the Buddha in Daoxin's teachings (chapter 12 above), which is very similar; this instruction probably comes from Daoxin's time rather than Guṇabhadra's.

37. The Tibetan translation of this chapter ends here.

38. Pelliot chinois 3436 has *fǎ* 法 ('dharma') instead of *cǐ* 此 ('this'); that version is followed by Cleary's and Faure's translations.

39. My translation here differs from Faure (1989: 111) and the passage is missing in Cleary (1986: 31). The key here is the character *zhēng* 徵, one of the meanings of which is 'look into, examine the situation; interrogate' (Kroll 2015: 601). The sentence seems to refer to a teaching practice attributed here to Guṇabhadra – approaching or pointing out a nearby object and asking questions about it.

40. These are everyday objects: the jar (or water bottle) is one of the monk's accessories; the pillar is a feature of the monastery. I give a tentative translation of *huǒ xuè* 火穴 as 'fire pit' because this fits with the other domestic objects mentioned by Guṇabhadra. However, I cannot incorporate the following character, *shān* 山, 'mountain'. Cleary (1986: 31) has 'Can you go through a mountain?' Faure, following Yanagida, reads this character as part of the next sentence, but has difficulty explaining the meaning of 'mountain staff' (1989: 113, n.49). I would break the lines so that the next phrase reads 'Can't this staff explain the dharma?' This phrase appears to be out of place here, belonging with Guṇabhadra's questions a little further on. In general, the order of these questions appears a bit haphazard, and one question is missing from Or.8210/S.2054. This suggests that they may have been annotations to earlier versions of the text that were copied into later versions.

41. This is a deliberate reversal of the usual metaphor of the body as vessel for the mind.

42. This line is missing in Taisho, taken from Pelliot chinois 3436. Note again these are everyday objects around the monastic teacher and students.

CHAPTER 9. BODHIDHARMA: SUDDEN AND GRADUAL

1. Translation based on McRae 1986: 17 and Dumoulin 1988: I.87. Dumoulin notes that this passage was first pointed out by Paul Pelliot.

2. Though many scholars accept that he was a direct student of Bodhidharma, Broughton (1999: 53) states that it is more likely that Tanlin was a student of Huike.

3. Broughton 1999: 54.
4. The Chinese versions of the *Masters of the Lanka* all state that Bodhidharma arrived at Wuyue. The Wuyue region was on the eastern coast of China. The Tibetan translation of the *Masters of the Lanka*, on the other hand, does not mention Wuyue and has instead Sang-chu, which might be Hangzhou (van Schaik 2015: 84).
5. These dates fit with the account of Bodhidharma's visit to Yongning monastery, which would have been between 516 and 526 (dates from McRae 1986: 17). A century later the monk Daoxuan wrote about Bodhidharma in his *Further Biographies of Eminent Monks*, stating that he travelled to southern China, arriving during the Liu Song dynasty (420–79). This dating is earlier than Tanlin's and accords less well with the *Masters of the Lanka* and other early sources, unless Bodhidharma spent decades in southern China before travelling north. Interestingly, in the *Masters of the Lanka* it is Guṇabhadra who arrives in southern China during the Liu Song dynasty. It almost seems that Daoxuan, though writing before the *Masters of the Lanka,* conflated the stories of Guṇabhadra and Bodhidharma – perhaps informed by the emerging tradition which associated Bodhidharma with the *Lankāvatāra sūtra.*
6. Adamek 2007: 311. Adamek suggests two sources in the sutras that may have served as an inspiration for this story. Interestingly, a Tibetan version of the same story appears alone in a compendium of Tibetan Zen texts; see van Schaik 2015: 71–2.
7. See Broughton 1999 for a translation and excellent study of this compendium.
8. John McRae (2003: 30) writes of *bìguān* 壁觀 that 'ultimately no one really knows what the term means'. See also McRae's earlier, more lengthy discussion in McRae 1986: 112–15, where he argues that the 'wall' may be metaphorical, as in one's mind being like a wall. It is interesting, though probably not relevant, that there is a homophone, *bìguān* 閉關, which means literally 'to shut the gates' but is used in the Buddhist context to refer to a meditation retreat. If this was Bodhidharma's original phrase, one would have to argue that it was misunderstood at a very early stage in the copying of the *Two Entrances and Four Practices.*
9. On techniques of meditation in Buddhism, from the Pali sources, see Shaw 2014: 21–3, and elsewhere. The word 'kaṣina' is Pali, the Sanskrit being *kṛtsnāya.*
10. See for example Anacker 2005: 282, n.48. McRae (1986: 306, n.21) mentions that the connection between wall gazing and the kaṣina was made in a paper by Lü Ch'eng. Heinrich Dumoulin (1988: I.18) does not connect the kaṣina objects with wall gazing, but mentions the similarity of a practice observed in later century Chinese Zen: 'Among the masters of the Igyō sect of Chinese Zen we encounter the practice of "circular figures", which is related to the practice of kaṣina.'
11. McRae 2003: 30–1.
12. Here, 'thusness' is translating Sanskrit *tathātā*, 'ultimate truth' is *paramārtha* and 'the nature of things' is *dharmatā.*
13. See Ziporyn 2003: 503. The character *lǐ* 理 is translated as 'reason' in Red Pine (1987: 3) and Baroni (2002: 361). The Tibetan translator of the *Masters of the Lanka* chose to translate *lǐ* with Tibetan *gzhung*, a word that is equally difficult to translate into English, but at this time carried the meanings of 'original', 'fundamental', 'central' and 'source'. In other Tibetan Zen texts, *gzhung* can also mean scriptures (as in original or fundamental source texts), but that does not apply

here; see van Schaik 2015: 123. In any case, it seems to be a mistake to translate *lǐ* in Bodhidharma's text as 'reason'.

14. This topic has been explored in detail in a series of lectures by Johannes Bronkhorst (Bronkhorst 2011).

15. The Tibetan translation goes into more detail about how Bodhidharma assessed the monks in a single day and then taught them the four practices; see van Schaik 2015: 84.

16. 'Bodhidharma said to Huike' is not in the Tibetan and somewhat contradicts the previous line's statement that he taught the two monks together.

17. The *Further Biographies of Eminent Monks* (*Xu Gaosengzhuan*) is a collection of biographies of Buddhist monks compiled by the monk Daoxuan (596–667). It is a continuation of the *Gaosengzhuan* which was compiled in the Liang period (502–57).

18. What follows is extracted from Tanlin's text, found in Xuzangjing vol. 63, no. 1217.

19. Literally 'Brahmin king', which is an oxymoron in the Indian caste system; however, in many Chinese sources all Indian teachers are called 'Brahmin'.

20. Here, 'inner and outer' probably means 'Buddhist and non-Buddhist'.

21. Literally, 'Han Wei'. Faure translates this as '[la région de] la Han et [de] la Wei'. I have taken the second character to refer to a dynasty, as it does at the beginning of the chapter. As discussed in the introduction to this chapter, Bodhidharma's main teaching activities are said to have been carried out in the city of Ye, which was the capital of the Eastern Wei, a Turkic dynasty, during this period.

22. The character *shì* 士 means 'elite', and more specifically, 'the nobility'. It is also in the Tibetan as *dra ma,* which means 'the elite', in terms of the nobility, the learned or simply those who excel.

23. Note that here the first entrance is linked to the practice of wall gazing.

24. This translation, similar to Cleary (1986: 33), is based on a medieval-period meaning of *zhuó* 著, 'make use of, ply'; see Kroll 2015: 620.I.

25. This is the end of Tanlin's preface (Xuzangjing vol. 63, no. 1217, p. 7a06), which has 'the above is a brief outline'.

26. Here 'guiding principle' is *zōng* 宗. In the Tibetan this is translated with *gzhung,* the same word used to translate *lǐ* 理, 'principle'.

27. Here, instead of *bì* 壁 ('wall'), S.2054 and Taisho have *bì* 辟, which seems to be a mistake.

28. This term *yuànxíng* 怨行, 'retribution for past wrongdoing', appears in the *Analects* of Confucius and elsewhere in early Chinese literature. In the *Analects* (*Xian wen*, 34) it refers to the question of how to respond to somebody who has hurt you; Confucius responds, not through kindness, but through justice. The term also appears in Buddhist translations, for Skt *pratyapakāra* and *vaira-nipīḍana*. In the context of this text, it is a contemplation of the fact that bad things that happen in one's life are the result of one's own previous non-virtuous actions, more informally known as 'payback'.

29. Literally, *suíyuán* 隨緣 is 'according to conditions' or 'in dependence'. This is translated by Cleary (1986: 34) as 'going along with the causal nexus', by Red Pine (1987: 5) as 'adapting to conditions' and by Faure (1989: 118) as 'être en accord avec les conditions'. I suggest that these translations all miss the point. The contemplation described in the text itself is that all occurrences of happiness and sorrow arise and pass away based on causes and conditions, i.e. dependent

arising (the usual Chinese term, *yuánshēng* 緣生, is used in the text of the contemplation itself). Therefore this is a contemplation of the doctrine that everything occurs through the process of dependent arising, rather than an injunction to 'go with the flow' as the other translations imply.

30. I have added the word 'contemplating' in the titles of the first and second practices to clarify that 'retribution for past wrongdoings' and 'dependence' are the subjects of contemplation, as is clear in the description of the practice itself.

31. This sutra has not been identified by Faure. A very similar line, with a different fourth character but the same meaning, is found in the *Dīrghāgama*, T.1, no. 1, p. 7a06: *féng kǔ bùqī* 逢苦不慼 'when you meet with suffering, do not sorrow'. And the *Mahāparinirvāṇa sūtra*, T.374, no. 374, p. 548b29 has *féng kǔ bùqī* 逢苦不戚, 'when you meet with suffering, do not be sad'. Given its influence in early Chan teachings, the latter is probably the source. Previous translations consider the quote to be continued in the next few lines, but four characters appear to be the full quotation; thus what follows them is Bodhidharma's explanation. Incidentally, the same line appears, though not as a citation, in T.2016, p. 939c11. This is a later work, the *Zongjing lu*, compiled by the Five Dynasties Chan figure Yongming Yanshou (904–76).

32. This translation, also in Faure (1989: 118), is based on a rare meaning of *tǐ* 體: 'realize, comprehend' (Kroll 2015: 449). The Tibetan, on the other hand, has 'angry thoughts do not occur and one yearns for the dharma path'.

33. The second half of this sentence is a little unclear in the Chinese versions; on the other hand, the Tibetan translation is clear: 'mind and the path are in accord'. While S.2054 has *tōng* 通 ('pass through; communicate') as the final character, this is clearly a mistake for *dào* 道 ('path'), which is the final character in Pelliot chinois 3436; this matches the Tibetan. However, the Chinese has 'profound' rather than 'mind' – thus 'profoundly in accord with the path'.

34. The Tibetan has, more specifically, 'to the five objects of desire' ('*dod pa lnga*).

35. I interpret *zhēn lǐ* 真理 as 'true principle' here, following the Tibetan (*yang dag pa'i gzhung*). Though this is a common Buddhist term, previous editions and translations do not read the characters together, splitting them across two sentences instead in order to preserve the metre. Also, I take *jí* 及 to belong to the beginning of the next sentence, a preposition roughly meaning 'when the time comes' or 'once . . .' (Kroll 2015: 184).

36. This is a difficult line to interpret, and previous translations vary. Faure (1989: 118) has 'et abandon le corps à son sort'. Cleary (1986: 35) has 'changing shape as they go'. Red Pine (1987: 5) has 'let their bodies change with the seasons'. The characters *suí yùn zhuǎn* 隨運轉 denote tractability, pliability and proceeding with ease; thus the general idea appears to be that an unchanging peace of mind allows the body to be adaptable and flexible. This is a continuation of the previous sentence about applying the true principle to worldly life.

37. Faure (1989: 119, n.24), quoting Yanagida, points out that 'good and bad' (or more literally, 'Merit and Darkness') may be a reference to the names of two gods in the *Mahāparinirvāṇa sūtra*.

38. Source not found, though it could be a paraphrase of T.1, n.49, where these two phrases appear several times.

39. The translation of this practice has varied depending on how translators have taken the character 稱 – either as *chèn*, 'accord with' or as *chēng*, 'praise' (the

former is more common). The essence of the practice is to see the principle in all phenomena, because the true nature of phenomena, as empty, *is* the principle.

40. This is the *Vimalakīrtinirdeśa sūtra*, T.14, no. 475, p. 540a4–5.

41. These are the six impurities of vexation, harm, resentment, flattery, deception and haughtiness.

42. Tibetan has 'body, life and possessions'.

43. The three aspects are the emptiness of the giver, the gift and the recipient. My translation of this passage is informed by the way the Tibetan breaks up the sentences, which is different from previous translations.

44. Here 'scroll' translates *juàn* 卷 (more technically rendered as 'fascicle') and 'sheets' translates *zhǐ* 紙. Chinese scrolls were made by pasting together rectangular sheets of paper. 'Bodhidharma Treatise' is *Damo Lun*. On the texts attributed to Bodhidharma from the Dunhuang manuscript collections, see Broughton 1999.

45. The Tibetan translation of this chapter ends here.

46. The term *yúnwù* 雲霧, here and in the next chapter, refers to a kind of cloud canopy, an overcast sky.

47. T.12, no. 374, p. 572a4–5.

CHAPTER 10. HUIKE: THE BUDDHA WITHIN

1. This appears towards the end of the chapter, just before the long quote from the *Avataṃsaka sūtra*, rather than in the biographical note at the beginning.

2. The *Anthology of Literary Texts* (*Yiwen leiju*) is one of the earliest examples of Chinese anthologies which present excerpts from texts arranged by subject matter. It was compiled over three years after a commission from the emperor Gaozu in 622 (Choo 2015: 454); though Endymion Wilkinson (2000: 602–3) gives the date of publication as either 604 or 624. The first phrase – 'though ice appears in water, it is able to stop water' – is very similar to one in the *Yiwen leiju* (vol. 9, *shuǐ bù xià, bīng* 6): 'Though ice appears in water, it is colder than water'. The original source of this phrase is a work attributed to the sage Xunzi (third century BC), which contains the line, 'Blue is taken from dark blue but it is bluer than dark blue; as for ice, it is water that produces it, yet it is colder than water'. The second phrase – 'When ice melts, water flows' – is similar to another line quoted in the *Yiwen leiju* (vol. 3, *shí shàng, chūn* 46): 'The ice melts, causing a subtle flow'. The phrase could also be an allusion to the words in the *Daodejing* (15) on the nature of the ancient sages: 'Loose like ice about to melt'.

3. The metaphor is also known in the Tibetan tradition, coming via the songs of the *mahāsiddha* Saraha; my thanks to Lama Jampa Thaye for this information. See the 'Royal Song' (*Do ha mdzod ces bya ba spyod pa'i glu*), v.17, my translation:

> When water is struck and stirred by the wind,
> Though water is soft, it takes the form of stone.
> When concepts stir up confusion, though it has no form,
> It becomes very hard and solid.

In the Dzogchen tradition, the metaphor appears in a popular text by Jigme Lingpa (1730–98), in which the basis of consciousness (*ālaya*) is likened to water, and the emergence of grasping consciousness (*ālaya-vijñāna*) is similar to ice on water (van Schaik 2004: 163).

4. See Wang and Ding 2010: 47–50. They write (p. 47): 'Zhang zai illustrates the interlocking of *taixu* and *qi* by again using the comparison of water and ice. Ice is solid or coalesced water just as *taixu* is coalesced *qi*.'

5. The passage is by Liu Yiming (1734–1821), translated in Cleary 2006: 13.

6. Translation in Tanahashi 2015: 96.

7. Beck 1995: 32.

8. This passage, like most Bruce Lee quotes, can be found in different forms in many places, especially on the internet. The quote in its original context, an essay on Jeet Kune Do, can be found in Little 2001: 121.

9. Though the influence of Daoism on Chinese Buddhism, and Zen in particular, is often mentioned, the picture was more complex. Daoism and Buddhism developed alongside each other in China, and the influence of Buddhism on organized Daoism was considerable, as scholars such as Christine Mollier (2008: 7) have shown:

> Buddhism not only deeply affected traditional Chinese religious life and mentality, but it also operated as a trigger for the native religion. Taoism owes part of the formation of its identity, as a fully structured and organized religion, to its face-to-face encounter with Mahāyāna Buddhism. In response to the sophisticated eschatological and soteriological concepts imported by its foreign rival, Taoist theologians had to formulate and define their own ideas of the after-life and human destiny, of moral precepts and ethical principles.

10. The city of Ye is near Lingzhang, Henan, and was important in this period (see Zürcher 2007: 181). Instead of Ye, the Tibetan states that Huike travelled to Tsang chu. The (Northern) Qi dynasty ruled from 550 to 577.

11. This sentence is not in the Tibetan translation.

12. The single vehicle (Ch. *yīshèng* 一乘, Skt *ekayāna*), as taught in several Mahayana sutras, is a way of condensing all the teachings of the Buddha, usually categorized in three vehicles, into a single path. In the *Laṅkāvatāra sūtra* LVI, the Buddha says that he teaches three vehicles because beings are different, but ultimately there is only a single vehicle, which is thusness:

> When I speak of the one path, I mean the one path to realization. And what does the one path to realization mean? Projections, such as projections of what grasps or what is grasped, do not arise in suchness. This is what the one path to realization means.

Translation in Red Pine 2013: 163.

13. The path of cultivation is the fourth of the five paths. This sentence can be read as referring to Huike's achievements or his teachings. The Tibetan translator (van Schaik 2015: 88) and Faure (1989: 124) take them as referring to Huike's achievements; however, it seems to me to make more sense to read them as introducing the following teaching by Huike that takes up the bulk of this chapter, as Cleary (1986: 38) does.

14. T.16, no. 670, p. 480b9–10. The line is from Mahāmāti's verses of praise to Śākyamuni at the beginning of chapter II.

15. 'Sitting meditation' (Ch. *zuòchán* 坐禪) is the usual way of referring to meditation practice in most later Zen traditions (Japanese Zen uses the same characters, pronounced 'zazen'). It does not feature prominently elsewhere in the *Masters of*

the Lanka, except in Daoxin's teachings for beginners, which starts, 'When you are beginning the practice of sitting meditation . . .' (see chapter 13 above). In the present case, the Tibetan translator simply translates *zuòchán* the same way as *chán*, i.e. with *bsam gtan*, 'meditation'.

16. Only the first line is found in the *Avataṃsaka sūtra*: T.9, no. 278, p. 624a14 and T.10, no. 279, p. 272c4. As Faure points out, the first six lines are similar to T.48, no. 2011, p. 377a24–26, which is also ostensibly a quotation from the *Daśabhūmika sūtra*. The last line of the quote ('So sentient beings cannot see it') is actually from the *Mahāparinirvāṇa sūtra* (T.12, no. 374, p. 523c20). The phrase 'vajra buddha' (*jīngāng fó* 金剛佛) is not in any of these texts, and is more associated with esoteric Buddhism. However, it can be an epithet of the buddha Vairocana, which is probably the case here.

17. T.9, no. 278, p. 542c21.

18. The passage from 'and not seen' to 'pure and unobscured' is in the Tibetan translation, but missing from both Chinese manuscripts which contain the text of this section (Or.8210/S.2054 and Pelliot chinois 3536). It seems to have been lost as a scribal error, skipping from one instance of the phrase 'sentient beings' to the next.

19. 'Wrong views' is literally 'all views' (*zhū jiàn* 諸見, Skt *sarvadṛṣṭi*); this phrase refers to the various non-Buddhist philosophical schools. The 'noble path' (*shèng dào* 聖道, Skt *āryamārga*) is the path followed by the bodhisattva. According to Muller (DDB), it is also a synonym for enlightenment and undefiled wisdom, which seems to be the case here.

20. The Tibetan has 'great wisdom' rather than 'great nirvana', and adds 'in harmony with stillness' at the end of the sentence; see van Schaik 2015: 89.

21. The sources of these two statements are not given here, but they are similar to two texts quoted in the the *Yiwen leiju*. See the introduction to this chapter for further details.

22. The passage from 'But when delusion' to 'empty and pure' is not present in the Tibetan.

23. The character *dēng* 燈 is usually translated as 'lamp' but here is better translated as 'candle' or 'flame', as the word 'lamp' may bring to mind a covered lantern, which would not be affected by the wind. In fact, the lamp in this analogy, and in the image of the 'transmission of the lamp', would have been an ancient open lamp, i.e. a bowl filled with oil with a wick in the middle. See Needham 1962: 78–80.

24. The Tibetan translation has a longer passage in place of 'then all desires' to 'further rebirths', as follows (van Schaik 2015: 89–90):

> Thus, when sentient beings are aware of the radiant purity of mind, they will be constantly merged with meditation. The blockages at the six gates will all flow, without being caught in the winds of error. Then the lamp of insight will be radiantly pure and will distinguish one thing from another. Thus buddhahood will be accomplished of itself, and the aspirations of your previous practice will be fully realized. Henceforth, you do not see the states of existence.

25. 'All the buddhas of the three times' refers to the buddhas of the past, present and future, i.e. all buddhas that have ever existed, exist now or will exist in the future.

26. The context of this statement is that every sentient being has already existed in the cycle of rebirth for an infinite amount of time, and therefore must already have met countless buddhas.

27. The lines from 'As the dharma scriptures say' to 'the ultimate path' are only found in the Tibetan translation; see van Schaik 2015: 90.

28. The phrase 'the sun and moon in the world' is from the *Sutra of the Great Conflagration* (*Daloutan jing*, T.1, no. 23) translated by Fali and Faju during the Western Jin dynasty. The sutra, which deals with cosmology, states that a very long time after the destruction of the world, a black wind arose and blew deep inside the ocean and took out the sun and moon and placed them on their current path, which is how there is 'the sun and moon in the world'. Thanks to Imre Galambos for clarifying this.

29. The second part of the sentence is missing in the Chinese manuscripts; taken from the Tibetan.

30. The lines from 'It is also like when' to 'remains unspoilt' are missing in Pelliot chinois 3436, and thus are found only in Or.8210/S.2054. The last statement ('just so, after the succession of lives and deaths of sentient beings has come to an end, the dharmakaya remains unspoilt') appears twice, which may have been the cause of eye-skip in the scribe of P.3436. This statement is not repeated in the Tibetan translation.

31. From 'I dispensed with' to 'who does this' is only in the Tibetan translation; see van Schaik 2015: 90–1.

32. The words 'As an old book says' appear only in the Tibetan translation; see van Schaik 2015: 91. The phrase may have been accidentally omitted from the Chinese texts because古書曰 ('an old book says') is graphically similar to what appears in the text (in S.2054), i.e. 故畫日 ('because all day'). Thanks to Imre Galambos for pointing this out.

33. This line is difficult to interpret, and though my translation is different from both Cleary's (1986: 40–1) and Faure's (1989: 127) interpretation, it accords with both the Chinese and the Tibetan. The intended meaning seems to be that the wrong kind of effort (i.e. in reading and study) only makes things worse.

34. T.9, no. 278, p. 429a3–4. Cleary (1986: 41) and Faure (1989: 128) do not include the fourth line within the quote, though it is in the *Avataṃsaka sūtra*.

35. The statement about the buddhas' teaching is similar to T.30, no. 1564, p. 24a1–2.

36. Literally, 'a thousand follow from this one'.

37. T.9, no. 262, p. 42c14–15.

38. In this and the following lines, 'absorption' translates *zhèngshòu* 正受 and 'samadhi' translates *sānmèi* 三昧 (which is the Chinese transliteration of the Sanskrit *samādhi*). The Tibetan translator uses *drang po tshor* ('direct attention') for *zhèngshòu* and *ting nge 'dzin*, (which is the usual equivalent for Skt *samādhi*) for *sānmèi*.

39. Literally, 'the dharma of form', which means the form aggregate (Skt *skāndha*). On the other hand, the Tibetan translation has 'colour'.

40. 'Concentration' translates *dìng* 定. The Tibetan translator uses an early term, *thub pa*.

41. Literally, 'the stages of learning and beyond learning'.

42. Literally, 'one enlightened by contemplation of dependent arising'.

43. This long passage is from T.9, no. 278, p. 438b27–p. 439b3, with some omissions. See also T.10, no. 279, p. 77c15–p. 78b29. Faure (1989: p. 130, n.32) points out that this was a popular passage in Chinese Buddhism. The general message is that

meditation on one object is the same as meditation on all objects, exemplified in the line: 'When you enter the state of absorption in a single mote of dust, / Samadhi arises in all motes of dust.'

44. The final words, 'the dharmakaya, the guiding principle' are only in the Tibetan translation; see van Schaik 2015: 92.

CHAPTER 11. SENGCAN: HEAVEN IN A GRAIN OF SAND

1. Adamek 2011: 81–2.
2. Ferguson 2011: 23.
3. Another version of the dialogue appears in the compendium known to contemporary scholars as the 'Long Scroll', in which Huike is named as the master, but the one who asks for absolution is anonymous. See Broughton 1999: 42.
4. Translation from Ferguson 2011: 23.
5. By contrast, the *Transmission of the Dharma Jewel* does not record any details about Sengcan's death. Here, Sengcan retires to the south, and the author states 'no-one ever knew where he ended up' (translation in McRae 1986: 261).
6. The original text, *Verses on Explaining the Hidden* (*Xiangxuanfu*), is found in T.52, no. 2103, p. 340a15–c9. See the discussion in Faure 1989: 134, n.10. Here, Faure also mentions another text attributed to Sengcan called 'Inscription on the Sprit of Faith' (T.48, no. 2010, p. 376b–377a), though he suggests caution in accepting this attribution.
7. Both verses translated in Cleary 1993: 1462. For an excellent discussion of the contents and context of the *Gaṇḍavyūha*, see Osto 2009. The *Gaṇḍavyūha* is contained within a larger, composite sutra, the *Avataṃsaka*.
8. Cleary 1993: 1490.
9. The Huayan school, named for the *Avataṃsaka sūtra*, became increasingly widespread during the Tang dynasty (though as I discuss elsewhere, 'school' should not be taken to imply an institutional structure). Teachers of this tradition explored similar themes to early Zen teachers, and in some cases belonged to both traditions, Zongmi being the most prominent example.
10. These similes are given at more length in the Tibetan translation, which I have drawn on here; see van Schaik 2015: 92.
11. In this sutra, the 'one true way' would normally refer to the single vehicle (*ekayāna*). The Tibetan translator, however, translated the phrase as 'mahayana'.
12. There is no exact correspondence in the sutra. Faure notes a similarity to T.9, no. 262, p. 8a18.
13. From 'The *Laṅkāvatāra*' to 'never taught in words' is only in the Tibetan translation; see van Schaik 2015: 93.
14. The Chinese literally says, 'samsara is liberated'. I am following the Tibetan translator here.
15. Cleary (1986: 44) has 'Nieshan temple'. The Tibetan translation has 'Huanggong temple' (Tib. *hwang kong*).
16. In the following sections, the original passages of Huiming's *Verses on Explaining the Hidden* are given first, followed by Sengcan's commentary (indented in the translation here). Although the original text is quite short, the commentary here is only on selected passages.
17. This line is missing two characters in S.2054 and Taisho, but the correct reading is found in P.3436.

18. Here all Chinese manuscripts actually have 'the sutra says', but this must be an error. The Tibetan has 'commentary'.
19. The character *qì* 器 is usually translated as 'vessel', but can mean any formed thing, and the simile in Sengcan's text is rings and bracelets, not vessels.
20. The 'precious palace' is a reference to Indra's palace, while the 'jade tower' is from Chinese mythology, in the realm of the immortals.
21. Literally, 'universal vision' – the way of seeing of a buddha or bodhisattva.
22. The Tibetan translation has: 'If you understand the true principle . . .' (van Schaik 2015: 94).
23. The Chinese text is difficult to interpret here. Faure (1989: 135) has 'sans éveiller l'attention'. I have followed the Tibetan translation.
24. Compare T.52, no. 2103, p. 340c2–3.
25. 'Concentration' here is *dìng* 定; however, the Tibetan translator chose *bsam gtan*, which usually renders *chán*. In general, the Tibetan translation is not very consistent when translating these terms; elsewhere *dìng* is rendered with Tib. *mi 'gyur* ('unmoving') and *thub pa* ('wisdom').
26. T.25, no. 1509, p. 234a19.
27. The relevance of this quote (T.16, no. 665, p. 409c24) is not entirely clear.

CHAPTER 12. DAOXIN I: HOW TO SIT

1. McRae 1986: 262.
2. For example, Sharf (2014) has the title as *Fundamental Expedient Teachings for Calming the Mind to Enter the Way*. The assumption that the current chapter of the *Masters of the Lanka* represents a single text by Daoxin led John McRae (1986: 142) to call it 'repetitive and occasionally confusing'.
3. The title *Methods for the Bodhisattva Precepts* translates *pú sà jiè fǎ* 菩薩戒法. If those characters are not read as a title, this could be translated as 'a book of dharma teachings [for] the bodhisattva precepts ceremony'. 'Also composed' is *jí zhì* 及制 and 'teachings for novices on methods for attaining peace of mind' is *rù dào ān xīn yào fāng biàn fǎ mén* 入道安心要方便法門. Here, *rù dào* means 'one who has entered the path' which in the Buddhist monastic context usually refers to novices.
4. Shuangfeng means 'Twin Peaks' (it was previously known as Potou, 'Broken Top').
5. T.16, no. 670, p. 481c2.
6. What Daoxin calls the *Wisdom Sutra Taught by Mañjuśrī* is the *Saptaśatika Prajñāpāramitā*, i.e. the Perfection of Wisdom in 700 lines, of which two translations (T.8, no. 232 and T.233) existed in Daoxin's time. What follows may be taken as Daoxin's summary of the passages of the *Saptaśatika* on the one practice concentration.
7. From 'If you' to 'single practice concentration' is missing in Or.8210/S.2054 and the Taisho edition.
8. See T.8, no. 232, p. 731a25–b9. The version in this text paraphrases the canonical sutra.
9. In this line, 'body and mind' translates *fāng cùn* 方寸, literally 'square inch'. In contexts such as this, 'square inch' refers to the physical heart as the centre of a human being's body and mind. In Daoxin's text (he uses the term again below) it appears to refer more generally to the mental and physical bundle that makes up a person. 'The site of awakening' is the *bodhimaṇḍa*, where Śākyamuni achieved enlightenment, and by extension, a place where the dharma is practised. In China,

it was also used to refer to the platform on which the precepts were conferred. Here, Daoxin is saying that every individual person is, at all times, a site of awakening.

10. See T.9, no. 277, p. 393b10–11. Faure (1989: 142) states that this sutra played an important role in the development of the ceremonies of the bodhisattva vow.

11. 'Judgements' here translates *jué guān* 覺觀; these two characters are equivalent to the Sanskrit *vitarka* and *vicāra* (DDB, Muller).

12. T.8, no. 223, p. 385c8.

13. This is the last line of the Tibetan translation of the *Masters of the Lanka*. Here, S.2054 (and Taisho) inserts 'has no shape' again, which does not appear in P.3436, so I have ignored it as a probable scribal error.

14. Note the similarity between this passage and the famous verse attributed to Shenxiu in the *Platform Sutra*.

15. This quote is slightly different from what appears in the canonical sutras. The first and third lines are both on T.9, no. 278, p. 623c28 and at T.10 no. 279, p. 272c8; the middle line, with a different final character, is at no. 278, p. 624a9 and a10, and at no. 279, p. 272c18.

16. This sentence suggests a question and answer session in the course of a sermon; though the character *jiǎ* 假 would usually indicate a condition, and therefore a rhetorical question from Daoxin ('if someone were to ask . . .'), I take it here to mean 'concede, grant' (Kroll 2015: 193), indicating Daoxin's graciousness in allowing questions from the younger members of the audience.

17. The text here has *fǎxìng zhī shēn* 法性之身, literally Skt *dharmatākāya*.

18. The *sphaṭika* crystal is a colourless transparent stone. It is used in India for religious objects of devotion.

19. Compare the *Laṅkāvatāra sūtra*, T.16, no. 670, p. 506c7. On the other hand, Faure (1989: p. 144, n.23) suggests a connection to the *Mahāparinirvāṇa sūtra*.

20. This quotation is from the *Amitartha sūtra*, T.9, no. 276, p. 385c23–26. Some lines from the canonical sutra are omitted in the quotation. I have followed the canonical version in the first four lines, as the version in the *Masters of the Lanka* seems to be garbled.

21. Being all knowing or omniscienct (*yīqiè zhì* 一切智) is one of the characteristics of a buddha's wisdom.

22. Literally, 'the single-form dharma method' (*yīxiàng fǎmén* 一相法門), this refers to a teaching based in the principle of nonduality.

23. See T.9, no. 262, p. 8a23–24.

24. This seems not to be a direct quote, though the first line occurs verbatim three times in T.9, no. 272, p. 349a29–b3. There is a similar metaphor in the *Mahāprajñāpāramitā sūtra*: see T.12, no. 375, p. 617c2–10.

25. To have slandered the three jewels and disrupted the harmony of the sangha are major violations of the monastic code. Here they stand for all negative actions in this and previous lives, which prevent sentient beings from realizing the nature of their minds.

26. This statement refers to the present context, the teaching on observing the mind. A little further in the text, Daoxin does teach analysis of the body as a preliminary practice.

27. T.9, no. 278, p. 672a27.

28. T.9, no. 278, p. 409b8–9.

29. Literally, 'when there is no reliance': *bù yī* 不依.

30. In both manuscript copies this second quotation from the *Avataṃsaka sūtra* and the following quotations from the *Mahāparinirvāṇa sūtra* appear slightly earlier, in the discussion of different types of students, after the sentence 'A person who wants to be a teacher must be capable of recognizing these differences', and before the sentence 'Among students there are four types of people'. However, it is clear that the quotations relate to the discussion of the pure lands, not to the different capacities of students. Thus they seem to have been copied into a slightly earlier part of the text by mistake at some point in the manuscript transmission.

31. The stages of further progress are the second level (Skt *bhūmi*) of the bodhisattva path.

32. See T.8, no. 235, p. 749a9, though the text is slightly different.

33. The path of practice (or 'cultivation') is the fourth of the five paths of progress for a bodhisattva.

34. Probably a reference to the *Heart Sutra*'s famous phrase, 'forms are nothing but emptiness; emptiness is nothing but form'.

35. 'Conditioned phenomena' (*yǒuwéi* 有爲) refers to all of the phenomena of saṃsāra; here Daoxin is saying that even the written teachings of the Buddha are conditioned phenomena, and one must realize for oneself the unconditioned state to which they point.

36. The text continues, 'Distressing: a great calamity.' I suspect this may be an explanatory gloss that has been copied into the main text.

37. The eye of the dharma (*fǎ yǎn* 法眼; Skt *dharmacakṣus*) is the ability to perceive all things clearly, and is one of the qualities a bodhisattva requires in order to aid all sentient beings.

38. I have added 'existent' here, which seems to be missing from this sentence, as a summary of the previous paragraph.

39. The text continues with a non-metrical line that may be another explanatory gloss: 'Ultimately they neither come into being nor cease to be.'

40. The adjectives 'wise and compassionate' (*zhì mǐn* 智愍) may be read as the personal name Zhimin. However, no such person has been identified. Chappell (1983: 113) reads it as referring to Zhiyi (538–97), but there is no other evidence that he was known as Zhimin. Faure (1989: 149, n.50) mentions Famin (597–652), but this figure was a contemporary of Daoxin and does not qualify as being from 'earlier times'.

41. This sentence contains two key terms in early Chinese Buddhist discussions of the mind. 'Mind's source' (*xīnyuán* 心源) refers to the true nature of mind, which is experienced when one's attention is turned upon mind itself; though Daoxin does not discuss this, it is important to other instructions on the practice of 'observing the mind' (see Meinert 2007: 12–15). The concept of essence and activity (*tǐyòng* 體用) goes back to early Chinese philosophy, and generally refers to the difference between the true nature of things and how they appear to be; see Cheng 2002.

42. See T.12, no. 366, p. 343a19. This is apparently a paraphrase rather than a direct quote.

43. Faure translates as five 'points' but the character used here, *zhǒng*, specifically means types or classes.

44. 'Awareness' is *jué* 覺. See the discussion of this term in chapter 5 above. As I mention there, this form of meditation seems to correspond to Daoxin's instructions earlier in the text on observing the mind (*kànxīn* 看心) and 'letting it be'.

45. The phrase 'maintain oneness' (*shǒu yī* 守一) may come from Daoism, as argued in McRae (1986: 138–9) and Sharf (2002: 182–4). This text is one of its earliest appearances in a Buddhist context. Here it refers to maintaining a single state of equanimity through both mental calmness (stillness) and turbulence (movement).

46. On Fu Dashi, or Fu Xi (497–569), see Broughton 2009: 283, n.344. Broughton translates a brief account of him from the *Xu gaoseng zhuan* (T.50 p. 650b1–6) and mentions that there are several manuscripts from Dunhuang containing his commentary on the *Vajracchedikā sūtra*. Here Daoxin states that Fu Dashi only taught the fifth method, but that he (Daoxin) will teach the fourth and fifth. Essentially Daoxin uses the fourth method of meditation as a preliminary practice to the fifth; this can be seen as a version of the classic pair of vipaśyanā and śamatha.

47. T.14, no. 475, p. 539b20.

48. While the previous passage establishes the physical body as composite, impermanent and lacking autonomy, this passage explains how to perceive one's own body as equivalent to the body of a buddha, empty but manifesting through the power of compassion.

49. Tathāgata means 'thus-come/gone' (Skt *tathā* + *āgata*). The Chinese translation, *rúlái* 如來, preserves this meaning.

50. This paragraph follows David Chappell's translation of *tā* 他 (literally 'other') as 'objectified'. Chappell states that many comparable uses of *tā* were discussed by John McRae in an unpublished translation of Hongren's *Treatise on the Essentials of Training the Mind*. See Chappell 1983: 125, n.46.

51. T.12, no. 389, p. 1110c19.

52. This is the end of the teaching of the fourth type of meditation practice, and the beginning of the fifth.

53. This is not a direct quotation.

54. T.9, no. 262; the first line appears on p. 41a, the other three on p. 45a.

55. T.12, no. 389, p. 1111a15–20.

56. 'Uncontaminated activity' (*wéilòuyè* 無漏業) is activity carried out without the conceptualization of actor, act and recipient. It does not generate further karma.

57. Though I take 'Listeners' (*wénzhě* 聞者) here as a direct address, other translators have not. Cleary (1986: 60) has 'those who hear' and Faure (1989: 154) 'ceux qui en ont pris connaissance'.

58. 'True mindfulness' (*zhèng niàn* 正念) is also translated 'right thought' in the context of the noble eightfold path.

59. This does not appear to be a direct quote. Compare *Mahāprajñāpāramitā sūtra*, T.6, no. 220, p. 700c3–6. Faure suggests a *Mahāprajñāpāramitā śāstra* 18 (T.25, no. 1509, p. 197c).

60. Literally 'a single word' (*yī yán* 一言). Faure (1997: 117) suggests that it refers to the visualization of a single syllable, as advocated by Hongren in the next chapter. However I think it can be safely translated as 'a single teaching' as in the Buddhist context *yī yán* can mean 'The same teaching, but which listeners may hear and interpret variously' (Muller, DDB).

61. As David Chappell (1983: 126, n.59) points out, this is very close to the closing lines of chapter 26 of the *Zhuangzi*.

CHAPTER 13. DAOXIN II: TEACHINGS FOR BEGINNERS

1. Adamek 2007: 318.

2. The Chinese translated by Adamek as 'someone who stays put' is *yǒurén chù* 有人處.

3. For an instruction on breathing in this way by a modern Japanese teacher, Maesumi Roshi, see 'What Are We Ignoring About Breathing?', in *Lion's Roar*, 16 April 2017 (http://www.lionsroar.com/what-are-we-ignoring-about-breathing/). Maesumi's life and teachings are discussed in Wright 2010.

4. Suzuki 1991: 27.

5. Hakuin's instructions are quoted in Mohr 2000: 257. Dogen's, in his *Eihei Kōruku*, are translated in Leighton and Okumura 2010: 349. While Daoxin uses the Chinese word *fù* 腹, in these examples the term used is *dāntián* 丹田 (*tanden* in Japanese), a more technical term indicating a point below the navel, which seems to be derived from Daoism.

6. 'Turn the mind within' translates *liàn xīn* 斂心. The character *liàn* means literally to fold back or withdraw. Again, translations of this passage seem to miss this subtlety; Chappell (1983: 19) has 'you collect the mind', and McRae (1986: 142) has 'mind [becomes] gradually regulated'. While *liàn* can certainly mean to collect or gather, the meaning of withdrawing or turning inwards accords better with the more detailed instructions in other early texts on the practice of observing the mind (*kànxīn* 看心).

7. Meinert 2007: 12.

8. The Chinese term used here by Daoxin is 'mind's ground' (*xīndì* 心地). In Wolun's *Dharma of Observing the Mind*, it is 'mind's source' (*xīnyuán* 心源); see Meinert 2007: 12. Both terms are synonymous with the *ālaya-vijñāna*. The use of the term 'ground' is paralleled in the Dzogchen tradition, where the basis of all existence is simply known as 'the ground' (Tib. *gzhi*).

9. Cuevas 2003: 63.

10. Eskilden 2006: 384–5. See also discussion in Cuevas 2003: 42–4.

11. Eskilden 2017: 130–42.

12. Translation in Ziporyn 2009: 12 (2.18–19).

13. Translation in Ziporyn 2009: 13 (2.19).

14. Yogācāra thinkers were criticized for positing an internal essence, in exactly the same way that Daoxin criticizes Laozi here. Nevertheless, the classic works of Yogācāra adhere to the principle of emptiness of all categories, including inner and outer. See for example the discussion in Gold 2017.

15. Note the equivalence of meditation with repentance here (cf. the meditation practice of the poṣadha ritual). Note also that meditation linked with repentance in the poṣadha ceremony and elsewhere in the early tradition involves the visualized deconstruction of one's body.

16. Here the instructions move from contemplation of the body to contemplation of the mind, a distinction most translators seem to have missed.

17. Deluded consciousness and perception are the fifth and third of the five aggregates.

18. Other translations do not mention letting the mind come to rest in the abdomen. For example John McRae has only 'force all the air out of your abdomen'. The same interpretation is found in Chappell 1983: 119 and Faure 1989: 157. The difference may be explained by their relying on a version of the text in which

the character *xīn* ('mind') is missing from this passage (it appears in S.2504 but not Pelliot chinois 3436).

19. Here, I translate *liàn xīn* 斂心 as 'turn the mind within'. 'Subtle and profound' is *yǎoyǎo míngmíng* 窈窈冥冥, a phrase from the *Zhuangzi*.

20. 'Energy' translates *yōulíng* 幽靈. Faure has 'esprit transcendent'.

21. T.14, no. 475, p. 541a8.

22. I presume the 'single phrase' mentioned in this quote is: 'realization is acquiring your original mind'. The actual quote here is not found in the *Vimalakīrti-nirdeśa sūtra*, however. Note the similarity of this 'single phrase' (*yī jù* 一句) to the 'single teaching' (*yī yán* 一言), literally 'single word', mentioned by Daoxin at the end of the *Methods for the Bodhisattva Precepts*.

23. The phrase *shě shēn* 捨身 is a reference to acts such as the bodhisattva giving up his body for the tigress and cubs; here, Daoxin seems to be using it as a euphemism for dying.

24. 'Mental attitude' here translates *xīn jìng* 心境, literally 'mind and its objects', indicating dualistic mental processes.

25. The tone of this sentence seems to be sarcasm, indicating that most people have a rigid, rule-based conception of what the dharma should be, and the remainder of the passage explains what dharma really means.

26. See the similar passage in the *Mahāprajñāpāramitā sūtra*, T.5, no. 220, p. 927c20, c23.

27. Here Daoxin appears to be suggesting that his teaching on dying ('the dharma of giving up the body') need not be taken literally, and can be applied to meditation practice generally.

28. The 'level of illumination' is the third of the ten bodhisattva levels (Skt *bhūmi*). 'Decide your own fate' translates *tuī cè* 推策, a phrase literally meaning 'to throw the divining sticks'. The meaning here is presumably an extension of the references above to not being compelled by karma into further rebirth in samsara.

29. T.85, no. 2901, p. 1435a24–25. On this text in early Zen, see McRae 1986: 202–5.

30. T.9, no. 278, p. 610a22.

31. T.14, no. 475, p. 541b19–20.

32. T.12, no. 374, p. 402c8–9.

CHAPTER 14. HONGREN: THE BUDDHA IN EVERYTHING

1. On the nine manuscript copies of the text, and the history of the (mainly Japanese) scholarship on them, see McRae 1986: 309–12, n.36.

2. McRae 1986: 119.

3. Wilkinson 2000: 267.

4. McRae 1986: 127. McRae also cites (p. 133) a passage from Yijing, where the buddha Vairocana is the sun.

5. McRae 1986: 130.

6. 'Single syllable' is *yī zì* 一字. In later Zen texts, there is much discussion of the single-syllable 'critical phrase' *mu* (*wú* 無). Faure (1989: p. 169, n.45) considers this to be 'sans doute' an allusion to the tantric practice of visualizing the letter 'a'. Note the similar terms used by Daoxin: 'single word/teaching' (*yī yán* 一言) and 'single phrase' (*yī jù* 一句); these seem to refer to essentialized teachings rather

than visualized syllables. A reference to the syllable 'a' appears in one of the Tibetan Zen texts from Dunhuang, a commentary on the 'Brief Precepts' (Tib. *lung chung*) found in Pelliot tibétain 699 (see van Schaik 2015: 189).

7. See Leighton 2015: 21ff.

8. Statements about animals and trees communicating the dharma occur in the longer and shorter *Sukhāvatīvyūha* sutras; see the translations in Gomez 1996: 16–18, 146–7, 180–1.

9. The title of the text is *Vajracchedikā-prajñāpāramitôpadeśa*, which appears in two canonical versions (T.25, no. 1511, p. 784b19; no. 1512, p. 819a29–b6). The two versions are different, but contain the same lines cited here. The citation is actually a quoted verse in the commentary itself, with no source; it is quoted in response to a similar question to the one here, i.e.: 'In that case, the buddha Śākyamuni is not a buddha, and does not teach the dharma. Is that right?'

10. See also the typically interesting discussion of nonsentient beings teaching the dharma in Dogen's *Shōbōgenzō*, 'Mujo Seppo' ('Nonsentient Beings Speak the Dharma'). See Tanahashi 2010: 548–57; Nearman 2007: 653–65; Nishijima and Cross 2006: III.95–104.

11. Faure (1989: 163, n.1) points out that Shuangfeng Mountain was known as 'West Mountain' while the neighbouring Mount Fengmao was known as 'East Mountain'. He believes that the *Masters of the Lanka* confuses East Mountain with Shuangfeng. However, it is clear from later in the chapter that the Youju monastery mentioned here is Daoxin's monastery on Shuangfeng, and it is also stated later in this chapter that Hongren was entombed in a stupa on Fengmao. Thus the use of 'East Mountain' here is meant to refer to the tradition established by Hongren in Fengmao, and not to Shuangfeng Mountain. The *Genealogy of the Dharma Jewel* states that Hongren initially travelled to Shuangfeng to study with Daoxin before moving to the Pingmao (not Fengmao), which it identifies as the East Mountain (see Adamek 2007: 85).

12. Here I am translating *mén* 門 as 'tradition' to give a sense somewhere in between a 'teaching method' or 'doctrine' and a 'school'. I think 'tradition' suggests both of these without the baggage of 'school' which suggests too much institutional presence.

13. There is a reference to ridgepoles and rafters in the *Dhammapada* (v.154, translation from Mascaró 1973: 56).

> But now I have seen thee, housebuilder: never more shalt thou build this house. The rafters of sins are broken, the ridge-pole of ignorance is destroyed.

14. The 'silent transmission' implies transmission of the nature of reality/mind through symbolic action, as in the story of the Buddha holding up the flower in silence to his students.

15. See McRae 1986: 90–1 for the text that was popularly attributed to Hongren (and partially appears in earlier chapters of this work).

16. The extent to which the following text was directly extracted from Xuanze's work, or whether it is a paraphrase, cannot be established in the absence of the original text. The character translated here as 'according to' is *àn* 按 (see Kroll 2015: 3.I). It is specifically used in the two citations from Xuanze's text, here and in the next chapter. The use of *àn* suggests that what follows is meant to draw

from that text, rather than to be a direct quote, as these are usually prefaced in this text with *yún* 云 or *yuē* 曰. The character *àn* can also indicate an author's or editor's aside (*nota bene*), and this is how Faure (1989: 163) takes it. Cleary (1986: 67) has 'according to'.

17. This is a direct expression of the Confucian ideal.

18. The suggestion here is that Hongren increased his community's practice of performing offering rituals (Ch. *gōngyǎng* 供養; Skt *pūja*), the usual way that Buddhist monks attract lay sponsorship. Just below in this chapter, an offering ritual is described, attended by laypeople and monastics, from whom Hongren receives the offerings.

19. The phrase *hún yí* 渾儀 here is difficult to translate in this context; I take *hún* to mean 'complete' and *yí* to mean 'observance' or 'ceremony'. According to DDB (Muller), it is equivalent to Skt *vidhi*, Tib. *cho ga*.

20. The four postures are walking, standing, sitting and lying down; the three activities are speech, thoughts and deeds.

21. Note the deliberate pattern of four, three, two, one here.

22. The nine kinds of disciples include all male and female, ordained and lay classes of Buddhist practitioner.

23. The Chinese *tǎ* 塔 usually means a stupa in a Buddhist context; in China and Japan, the same word was used for the tombs of abbots of monasteries. Here, the implication is that Hongren is commissioning his own memorial.

24. It appears that Hongren is here predicting that he will die on or after the next anniversary of the Buddha's parinirvāṇa, and saying that after his death his residence should be converted into a monastery. The parinirvāṇa was traditionally celebrated on the fifteenth day of the second month. The implication of the text is that the stupa was intended by Hongren as a memorial for himself. Faure seems to agree with this but he only has the first statement as the direct speech of Hongren and therefore makes the intent unclear. A similar passage occurs in the *Genealogy of the Dharma Jewel* and Adamek (2007: 320) translates it as 'I can't very well enter *parinirvāṇa* on the fifteenth day of the second month, the same as the Buddha.' According to Faure (1989: 164, n.21), the residence mentioned here was 'sans doute' Hongren's family home in Huangmei. He cites the comparable cases where Huike's and Shenxiu's family homes were converted into monasteries. However, in the present context, it seems that Hongren is meant to be speaking to his students on Mount Fengmao, and it is his residence there, at the centre of a meditation teaching retreat setting, that he is asking to have converted into a monastery.

25. See Adamek 2007: 164–5; she says that lists of ten disciples of Hongren occur in several Chan histories; in others, from the *Genealogy of the Dharma Jewel* onwards, Huineng is made the prime disciple. Adamek suggests that the *Masters of the Lanka* is the more accurate of the two texts in some areas. See also Adamek 2007: 166, on the preface to Jingjue's commentary on the *Heart Sutra*, in which Jingjue states that his three main teachers were Shenxiu, Huian (i.e. Laoan) and Xuanze.

26. On Zhishen from Zizhou see also the *Genealogy of the Dharma Jewel* (Adamek 2007: 330–4). According to Faure (1989: 165, n.25), he is also the author of commentaries found in the Dunhuang manuscripts. Hongren's calling them both 'educated people' would seem to be a double-edged compliment or even a mild criticism, given the account of his attitude to book learning.

27. Laoan means 'Old An'. His dates are usually given as 582–709, and he was also known as Huian. See Adamek 2007: 165.

28. Faru is an important figure for historians of Chan, because his epitaph has survived (see Adamek 2007: 161, as well as McRae 1986: 85–6). The epitaph has Faru as Hongren's prime disciple. The inscription identifies the mind-to-mind silent transmission as the single practice concentration, and an inscription for one of Faru's disciples identifies this lineage with the *Laṅkāvatāra sūtra*. In the *Transmission of the Dharma Jewel*, Faru is also presented as the main disciple of Hongren and his biography is in between Hongren's and Shenxiu's (see translation in McRae 1986: 264–5).

29. Huineng is of course the figure who was accepted as Hongren's true successor by Shenhui and those who followed his lead; later, this became orthodoxy.

30. 'Simultaneous practice' (*jiān xíng*, 兼行) is the practice of the six perfections all at once. This seems to be the practice that Hongren is asking Xuanze to cultivate and teach. Teachings on how the six perfections are present in the act of nonceptual meditation are found in a number of early Zen texts; see for example van Schaik 2015: 50–1 and 124–5.

31. There is probably some wordplay suggested here, also present in the English, where Hongren is asking Xuanze if he knows his wants and needs, while at the same time asking if he understands the nature of his (enlightened) mind. Thanks to Imre Galambos for this suggestion.

32. 'Springs and autumns' (*chūn qiū* 春秋) can also be translated simply as 'years' or 'age' but it is a nice image. It is also the name of a chapter of the *Shōbōgenzō*: 'Shunju'.

33. Cleary (1986: 69) translates this to mean that Hongren's body remained the same, but there is no other case of Hongren being said to be mummified.

34. This was a high-level post, with only one higher command level beneath the emperor.

35. This literally means: 'cut off wisdom'. It is possibly a reference to the *Daodejing* which has the words: 'If we could renounce our sageness and discard our wisdom, it would be better for the people a hundredfold.' Thanks to Imre Galambos for pointing this out.

36. The lamp is often used as a simile for the mind in Yogācāra Buddhist texts; this statement is a reference to how the mind creates the objects of perception.

37. According to Faure (1989: 169, n.51), this phrase occurs word for word in Jingjue's commentary on the *Heart Sutra*. Faure puts only this line in quotation marks.

38. The text is the *Mūlamadhyamakakārikā*, translated into Chinese by Kumarajiva, and this is the first verse after the dedication (T.30, no. 1564, p. 2b6–7).

39. These two lines are a direct quote from the *Sarvabuddha-viṣayāvatāra-jñānālokā-laṃkāra sūtra* (T.12, no. 35, p. 262c6).

CHAPTER 15. SHENXIU: ZEN IN THE WORLD

1. The best source in English on Shenxiu and his works remains John McRae's *The Northern School and the Formation of Early Ch'an Buddhism* (McRae 1986). This work contains complete translations of the *Treatise on Original Luminosity* (*Yuánmíng lùn*) and *Five Skilful Means* (*Wǔ fāngbiàn*), as well as excerpts from the *Treatise on Contemplating the Mind* (*Guānxīn lùn*).

2. 'Imperial Preceptor' is *dìshī* 帝師, and 'National Preceptor' is *guóshī* 國師. While the post of National Preceptor has been shown to go back as far as the Northern Qi dynasty (550–77), modern scholarship generally discusses the origins of the Imperial Preceptor post during the Tangut kingdom in the late twelfth century (Dunnell 1992). The post became famous soon after this during the reign of the Mongols, particularly with Kublai Khan's appointment of Chogyal Pagpa (1230–85) to the role of Imperial Preceptor. The appointment of Shenxiu by Wu Zetian to a post of the same name several centuries earlier seems to have been missed in these discussions.

3. The five skilful means are the five chapters of the text itself; they are (i) explaining the essence of buddhahood, or teaching the transcendence of thought; (ii) opening the gates of wisdom, or teaching motionlessness; (iii) the teaching on manifesting the inconceivable; (iv) elucidating the true nature of entities; (v) the naturally unobstructed path of liberation. Fivefold structures are particularly popular in early Zen; we have already seen the five types of meditation used by Daoxin. The eighth-century teacher Moheyan taught five levels of meditation as well (van Schaik 2015: 146):

    1. If you experience the movements of the deluded mind, this is a neutral state.
    2. If you experience the movements of the deluded mind and you follow that experience, this is the state of an ordinary sentient being.
    3. If you experience the movements of the deluded mind and you understand that movement as a fault, then that experience will stop the various movements.
    4. If you experience the movements of the deluded mind and know that they are without self, then this is one-sided peace, quiescent in emptiness.
    5. If you experience the movements of the deluded mind and do not conceptualize or follow them, then each thought is liberated as soon as it comes. This is the correct meditation.

    Five levels of realization are also attributed to Dongshan Liangjie (807–69). See the discussion of these in Leighton 2015.

4. McRae 1986: 172.
5. McRae 2003: 92–3.
6. McRae 1986: 180.
7. Red Pine 2006: 36.
8. The distinction between direct and indirect teachings is an important one in Mahayana Buddhism. A number of sutras – such as the *Saṃdhinirmocana* – and exegetical works distinguish between statements of the Buddha that expressed the truth directly (Skt *nītārtha*) and those statements which were meant for students for whom the direct truth is not appropriate, and therefore require interpretation (Skt *neyārtha*).
9. Red Pine 2006: 34.
10. Cleary 1986: 74; McRae 1986: 54–5.
11. Faure 1989: 174.
12. *Liji* (Yueji 30), translation in Legge 1990a: 110; Chinese text consulted in http://ctext.org/shang-shu/great-plan. *Shangshu* (IV.3), translation in Legge 1990b: 141; Chinese text consulted in http://ctext.org/liji/yue-ji.

13. Nishiyama and Stevens 1975: I.xvi. 'Soft and flexible mind' translates Japanese *nyūnan shin* 柔軟心.
14. See Faure 1997: 93–6.
15. Wu Zetian reigned from 690 to 705. She was followed by Zhongzong (r. 684; 705–10), also known as Yingwang, Prince of Ying, and a period of his reign was known as Shenlong (705–7). The period of his rule from 705–710 was dominated by Empress Wei (d. 710), his consort. He was followed by Ruizong (r. 684–90; 710–12); Emperor Taishang is an honorific title meaning 'retired emperor'. Another influential figure during both of these emperors' reigns was Princess Taiping (d. 713), youngest daughter of Wu Zetian. This period was followed by the reign of Emperor Xuanzong (r. 712–56). Cleary (1986: 72) misses out the other two emperors in his translation. Faure (1989: 171) omits some of the text, perhaps partially following an ellipsis in Pelliot chinois 3703. 'National Preceptor' here translates *guóshī*.
16. 'Prediction' is *shòujì* 授記 (Skt *vyākaraṇa*) which in Buddhist scriptures refers specifically to a guarantee from the Buddha that a person will attain enlightenment.
17. Bianzhou was a prefecture in modern Kaifeng from the sixth to the tenth century. Present-day Weishi County is in Henan, under the administration of Kaifeng.
18. 'Abandoned the methods of verbal expression' is *yányǔ dào duàn* 言語道斷, a phrase that became popular in Zen, and was earlier used by Zhiyi.
19. 'Put an end to the operation of his mental functions' is *xīnxíng chù miè* 心行處滅, a common phrase.
20. Cleary (1986: 72–3) and Faure (1989: 172) translate these four lines as describing Shenxiu; however, the last line about not producing any writings suggests they are about Hongren. Also, the two commonly used four-character phrases *yányǔ dào duàn* 言語道斷 and *xīnxíng chù miè* 心行處滅 refer to enlightened beings, so may be more applicable at this point in the narrative to Shenxiu's teacher.
21. At the beginning of the text the only post mentioned is National Preceptor: *guóshī* 國師. So either the titles are being used interchangeably, or Shenxiu was the only one of the three teachers mentioned at the beginning who was granted the role of Imperial Preceptor as well as (or subsequent to) having the role of National Preceptor.
22. Here, 'school of thought' is a translation of *jiā zōngzhǐ* 家宗旨.
23. Neither Cleary (1986: 73) nor Faure (1989: 173) makes these two lines part of Zetian's speech.
24. As mentioned earlier, this is Zhongzong (r. 684; 705–10).
25. Literally, 'hoping to go to the beginning point of the path'. On the other hand, Cleary (1986: 73) and Faure (1989: 174) translated this as a 'leader' or 'guide' on the path.
26. As Faure (1989: 174, n.14) points out, this is an allusion to a story about the emperor Gaozu (206–195 BC), who had the elm trees of his home village transplanted to his new palace.
27. This looks like a letter of passage; for other examples in a Dunhuang manuscript, see van Schaik and Galambos 2011.
28. Faure (1989: 174) has 'three emperors' based on Pelliot chinois 3703, but as only two are mentioned and 'three' is actually an insertion in Pelliot chinois 3703, I follow Pelliot chinois 3646 here.

29. The phrase 'court and countryside' (*cháo yě* 朝野) refers to the aristocracy and the ordinary people.

30. According to McRae (1986: 46), Li was actually the name of Shenxiu's family, and it was the family residence that was converted into a monastery as a result of the emperor's decree.

31. On the interpretation of this enigmatic phrase, see the introduction to this chapter.

32. 'Monastic and lay devotees' is literally 'the four orders', i.e. *bhikṣu, bhikṣuṇī, upāsaka* and *upāsikā*.

33. The rank of 'emperor's son-in-law' is *fùmǎ* 駙馬. The 'imperial princess' is *gōngzhǔ* 公主, as for example Wencheng Gongzhu, the princess who married the Tibetan emperor Songtsen Gampo in the early seventh century.

34. The 'topknot jewel' is *jìzhū* 髻珠, the king's most prized possession in the *Lotus Sutra* parable (Muller, DDB).

35. This is a play on the popular metaphor of a network of hanging mirrors, all reflecting each other, which appears in Sengcan's chapter. Here, Shenxiu's unique nature is conveyed with the image of a mirror hanging alone.

36. 'Luminous spirit' is *shénmíng* 神明. Though the term's origins predate Buddhism in China, later it came to be a synonym for the Buddha nature.

37. This line is difficult to translate as it stands. Here I read the character *qián* 前 ('in front; preceding') as a scribal error for *qián* 潛, meaning 'to plumb the depths, probe'. Middle Chinese pronunciations are the near homophones *dzen* and *dzjem* respectively (Kroll 2015: 361).

38. Here I am substituting *yīqiè* 一切 ('everyone') for *yīshāng* 一傷 ('single suffering'). If we keep the original character, a translation could be 'he set his heart on the nirvana of a single suffering [being]'. On the other hand, Faure has the emperor's speech moving into the first person to say he was upset at the thought of the death of Shenxiu.

39. This is Shenxiu's official title. Literally, *dàtōng* 大通 means 'vastly pervasive' (compare the Tibetan title *Longchen*).

40. For the name of the monastery, Pelliot chinois 3436 has Dumensi, while Pelliot chinois 3703 has Duren. The name of Shenxiu's monastery, from other sources, is Dumen, and I use that here. See McRae (1989: 50, 55–6) on this monastery, and the full ceremonies around Shenxiu's death. Faure's (1989: 175) translation states that the officer was told to establish the monastery, as well as the stele, which seems to be wrong.

41. *Mahāparinirvāṇa sūtra*: T.12, no. 374, p. 384, c16.

42. Literally 'the universe of the ten directions'.

43. 'Reflection' (or shadow) is *yǐng* 影, which can also mean 'portrait', which does remain after the body is gone. However, the line is probably meant to be contradictory. As Faure (1989: 177, n.28) points out, this reverses the usual order of things, in which the body is primary and the shadow dependent on it. This theme continues in the next line, 'The bridge flows but the water does not'.

44. 'Essence and activity' is *tǐyòng* 體用. The concept appears frequently in Shenxiu's works; see for example McRae 1986: 178.

45. The 'twofold mystery' (*chóngxuán* 重玄) was the name of a school of Daoism (see Pregadio 2008: 1.274ff.). The term is derived from Laozi; as the name for a school, it apparently goes back to the sixth century but reached its apogee during the Tang dynasty. The Daoist context of the term was known to Buddhist writers

well before this: 'Buddhist thinkers such as Zhi Dun (314–66), Sengzhou (374–414), and Jizang (549–623) used the expression *chongxuan* to speak of Laozi's truth, and identify it as a Taoist usage' (Pregadio 2008: 275). Thus Shenxiu is, at least as an allusion, refering to a Daoist concept here.

46. This seems to be a reference to the abhidharma doctrine that everything is renewed in every instant. The same point is made in a dialogue between a teacher and student in one of the Dunhuang Tibetan Zen texts (see van Schaik 2015: 106–7). Note that Cleary (1986: 76) and Faure (1989: 177) both translate this differently, leaving out the character *jì* 寂 ('peace, cessation') which is in Pelliot chinois 3436 but missing in the Taisho edition.

47. Chapter 28 of the *Mahāparinirvāṇa sūtra* (T.12, no. 374) addresses the nature of the Buddha, including the idea that the Buddha came from eastern India, but also that his body fills all of space.

48. Faure (1997: 207, n.33) discusses Jingxian and also suggests that this eighth chapter is a later addition by a disciple of one of these four figures, and because Jingxian is obscure, he suggests it could be one of his disciples. However, there is no compelling reason to think that this is the case.

49. In this metaphor, it seems that the lamp is the teachings, and the mirror the clear minds of the disciples.

50. 'Eminent' is *dàdé* 大德, literally 'of great virtue'. It is a term of respect for senior monks.

51. The twenty-four are: eleven masters at the head of the eight chapters; Bodhidharma's other two students Daoyu and Tanlin (excluding Huike who is already counted); Hongren's other nine main disciples (i.e. excluding Shenxiu who is already counted); Xuanze and Jingjue.

REFERENCES

Adamek, Wendi L. 2007. *The Mystique of Transmission: On an Early Chan History and its Contexts*. New York: Columbia University Press.
—— 2011. *The Teachings of Master Wuzhu: Zen and Religion of No-Religion*. New York: Columbia University Press.
Aitken, Robert. 1982. *Taking the Path of Zen*. New York: North Point Press.
Allen, Sarah. 2015. *Buried Ideas: Legends of Abdication and Ideal Government in Early Chinese Bamboo-Slip Manuscripts*. New York: State University of New York Press.
Baier, Annette. 2009. *Reflections on How We Live*. New York: Oxford University Press.
Baroni, Helen. 2002. *The Illustrated Encyclopedia of Zen Buddhism*. New York: The Rosen Publishing Group.
Barrett, Timothy. 1991. 'The Date of the *Leng-chia shih-tzu chi*'. *Journal of the Royal Asiatic Society*, 3rd Series, 1.2: 255–9.
—— 2008. *The Woman Who Discovered Printing*. London: Yale University Press.
Batchelor, Martine. 2008. 'What is This?', *Tricycle Magazine* 18.1.
Beck, Charlotte Joko. 1995. *Nothing Special: Living Zen*. New York: HarperCollins.
Bingenheimer, Marcus and Chang Po-Yung (eds). 2018. *Four Early Chan Texts from Dunhuang – A TEI-based Edition*. Taipei: Shin Wen Feng.
Braarvig, Jens. 2000. 'Sarvadharmāpravṛttinirdeśa'. In Jens Braarvig (ed.), *Buddhist Manuscripts in the Schøyen Collection, vol. I*. Oslo: Hermes Publishing. 81–166.
Bronkhorst, Johannes. 2011. *Language and Reality: On an Episode in Indian Thought*. Leiden: Brill.
Broughton, Jeffrey L. 1999. *The Bodhidharma Anthology: The Earliest Records of Zen*. Berkeley: University of California Press.
—— 2009. *Zongmi on Chan*. New York: Columbia University Press.
Brown, Brian Edward. 1991. *A Study of the Tathāgatagarbha and Ālaya-vijñāna*. New Delhi: Motilal Banarsidass.
Buswell, Robert. 1983. *The Korean Approach to Zen: The Collected Works of Chinul*. Honolulu: University of Hawai'i Press.
—— 1987. 'The "Short-cut" Approach of K'an-hua Meditation: The Evolution of a Practical Subitism in Chinese Ch'an Buddhism'. In Peter Gregory (ed.), *Sudden and Gradual: Approaches to Enlightenment in Chinese Thought*. Honolulu: University of Hawai'i Press. 321–77.
Chang, Garma C.C. 1983. *A Treasury of Mahayana Sutras: Selections from the Mahāratnakūṭa Sūtra*. University Park: Pennsylvania State University Press.
Chappell, David. 1983. 'The Teachings of the Fourth Ch'an Patriarch Tao-hsin (580–651)'. In Lewis Lancaster and Whalen Lai (eds), *Early Ch'an in China and*

Tibet. Berkeley Buddhist Studies Series 5. Berkeley: University of California Press. 89–129.

Cheng, Chung–Ying. 2002. 'On the Metaphysical Significance of *Ti* (Body-Embodiment) in Chinese Philosophy: *Benti* (Origin-Substance) and *Ti-Yong* (Substance and Function)'. *Journal of Chinese Philosophy* 29.2: 145–61.

Choo, Jessey. 2015. 'Yiwen Leiju.' In Cynthia Chennault et al (eds), *Early Medieval Chinese Texts: A Bibliographical Guide.* Berkeley: Institute of East Asian Studies. 454–64.

Cleary, J.C. 1986. *Zen Dawn: Early Zen Texts from Tun Huang.* Boston: Shambhala.

Cleary, Thomas. 1993. *The Flower Ornament Scripture.* Boston: Shambhala.

———— 2006. *Awakening to the Tao.* Boston: Shambhala.

Cole, Alan. 2009. *Fathering Your Father: The Zen of Fabrication in Tang Buddhism.* Berkeley: University of California Press.

Cuevas, Bryan. 2003. *The Hidden History of the Tibetan Book of the Dead.* New York: Oxford University Press.

Deleanu, Florin. 1992. 'Mindfulness of Breathing in the *Dhyāna Sūtras*'. *Transactions of the International Conference of Orientalists in Japan* 37: 42–57.

Drikung Kyabgön Chetsang. 2010. *Lanka'i mkhan po dang slob ma'i mdo: Bod rgya shan sbyor.* Dehradun: Songtsen Library.

Dumoulin, Heinrich. 1988. *Zen Buddhism: A History, Volume 1: India and China.* New York: Macmillan.

Dunnell, Ruth. 1992. 'The Hsia Origins of the Yüan Institution of Imperial Preceptor.' *Asia Major* 5.1: 85–111.

Eskilden, Stephen. 2006. 'Emergency Death Meditations for Internal Alchemists'. *T'oung Pao,* Second Series, 92.4/5: 373–409.

———— 2017. 'Bodhidharma Outside Chan Literature: Immortal, Inner Alchemist, and Emissary from the Eternal Realm'. *Journal of Chinese Religions* 45.2: 119–50.

Faure, Bernard. 1989. *Le Bouddhisme Ch'an en mal d'histoire: genèse d'une tradition religieuse dans la Chine des T'ang.* Paris: Ecole française d'Extrême-Orient.

———— 1997. *The Will to Orthodoxy: A Critical Genealogy of Northern Chan Buddhism.* Stanford, CA: Stanford University Press.

———— 1998. 'Voices of Dissent: Women in Early Chan and Tiantai'. *Annual Report, The Institute for Zen Studies* 24: 25–42.

Ferguson, Andrew. 2011. *Zen's Chinese Heritage: The Masters and Their Teachings* (Expanded Edition). Somerville, MA: Wisdom.

Ford, James Ishmael. 2006. *Zen Master Who? A Guide to the People and Stories of Zen.* Boston: Wisdom.

———— 2012. *If You're Lucky, Your Heart Will Break: Field Notes from a Zen Life.* Boston: Wisdom.

Foulk, T. Griffith. 1999. 'Sung Controversies Concerning the "Separate Transmission" of Chan'. In Peter Gregory and Daniel Katz (eds), *Buddhism in the Sung.* Honolulu: University of Hawai'i Press. 220–94.

———— 2006. 'Rules of Purity in Japanese Zen'. In Steven Heine and Dale S. Wright (eds), *Zen Classics: Formative Texts in the History of Zen Buddhism.* New York: Oxford University Press. 137–69.

Fuller Sasaki, Ruth and Isshū Miura. 1965. *Zen Dust: The History of the Koan and Koan Study in Rinzai (Linji) Zen.* New York: Harcourt, Brace & World.

Garfield, Jay. 1995. *The Fundamental Wisdom of the Middle Way: Nāgārjuna's Mūlamadhyamakakārikā.* New York: Oxford University Press.

Glass, Andrew and Mark Allon. 2007. *Four Gandhari Samyuktagama Sutras: Senior Kharosthi Fragment 5*. Seattle: University of Washington Press.

Gold, Jonathan C. 2017. 'Vasubandhu'. In Edward N. Zalta (ed.), *The Stanford Encyclopedia of Philosophy* (Spring Edition), URL: plato.stanford.edu/archives/spr2017/entries/vasubandhu/.

Gomez, Luis. 1996. *Land of Bliss: The Paradise of the Buddha of Measureless Light*. Honolulu: University of Hawai'i Press.

Greene, Eric. 2012. 'Meditation, Repentance, and Visionary Experience in Early Medieval Chinese Buddhism'. Ph.D. Thesis, University of California, Berkeley.

Gregory, Peter. 2002. *Tsung-mi and the Sinification of Buddhism*. Honolulu: University of Hawai'i Press.

Harris, Sam. 2014. *Waking Up: Searching for Spirituality Without Religion*. London: Bantam Press.

Herrigel, Eugen. 1953. *Zen in the Art of Archery*. Tr. R. F. C. Hull. London: Routledge & Kegan Paul.

Huxley, Aldous. 2009 [1945]. *The Perennial Philosophy*. New York: HarperCollins.

Imaeda, Yoshiro. 2008. 'The Provenance and Character of the Dunhuang Documents'. *Memoirs of the Toyo Bunko* 66: 81–102.

Ives, Christopher. 2009. 'In Search of a Green Dharma: Philosophical Issues in Buddhist Environmental Ethics'. In John Powers and Charles S. Prebish (eds), *Destroying Mara Forever: Buddhist Ethics Essays in Honour of Damien Keown*. Ithaca, NY: Snow Lion. 165–86.

Jaffe, Richard. 2001. *Neither Monk nor Layman*. Princeton, NJ: Princeton University Press.

James, William. 1982 [1902]. *The Varieties of Religious Experience: A Study in Human Nature*. London: Penguin.

Jorgensen, John. 2012. 'The Figure of Huineng'. In Morten Schlütter and Stephen Teiser (eds), *Readings of the Platform Sutra*. New York: Columbia University Press. 25–52.

Kapleau, Philip. 1989. *The Three Pillars of Zen (25th Anniversary Edition)*. New York: Doubleday.

Kapstein, Matthew. 2004. 'The Strange Death of Pema the Demon Tamer'. In Matthew Kapstein (ed.), *The Presence of Light: Divine Radiance and Religious Experience*. Chicago: University of Chicago Press. 119–56.

Kroll, Paul. 2015. *A Student's Dictionary of Classical and Medieval Chinese*. Leiden: Brill.

Legge, James. 1990a [1885]. *The Sacred Books of China, Part I, The Shu King*. New Delhi: Atlantic Publishers.

Legge, James. 1990b [1885]. *The Sacred Books of China, Part IV, The Lī Kī, XI–XLVI*. New Delhi: Atlantic Publishers.

Leighton, Taigen Dan. 2000. *Cultivating the Empty Field: The Silent Illumination of Zen Master Hongzhi*. North Clarendon, VT: Tuttle.

———— 2015. *Just This Is It: Dongshan and the Practice of Suchness*. Boston: Shambhala.

Leighton, Taigen Dan and Shohaku Okumura. 2010. *Dōgen's Extensive Record: A Translation of the Eihei Kōruko*. Boston: Wisdom.

Little, John (ed.). 2001. *Bruce Lee: Artist of Life*. Boston: Tuttle.

MacIntyre, Alasdair. 2011 [1981]. *After Virtue: A Study in Moral Theory*. London: Bloomsbury.

Mascaró, Juan (tr.). 1973. *The Dhammapada: The Path of Perfection*. London: Penguin.

McMahan, David L. 2008. *The Making of Buddhist Modernism*. New York: Oxford University Press.

McRae, John. 1986. *The Northern School and the Formation of Early Ch'an Buddhism*. Honolulu: University of Hawai'i Press.

———— 2003. *Seeing Through Zen: Encounter, Transformation, and Geneaology in Chinese Chan Buddhism*. Berkeley: University of California Press.

Meinert, Carmen. 2007. 'The Legend of *Cig car ba* Criticism in Tibet: A List of Six *Cig car ba* Titles in the *Chos 'byung me tog snying po* of Nyang Nyi ma 'od zer (12th Century)'. In Ronald Davidson and Christian Wedermeyer (eds), *Tibetan Buddhist Literature and Praxis*. Leiden: Brill. 31–54.

Midgley, Mary. 1996. *Utopias, Dolphins and Computers: Problems of Philosophical Plumbing*. London: Routledge.

Mohr, Michel. 2000. 'Emerging from Nonduality: Kōan Practice in the Rinzai Tradition since Hakuin'. In Steven Heine and Dale Wright (eds), *The Kōan: Texts and Contexts in Zen Buddhism*. New York: Oxford University Press. 244–79.

Mohr, Michel. 2008. 'Invocation of the Sage: The Ritual to Glorify the Emperor'. In Steven Heine and Dale Wright (eds), *Zen Ritual: Studies of Zen Buddhist Theory in Practice*. New York: Oxford University Press. 205–22.

Mollier, Christine. 2008. *Buddhism and Taoism Face to Face: Scripture, Ritual, and Iconographic Exchange in Medieval China*. Honolulu: University of Hawai'i Press.

Monier-Williams, M. 1998 [1899]. *A Sanskrit–English Dictionary*. Oxford: Oxford University Press.

Nearman, Hubert (tr.). 2007. *Shōbōgenzō: The Treasure House of the Eye of the True Teaching*. Mount Shasta, CA: Shasta Abbey Press. https://www.shastaabbey.org/pdf/shoboAll.pdf.

Needham, Joseph. 1962. *Science and Civilization in China, Vol. 4: Physics and Physical Technology, Part 1: Physics*. Cambridge: Cambridge University Press.

Nishijima, Gūdo and Chodo Cross (tr.). 2006. *Master Dogen's Shobogenzo*. 2nd ed., 4 vols. Charleston, SC: Booksurge Publishing.

Nishiyama, Kosen and John Stevens (tr.). 1975–83. *A Complete English Translation of Dōgen Zenji's Shōbōgenzō*. 4 Vols. Tokyo: Nakayama Shobō.

Okumura, Shohaku. 2012. *Living by Vow: A Practical Introduction to Eight Essential Zen Chants and Texts*. Somerville, MA: Wisdom.

Osto, Douglas. 2009. *Power, Wealth and Women in Indian Mahāyāna Buddhism: The Gaṇḍavyūha-sūtra*. London: Routledge.

Pirsig, Robert. 1974. *Zen and the Art of Motorcycle Maintenance: An Enquiry into Values*. London: The Bodley Head.

Poceski, Mario. 2010. 'Monastic Innovator, Iconoclast, and Teacher of Doctrine: The Varied Images of Chan Master Baizhang'. In Steven Heine and Dale Wright (eds), *Zen Masters*. New York: Oxford University Press. 3–32.

———— 2015. 'Conceptions and Attitudes towards Contemplative Practice within the Early Traditions of Chan Buddhism'. *Journal of Chinese Buddhist Studies* 28: 67–116.

Pregadio, Fabrizio (ed.). 2008. *Encyclopedia of Taoism*. London: Routledge.

Raymond, Eric. 2003. 'Jargon File (version 4.4.7)'. URL: www.catb.org/jargon/html/

———— 2015. 'How to Become a Hacker (Version 1.50)'. URL: www.catb.org/esr/faqs/hacker-howto.html

Red Pine. 1987. *The Zen Teaching of Bodhidharma*. New York: North Point Press.

———— 2006. *The Platform Sutra: The Zen Teaching of Huineng*. Berkeley: Counterpoint.

———— 2013. *The Lankavatara Sutra: A Zen Text*. Berkeley: Counterpoint.

Robson, James. 2011. 'Formation and Fabrication in the History and Historiography of Chan Buddhism'. *Harvard Journal of Asiatic Studies* 71.2: 311–49.

Rong Xinjiang. 2000. 'The Nature of the Dunhuang Library Cave and the Reasons for its Sealing'. In *Cahiers d'Extrême-Asie* 11: 247–75.

Rosenbaum, Robert and Barry Magid (eds). 2016. *What's Wrong With Mindfulness (And What Isn't): Zen Perspectives*. Boston: Wisdom.

Salomon, Richard. 2011. 'Why did the Gandhāran Buddhists Bury Their Manuscripts?'. In Stephen Berkwitz, Juliane Schober and Claudia Brown (eds), *Buddhist Manuscript Cultures*. Abingdon: Routledge. 19–34.

Satō Giei and Nishimura Eshin. 1973. *Unsui: A Diary of Zen Monastic Life*. Honolulu: University of Hawai'i Press.

Schlingloff, Dieter. 2006. *Ein buddhistisches Yogalehrbuch: unveränderter Nachdruck der Ausgabe von 1964 unter Beigabe aller seither bekannt gewordenen Fragmente*. Düsseldorf: Haus der Japanischen Kultur.

Schlütter, Morten. 2008: *How Zen Became Zen: The Dispute Over Enlightenment and the Formation of Chán Buddhism in Sòng-Dynasty China*. Honolulu: University of Hawai'i Press.

———— 2012. 'The Platform Sūtra, Buddhism and Chinese Religion'. In Morten Schlütter and Stephen Teiser (eds), *Readings of the Platform Sutra*. New York: Columbia University Press. 1–24.

Sharf, Robert. 1993. 'The Zen of Japanese Nationalism'. *History of Religions* 33.1: 1–43.

———— 2002. *Coming to Terms with Chinese Buddhism: A Reading of the Treasure Store Treatise*. Honolulu: University of Hawai'i Press.

———— 2014. 'Mindfulness and Mindlessness in Early Ch'an'. *Philosophy East and West* 64.4: 933–64.

Shaw, Sarah. 2014. *The Spirit of Buddhist Meditation*. London: Yale University Press.

Sheng Yen. 2008. *The Method of No-method: The Chan Practice of Silent Illumination*. Boston: Shambhala.

Shibayama Zenkei. 1974. *Zen Comments on the Mumonkan*. New York: Harper & Row.

Sørensen, Henrik H. 1989. 'Observations on the Characteristics of the Chinese Chan Manuscripts from Dunhuang'. *Studies in Central and East Asian Religions* 2: 115–39.

Stein, Marc Aurel. 1921. *Serindia: Detailed Report of Explorations in Central Asia and Westernmost China* [5 vols]. Oxford: Clarendon Press.

Stevenson, Daniel. 1987. 'The T'ien-t'ai Four Forms of Samādhi and Late North–South Dynasties, Sui, and early T'ang Buddhist Devotionalism'. Ph.D. dissertation, Columbia University, New York.

Suzuki Shunryu. 1991 [1970]. *Zen Mind, Beginner's Mind*. New York: Weatherhill.

Tanahashi Kazuaki. 2010. *Treasury of the Dharma Eye: Zen Master Dogen's Shobo Genzo*. Boston: Shambhala.

———— 2015. *Zen Chants: Thirty-Five Essential Texts in New Translations with Commentary*. Boston: Shambhala.

Thich Nhat Hanh. 1995. *Zen Keys*. New York: Doubleday.

Thich Thien-An. 1975. *Buddhism and Zen in Vietnam in Relation to the Development of Buddhism in Asia*. Los Angeles: College of Oriental Studies, Graduate School.

van Schaik, Sam. 2004. *Approaching the Great Perfection: Simultaneous and Gradual Methods of Dzogchen Practice in the Longchen Nyingtig*. Somerville, MA: Wisdom.

—— 2015. *Tibetan Zen: Discovering a Lost Tradition*. Boston: Shambhala.

—— 2016. *The Spirit of Tibetan Buddhism*. London: Yale University Press.

van Schaik, Sam and Imre Galambos. 2011. *Manuscripts and Travellers: The Sino-Tibetan Documents of a Tenth-century Buddhist Pilgrim*. Berlin: de Gruyter.

Victoria, Brian. 2006. *Zen at War* (2nd edn). Lanham, MD: Rowman & Littlefield.

Wang, Robin and Ding Weixiang. 2010. 'Zhang Zai's Theory of Vital Energy'. In John Makeham (ed.), *Dao Companion to Neo-Confucian Philosophy*. 47–50.

Watts, Alan. 1991 [1936]. *The Spirit of Zen*. London: HarperCollins.

Welch, Holmes. 1967. *The Practice of Chinese Buddhism: 1900–1950*. Cambridge, MA: Harvard University Press.

Welter, Albert. 2000. 'Mahākāśyapa's Smile: Silent Transmission and the Kung-an (Koan) Tradition'. In Steven Heine and Dale Wright (eds), *The Kōan: Texts and Contexts in Zen Buddhism*. New York: Oxford University Press. 75–109.

—— 2008. 'Buddhist Rituals for Protecting the Country in Medieval Japan: Myōan Eisai's "Regulations of the Zen School"'. In Steven Heine and Dale S. Wright (eds), *Zen Ritual: Studies of Zen Theory in Practice*. New York: Oxford University Press.

Wilkinson, Endymion. 2000. *Chinese History: A Manual (Revised and Enlarged)*. Cambridge, MA: Harvard University Press.

Wittgenstein, Ludwig. 1922. *Tractatus Logico-Philosophicus*. London: Kegan Paul.

Wright, Dale. 2010. 'Humanizing the Image of a Zen Master: Taizan Maezumi Roshi'. In Steven Heine and Dale Wright (eds), *Zen Masters*. New York: Oxford University Press. 239–66.

Yamada Shōji. 2001. 'The Myth of Zen in the Art of Archery'. *Japanese Journal of Religious Studies* 28.1–2: 1–30.

Yampolsky, Philip. 2012 [1967]. *The Platform Sutra of the Sixth Patriarch: The Text of the Tun-Huang Manuscript*. New York: Columbia University Press.

Yanagida Seizan. 1971. *Shoki no Zenshi 1: Ryōgashijiki; Denhōbōki*. Tokyo: Chikuma shobō.

Yoshida, Yutaka. 2015. 'A Handlist of Buddhist Sogdian Texts'. Memoirs of the Faculty of Letters, Kyoto University 54: 167–80. http://hdl.handle.net/2433/197456.

Yu, Jimmy. 2006. 'Bodies of Sanctity: Ascetic Practices in Late Imperial China'. Ph.D. dissertation, Princeton University.

Ziporyn, Brook. 2003. '*Li* (Principle, Coherence) in Chinese Buddhism'. *Journal of Chinese Philosophy* 30.3–4: 501–24.

—— 2009. *Zhuangzi: The Essential Writings, With Selections from Traditional Commentaries*. Indianapolis, IN: Hackett.

Zürcher, Eric. 2007. *The Buddhist Conquest of China: The Spread and Adaptation of Buddhism in Early Medieval China* (2nd edn). Leiden: Brill.

ONLINE RESOURCES

Chinese Text Project: https://ctext.org

Digital Dictionary of Buddhism (DDB): http://www.buddhism.dict.net

Dunhuang Manuscript Full Text Digitization Project: http://dev.ddbc.edu.tw/Dunhuang_Manuscripts

International Dunhuang Project (IDP): http://idp.bl.uk

INDEX

Note: Sanskrit words are given here with diacritical marks, even when this is not the case in the main text. The Chinese equivalents provided for Sanskrit Buddhist words are those most commonly found in the *Masters of the Lanka*.